Writing in the Disciplines

Universities into the 21st Century

Series Editors: Noel Entwistle and Roger King

Further titles are in preparation

Writing in the Disciplines

Edited by
Mary Deane and Peter O'Neill

Selection, editorial matter, Introduction © Mary Deane and
Peter O'Neill 2011
Individual chapters © the contributors 2011
Preface © Jonathan Monroe

First published 2011 by
PALGRAVE MACMILLAN

Palgrave Macmillan in the UK is an imprint of Macmillan Publishers Limited,
registered in England, company number 785998, of Houndmills, Basingstoke,
Hampshire RG21 6XS.

Palgrave Macmillan in the US is a division of St Martin's Press LLC,
175 Fifth Avenue, New York, NY 10010.

Palgrave Macmillan is the global academic imprint of the above companies
and has companies and representatives throughout the world.

Palgrave® and Macmillan® are registered trademarks in the United States,
the United Kingdom, Europe and other countries.

ISBN 978–0–230–23708–7

Library of Congress Cataloging-in-Publication Data
Writing in the disciplines / [edited by] Mary Deane and Peter O'Neill.
       p. cm.
    Includes index.
    Summary: "Writing in the Disciplines is an expanding field in which subject
    specialists and writing specialists collaborate to provide academic writing
    tuition to student writers. This book places WiD in its theoretical and
    cultural contexts and reports on initiatives taking place at a range of
    UK Higher Education Institutions"—Provided by publisher.
    ISBN 978–0–230–23708–7 (pbk.)
    1. English language—Rhetoric—Study and teaching.   2. Interdisciplinary
    approach in education.   I. Deane, Mary, 1975–   II. O'Neill, Peter, Dr.
    PE1404W7264 2011
    808′.066—dc23   2011016923

10   9   8   7   6   5   4   3   2   1
20   19   18   17   16   15   14   13   12   11

Printed and bound by CPI Group (UK), Croydon, CR0 4YY

Contents

Part I Contexts

Part II Collaborating to Support Student Writers

Part III WiD and the Institution

List of Tables and Figures

Tables

Figures

Preface

Jonathan Monroe

▶ Explicit knowledge: writing in the disciplines as higher education

As the costs of higher education in the twenty-first century continue to increase, along with accelerating demand for broader access to the benefits higher education can provide, academic disciplines face growing pressure to demonstrate their relevance and usefulness to the world beyond the university. Recognising the integral importance of writing to the production and sharing of knowledge in all areas of academic specialisation, Writing in the Disciplines (WiD) has come to play an increasingly influential role at the front lines of higher education's efforts to make the strongest possible case for its value and importance through explicit recognition that disciplinary knowledge is inseparable from the writing practices specific to each discipline. Since the knowledge specific to particular disciplines is unavailable, if not quite literally unthinkable, apart from such disciplinary practices, the integral role of writing in higher education merits the highest priority in university funding and support at all levels of the curriculum, in undergraduate as well as postgraduate education, across all disciplines.

Underlying the outstanding contributions Mary Deane and Peter O'Neill have brought together in the present collection is a shared recognition at the heart of all higher education: Knowledge, as writing, as articulation, is explicitation. At all levels of undergraduate and graduate research and teaching, whatever the discipline, making knowledge explicit is at once means and end of an enlightened pedagogy, as it is also of the most rigorous, self-questioning research. Cultivating such disciplinary self-reflexivity—about the conditions, protocols, procedures, and limits of the production of knowledge, all of which play a role in what is sometimes called a rhetorical understanding or understanding of rhetoric, in its most encompassing implications—is the indissoluble link between knowledge and writing. When students write within particular disciplinary contexts, the self they bring to the diverse practices of disciplinary writing becomes at once suspended, dispersed, and concentrated through the discursive options each discipline makes available. Whether students ultimately align themselves with or call into question the disciplinary practices they encounter, making the character of those practices explicit can prove of great, if not indispensable value. While some students learn well through processes of acculturation and emulation without manifest explicitation, others may require, and all stand to benefit from, as high a level as possible of explicit understanding. Although the level of engagement necessarily varies, making knowledge explicit is the shared challenge of every writer at each moment of writing, from the novice first-year university undergraduate to a discipline's most renowned representative.

While practitioners at the highest levels of disciplinary practices may well want to demand what the capaciously multi- and cross-disciplinary Martinican writer Edouard Glissant has aptly called "the right to opacity", we understand the power of Glissant's affirmation of such knowledge through its elegant, precise articulation. As his complex, remarkably varied writings make manifest, the drive to write self-reflexively within and across diverse disciplinary practices does not in itself require students—as themselves "researchers"—to agree to a false choice between opacity and clarity, between "jargon" and "ordinary language". As anyone who has developed substantial disciplinary expertise understands, such a false choice may prove as unhelpful and limiting to the production of knowledge as that between writing for a "general reader" or "lay audience", on the one hand, and, on the other, writing for a cognoscenti of the narrowest of disciplinary specialisations.

As a movement within higher education, Writing in the Disciplines has helped make explicit the extent to which "common knowledge" and "disciplinary knowledge" remain in constant conversation with each other, even when readers who might situate themselves at one end or the other of the continuum seem not to be listening to one another. Complex, multi-layered, heterogeneous, internally fractured, various, overlapping, contradictory, at times stagnant, yet ever-evolving, practices of disciplinary knowledge remain, even when they seem to be separate within the university or from broader discursive practices beyond the university's increasingly porous borders, inseparable from their articulation, from acts of writing and speaking that make their knowledge explicit to all who would understand them, so much so that we may fairly say, as the writers of the present volume make clear in prismatic fashion, that knowledge and explicitation—the "bringing to light" of knowledge—are one.

If the frontiers of knowledge are always, by definition, opaque, the most advanced researchers in a given field and the novice student writer share a common challenge. While clarity is often claimed to be one of the hallmarks of good writing, advances in the thinking and writing of a discipline—of writing as thinking and thinking as writing—frequently strike the discipline's gatekeepers as scandalously incomprehensible. There is, in this sense, a perfectly understandable, even necessary connection between advances in knowledge within and across fields and a certain difficulty, even impenetrability. The greater the advance, perhaps calling into question everything once thought to be true and clear, the more likely it may be to strike the entrusted guardians of disciplinary knowledge as bordering on complete opacity. Remembering the opacity of the difficult knowledge they have acquired in their respective fields, researchers across the disciplines can better put into practice an approach to writing and learning that doesn't underestimate how much students need them to make explicit the underlying assumptions and procedures they take for granted and how context-specific that knowledge is to their particular ways of making meaning. What is called "writing" is nothing more, and nothing less, than the means and end of that process without which disciplinary knowledge remains literally incommunicable.

Perhaps the greatest challenge at all levels of learning within and across disciplines, experienced by both teachers and students, who are all in this sense researchers, is that so much typically remains implicit, in need of clarification, distillation, elaboration, and amplification, in the production and sharing of knowledge. To place on the margins of the curriculum writing's integral relationship to learning and the production of knowledge, given this understanding, would be to undervalue its central role not only in the first year of a student's higher education, but in higher education generally. While researchers in all fields share this understanding more or less implicitly, its explicit recognition lags behind in the degree of support (financial, bureaucratic, etc.) it receives in virtually every institution of higher learning.

While the movement known as Writing in the Disciplines has made progress over the past several decades, there is still a long way to go to realise its promise. Yet as the present volume makes clear in its adaptation of WiD principles, ours is a time of increasing reflection on the explicit conditions and practices of disciplinary knowledge. Bridging WiD theory and practice between the UK and the US in particular, with useful forays as well into Australian, Irish, and French contexts, *Writing in the Disciplines* offers a timely contribution that will resonate locally and globally for years to come.

As much as thinking about writing in higher education in the UK and elsewhere may have benefited from examples of such thinking in the US, and as generous as this volume's contributors are in acknowledging specific influences, it is exciting to see the process in reverse in the increasingly international conversation it both stages and encourages. Representing disciplines as distinct from one another as business and geography, mathematics and political theory, as well as more traditionally writing-aligned fields such as law, the collection offers an impressive range of theoretical and practical inquiry, including reflection on the theory and practice of WiD, WAC (Writing across the Curriculum), and their relation to the burgeoning composition industry that has come to play such a powerful role in the shaping of higher education in the US over the past several decades. Especially powerful is the volume's sense of urgency in making explicit connections between disciplinary knowledge and discipline-specific writing practices both within and beyond the university, where the boundaries between these increasingly overlapping, interpenetrating sites become increasingly difficult to discern.

In an article published May 28, 2010, entitled "Oxford Tradition Comes to this: 'Death' (Expound)", Sarah Lawall of *The New York Times* reports the decision to eliminate an annual essay exam required of all applicants to All Souls College since 1932, and in one form or another since 1878, the sole explicit prompt for which consisted of a single noun. Intended to test the "intellectual agility" and "acrobatic flexibility" of a prospective Fellow's intellect, the exam's approach, with its much-anticipated "unveiling of the word," has seen its last days as a measure of each candidate's potential. The current collection's contributions from five UK universities—Coventry, London Metropolitan, King's College London, Queen Mary of London, Nottingham Trent—as well as Saint Mary's College Belfast (Ireland), University of Wollongong (Australia), Seattle University and Dartmouth College (US)—attest to great strides throughout higher education in making processes of research, teaching, and evaluation more accessible. Bringing to light the disciplinary, multi-disciplinary opacities that can be packed into a single word, as in the name of an academic discipline—"business," "design," "politics," "law"—they help foster an approach to learning at all levels that will be less veiled, less shrouded in mystery, and more manifestly engaged. Through explicit attention to the full range of academic writing in all its discipline-specific forms, they encourage access to disciplinary knowledge in the service of a higher education—more broadly democratic, more openly dialogical—that knows no end.

▶ References

Glissant, Edouard. *Poetics of Relation.* Trans. Betsy Wing. Ann Arbor: University of Michigan, 1997; *Poétique de la relation* 1990, 194.

Lawall, Sarah. "Oxford Tradition Comes to this: 'Death' (Expound)". *The New York Times.* May 28, 2010, A1.

Acknowledgements

Mary wishes to thank Sam Mason for his expertise as a reader and his generosity in compiling the book's index, but most of all for his exceptional support.

Mary would like to thank Jonathan Monroe and Cheryl Glenn for sharing their scholarship on disciplinary writing development and contributing to this collection. She is also grateful to Rowena Murray for her advice. Mary is particularly indebted to the Australian scholar Jan Skillen, whose pioneering leadership of discipline-based writing development deeply influences this book.

Mary is grateful to her family and friends, especially Moira, Pat, Elaine, Teresa, Tim, Lottie, Charley, Tom, Paul, Joe, Sarah, Emma, Mollie, Jen, Sally, and Gwen. She has been generously guided by her colleagues, Adam, Arina, Catalina, Caroline, Clare, Claudia, Cynthia, Dimitar, Elizabeth, Erik, Hilary, Holly, Janet, Jon, Juan Antonio, Lisa, Liz, Magda, Mike, Miriam, Monica, Neil, Paul, Penny, Sarah, Sheila, and Tom. She wishes to express her appreciation to the legal writing expert Steve Foster and the Mathematics Education specialist Peter Samuels for being such impeccable collaborators. Special thanks are due to Ray Summers for his guidance on Chapter 13 and his technical expertise.

Peter wishes to thank his colleagues at the Write Now Centre for Excellence in Teaching and Learning and the London Metropolitan University Writing Centre, Martin Agombar, Savita Bakhshi, Jane Ferguson, Emma Greenough, Kathy Harrington, Katerina Koutsantoni, Celine Llewellyn-Jones, and Lynn Reynolds. He is grateful for the hard work and enthusiasm of all the London Met Writing Mentors from 2006–2011. He would also like to thank friends and colleagues at London Met, in particular, Dipti Bhagat, Myrtle Emmanuel, Sandra Sinfield and Rosemary Stott.

Thanks to his family for continuing love and support and to Michele Sisto for being such a patient and enduring listener while this book was in gestation.

Mary and Peter are both grateful for the expertise of Suzannah Burywood, Jennifer Schmidt, Cecily Wilson, Priya Venkat, and Della Oliver of Palgrave Macmillan.

The editors and publishers wish to thank the following for permission to reproduce copyright material:

King's College London and Blackboard Inc for 'screenshot of list of tutor comments' from King's College London university website © 2011.

Lawrence Erlbaum Associates, for Table 12.2, from J. Bizup (2008) 'BEAM: A Rhetorical Vocabulary for Teaching Research-Based Writing', *Rhetoric Review* vol. 27, no. 1.

NCTE, for Table 12.1, from M Carter (2007) 'Ways of Knowing, Doing, and Writing in the Disciplines', *Journal of College Composition and Communication*, vol. 58, no. 3.

Queen Mary University London for 'Typical Outline for the Hazards Module,' 'Category B of MASUS Assessment Criteria,' 'Annotated Example of Student Writing to Illustrate Category B of Assessment Criteria' and 'Hazards Briefing Paper Coursework' by Dave Horne from course materials, 2011.

SEDA, for Figure 13.1, from M Oliver (2002) 'What Do Learning Technologists Do?', *Innovations in Education and Teaching International*, vol. 39, no. 4.

The University of Coventry for 'An Annotated Sample Law Essay' and 'The Related Roles of Writing Specialist, Disciplinary Expert, and Learning Technologist' by Mary Deane from course materials, 2011.

The Victoria and Albert Museum, London, for the image used in Figure 10.2.

Every effort has been made to trace rights holders, but if any have been inadvertently overlooked the publishers would be pleased to make the necessary arrangements at the first opportunity.

Series Editors' Preface

The series is designed to fill a niche between publications about universities and colleges that focus exclusively on the practical concerns of university teachers, managers or policy makers and those which are written with an academic, research-based audience in mind that provide detailed evidence, argument, and conclusions. The books in this series are intended to build upon evidence and conceptual frameworks in discussing issues which are of direct interest to those concerned with universities. The issues in the series will cover a broad range, from the activities of teachers and students, to wider developments in policy, at local, national, and international levels.

The current pressures on academic and administrative staff, and university managers, mean that, only rarely, can they justify the time needed to read lengthy descriptions of research findings. The aim, therefore, is to produce compact, readable books that in many parts provide a synthesis and overview of often seemingly disparate issues.

Some of the books, such as the first in the series—*The University in the Global Age*, are deliberatively broad in focus and conceptualisation, looking at the system as a whole in an international perspective, and are a collection of integrated chapters, written by specialist authors. In other books, such as *Research and Teaching: Beyond the Divide*, the author looks within universities at a specific issue to examine what constitutes "best practice" through a lens of available theory and research evidence.

Underpinning arguments, where appropriate with research-based conceptual analysis, makes the books more convincing to an academic audience, while the link to "good practice and policy" avoids the remoteness that comes from an over-abstract approach. The series will thus appeal not just to those working within higher education, but also to a wider audience interested in knowing more about an organisation that is attracting increasing government and media attention.

NOEL ENTWISTLE
ROGER KING

Notes on Contributors

Martin Agombar is a Learning Technologist at London Metropolitan University, where he collaborates with academics to support students' academic writing in the disciplines. His specialisms include using technologies to enhance students' learning and the potential of reusable learning objects. Martin has a PGCE in Media with English and CMALT accreditation.

Julius Ayodeji is a Playwright and Senior Lecturer at Nottingham Trent University. Over the last 10 years he has written for radio, the stage, and short film scripts. He has also written and presented a number of papers for academic conferences. His subject specialisms are multimedia, writing as a way of thinking, and how technology might be used to express that thinking.

John Bean is a Professor of English at Seattle University. He is the author of *Engaging Ideas: The Professor's Guide to Writing, Critical Thinking and Active Learning in the Classroom*, 2nd ed. (2010) as well as the co-author of four textbooks. In 2010, his co-authored article "Messy Problems and Lay Audiences: Teaching Critical Thinking within the Finance Curriculum" won the 2009 McGraw-Hill—Magna Publications Award for the year's best "scholarly work on teaching and learning".

Rebecca Bell is a Learning and Teaching Officer at Nottingham Trent University. Her work involves supporting students with their academic writing, primarily through Writing Across the Curriculum (WAC) and Writing in the Disciplines (WiD). Rebecca is interested in developing staff perceptions of student academic writing, organising events, and developing resources to help lecturers embed academic writing into their teaching and learning practice. She worked as part of the LearnHigher CETL and has summarised her involvement in *Learning Development in Higher Education*.

Dipti Bhagat is a Design Historian and Senior Lecturer. She leads the design history and theory curriculum for undergraduate and postgraduate courses in design in the Faculty of Art, Media and Design at

London Metropolitan University. She has published in design history and researches (with Peter O'Neill) inclusive pedagogies and widening participation in art and design higher education in the UK.

Sarah Broadberry is Senior Lecturer in Animal Science at Nottingham Trent University and is programme leader for the BSc (Hons) Zoo Biology degree. She recently completed her PGCHE, which developed her interest in pedagogical research, and specifically "Writing in the Disciplines" (WiD). Sarah is currently establishing a research project which aims to quantify learning in the zoo environment.

Mary Deane is Senior Lecturer in academic writing at Coventry University's Centre for Academic Writing (CAW). Her publications include *Academic Research, Writing, and Referencing*, *Critical Thinking and Analysis*, and "Measuring the Outcomes of Individualised Writing Instruction". Her specialisms include technologies for teaching writing, disciplinary writing development, and publication strategies. Mary won a Teaching Excellence Award in 2008, and since 2009 she has been an Executive Board member of the European Writing Centers Association (EWCA) and the International Writing Centers Association (IWCA).

Christiane Donahue is the Director of the Institute for Writing and Rhetoric at Dartmouth College. She is a member of the Théodile-CIREL research group at l'Universite´ de Lille III, and she publishes on writing, disciplinarity, transfer of knowledge, and cross-cultural issues in writing and instruction. Her recent publications include " 'Internationalization' and composition studies: re-orienting the discourse" and "Transfer, portability, generalization: (How) does composition expertise 'carry'?"

Myrtle Emmanuel is a Principal Lecturer in Learning and Teaching at LMBS and a writing specialist in the disciplines specialist with the HRM and Management subject fields. She has recently written "Reading and writing skills for business: the students' voice" with co-authors at London Metropolitan University. Myrtle is currently working towards completing her PhD study on "the relational nature of undergraduates' career management and career success".

Steve Foster has taught law to undergraduates and postgraduates for over 30 years. He specialises in human rights law, prisoners' rights, legal skills, and academic legal writing. Steve has published widely in various journals in those fields and is the author of *How to Write Better Law Essays* (2009, 2nd ed.), a bestselling text dedicated to academic writing style in legal assessments. He has also written two textbooks on human rights law in the UK.

Lisa Ganobcsik-Williams is the Head of the Centre for Academic Writing at Coventry University. Her publications include *A Report on the Teaching of Academic Writing in UK Higher Education* (2004) and *Teaching Academic Writing in UK Higher Education: Theories, Practices and Models* (2006). Her current research focuses on the Coventry Online Writing Lab (COWL). Formerly Executive Board member of the European and International Writing Centers Associations (EWCA/IWCA), she serves as Chair of the European Association for the Teaching of Academic Writing (EATAW).

Cheryl Glenn is Liberal Arts Research Professor of English and Women's Studies, and Co-director of the Center for Democratic Deliberation at Pennsylvania State University. She is author of the award-winning *Rhetoric Retold: Regendering the Tradition from Antiquity Through the Renaissance, Unspoken: A Rhetoric of Silence, Rhetorical Education in America*, and several other titles, including *The Harbrace Guide to Writing, the Writer's Harbrace Handbook*, and *Hodge's Harbrace Handbook*. Her research interests include rhetorical history and theory, feminist historiography, the ever-expanding feminist rhetorical project, and delivery systems for the teaching of writing.

Katherine Harrington is the Director of the Write Now Centre for Excellence in Teaching and Learning at London Metropolitan University, which develops evidence-based approaches to supporting students' learning and writing within disciplines. She has published in the areas of writing and curriculum development, student learning, and assessment in higher education, and has particular interests in peer and collaborative learning and evaluating the efficacy of writing development programmes.

Debbie Holley is a Principal Lecturer in the Faculty of Education at Anglia Ruskin University. Previously working at London Metropolitan University Business School, Debbie is interested in blended learning and pedagogic design. With the student experience at the heart of her research and teaching, she has contributed to the work of three Centres of Excellence in Teaching and Learning: Reusable Learning Object CETL (www.rlo-cetl.ac.uk); the Write Now CETL.

David Horne is Reader in Environmental Change in the School of Geography, Queen Mary University of London, where his efforts to improve student writing skills have included participation in the *DALiC* project and an HEA-supported project on *Widening Participation and Student Writing in the Disciplines* as well as membership of a recent *Working Group on Development of Students' Writing*. He collaborates internationally in research on past climates and environmental change, and has published more than 120 scientific journal articles and books.

Linda Johnson is the Head of Learning and Teaching at London Metropolitan Business School. She has been teaching Business Law and academic study skills for around 25 years. Linda is particularly interested in strategies to engage and motivate students and is presently conducting research with colleagues from two Universities on the notion of 'Student Belonging' at University.

Celine Llewellyn-Jones is a Learning Technologist for the Writing Centre at London Metropolitan University and a Research Fellow at SMARTlab, University of East London. She has a special interest in mobile and location-based learning and is currently working towards a PhD in using new technologies to support full-body learning.

Jonathan Monroe is Director of Graduate Studies in Comparative Literature in the Department of Comparative Literature at Cornell University. He is an affiliated member of the Graduate Field of English, a former Associate Dean of Arts and Sciences, George Reed Professor of Writing and Rhetoric, and Director of the John S. Knight Institute for Writing in the Disciplines. Jonathan has led the field of disciplinary writing development, with seminal publications including *Writing and Revising the Disciplines* (2002) and *Local Knowledges, Local Practices: Writing in the Disciplines at Cornell* (2003).

Peter O'Neill is Senior Lecturer in academic writing at the Write Now Centre for Excellence in Teaching and Learning, London Metropolitan University. He works with staff who are interested in teaching writing in the disciplines, helping them to develop effective techniques for teaching writing and to incorporate 'writing to learn' activities within their courses.

Kelly Peake is a Project Advisor at the Thinking Writing programme, Queen Mary University of London. Her interests include argumentative skills in first-year undergraduates and staff development in teaching writing. She was a key contributor to the University of Wollongong's "Developing Academic Literacy in Context" (DALiC) project. Kelly has a BA in English and Linguistics from the University of Cape Town, South Africa, and an MSc in Applied Linguistics from the University of Edinburgh.

Emily Purser teaches in the Learning Development (LD) unit at the University of Wollongong. Her specialisms are English language teaching, educational linguistics, materials writing, and editing. Her work focuses on the learning needs of international students in Commerce and Informatics and her interests include language and literacy support in online learning environments. Emily also provides outreach support in LD to the Moss Vale Education Centre.

Peter Samuels is an Academic Skills Tutor in Mathematics at Birmingham City University. He has a research background in university-level mathematics education with the sigma Centre for Excellence in Teaching and Learning at Coventry University, especially the use of technology in extra-curricular mathematics education, known as mathematics support. Peter has been involved in serious games research at Coventry University since 2006, and in 2007 he set up the Serious Games Applied Research Group at the University.

Birgit Schippers is Senior Lecturer in Politics at St Mary's University College Belfast, where she teaches modern and contemporary social and political theory. Her research interests focus on feminist theory, citizenship and democratic theory, and identity politics. She is the author of *Julia Kristeva and Feminist Thought* (2011) and is currently researching a book on the political thought of Judith Butler.

Sandra Sinfield is a Teaching Fellow at London Metropolitan University, co-ordinator for Learning Development, and a member of the Steering Group of the Association for Learning Development in Higher Education (ALDinHE). Sandra won the 1998 IVCA gold award for education with Tom Burns, for *Everything You Wanted to Know about Studying but Were too Afraid to Ask*. They have also co-written *Teaching, Learning and Study Skills: A Guide for Tutors* and *Essential Study Skills: The Complete Guide to Success at University*.

Ursula Wingate is a Lecturer in Language in Education in the Department of Education and Professional Studies, King's College London. Among her research interests are students' transition from school to university, theoretical and pedagogic approaches to teaching academic writing, and e-learning. She has carried out several research projects concerned with the development of writing in higher education.

Jonathan Worley is the Writing Centre Director at St Mary's University College Belfast. His research interests include writing centre pedagogy, teaching of writing, and writing theory. Jonathan has published on peer tutoring and learning and teaching enhancement. He is currently researching writing in the disciplines pedagogies.

Part I

Contexts

Writing in the Disciplines: Beyond Remediality

Mary Deane and Peter O'Neill

Writing in the Disciplines reports on the developing movement to embed writing instruction into British degree programmes to enhance students' confidence as subject specialists. This book's premise is that the quicker students engage with disciplinary discourse, the more likely they are to succeed. Students' success can be improved by increasing their awareness of the genres in their subject areas, rather than leaving them to discover writing cultures and conventions through trial and error. This explicit teaching of disciplinary writing practices does not imply prescribing ways of communicating or imposing ideologies, but instead, helping students to become proficient writers in their fields can liberate them to experiment with language and develop fresh perspectives.

This book aims to stimulate debate about ways of supporting student writers within their subject studies. Although many academics naturally appreciate the role of writing in the process of developing disciplinary understanding, finding practical ways of applying this insight to teaching in higher education is another matter. So, *Writing in the Disciplines* brings together a range of ideas that can be adapted for other contexts. The volume is divided into three parts. Part I, "Contexts", introduces approaches to enhancing students' academic writing in the US, Australia, and the UK. Part II, "Collaborating to Support Student Writers", contains case studies of pedagogic collaborations between subject experts, writing developers, and learning technologists in a range of subjects. Part III, "WiD and the Institution", addresses the wider themes of staff development, curricula design, using technologies, and the role of the British Writing Centre as a base for research and staff development.

▶ Discipline-based writing instruction

Discipline-based writing development builds constructively on British research into academic literacies (Street, 1995; Ivanic, 1998; Lea and

Street, 1998; Lillis, 2006). Disciplinary writing instruction offers a flexible approach whereby such literature can be implemented pragmatically to benefit student writing and learning. British Writing in the Disciplines (WiD) work is also indebted to Jonathan Monroe's emphasis on the fact that thinking and writing are integral and cannot be divorced from the epistemologies and discourses students need to learn about in their disciplines (Monroe, 2002, 2003, pp. xi–xiii). In addition, the British WiD movement is influenced by John Bean, who argues that integrating "writing and other critical thinking activities into a course increases students' learning while teaching them thinking skills for posing questions, proposing hypotheses, gathering and analyzing data, and making arguments" (Bean, 2001, p. 1). UK-based disciplinary writing development also draws on an Australian pedagogic approach that highlights the epistemological aspects of academic writing in context called "Developing Academic Literacy in Context" (DALiC) (Skillen et al., 1999; Purser et al., 2008).[1]

During the last two decades, as UK university populations have changed and become more representative of the population at large, writing development has become an increasingly energetic field of practice. Writing development practitioners in the UK can be found working in a variety of institutional spaces, including EAP (English for Academic Purposes), EFL (English as a Foreign Language), Learning Development and Study Skills units, and more recently Royal Literary Fellows and Writing Centres. However, in one respect WiD is perhaps distinctive: in its insistence that taking responsibility for student writing in the discipline is ultimately the role and responsibility of subject specialists.

In tackling academic writing in the various disciplines, it is clearly subject experts who are best placed to inform students of the conventions in their fields. Students are likely to be most engaged by discipline-relevant teaching rather than generic instruction about academic writing that is at times divorced from their degree programmes. But while we emphasise the role of subject specialists, we also suggest that staff in EAP, EFL, or Learning Development Units, along with dedicated writing specialists, are very well-placed to carry out the kind of collaborative WiD work with academic staff called for in this book. Indeed, there is already a great deal of interest amongst learning developers in embedding the good practice they advocate within disciplinary courses (Mitchell and Evison, 2006).

The WiD approach is antithetical to deficit models of writing instruction, which tend to isolate individuals or groups of students in order to provide them with remedial teaching that is unrelated to degree programmes (Wingate, 2006). Through disciplinary writing development, all students receive explicit instruction as an integral part of their cognitive development and acquisition of disciplinary knowledge. At university this may involve using informal writing activities to help students generate arguments and responses to topics, or staging the production of written assessments so there is dedicated time for planning and drafting as part of the learning, thinking, and writing processes. This encourages student writers to investigate the repertoire of rhetorical and linguistic devices used within their discourse communities (Bazerman, 1988).

A potential challenge of WiD work is that lecturers may find it hard to dedicate time to focusing on disciplinary writing conventions alongside teaching course content. However, we argue that the rewards of doing so are great because teaching about both the content and the form of scholarly genres can benefit learners at various levels of ability. High achievers are often stimulated by close attention to the nuances of disciplinary writing; students who lack confidence can respond well to the formative feedback opportunities that are often part of WiD work; and students who struggle with written assessment usually appreciate explicit tuition in disciplinary conventions. Increasingly, academics are being held accountable for the completion rates and performance of their students, so finding ways of working to improve these can be advantageous for teachers, and this is likely to become more of an expectation as part of effective academic practice.

▶ The origins of WiD

Writing developers in the UK often look to the US for lessons, since North Americans have long been grappling with student writing. In the US, the massification of higher education was experienced much earlier than in the UK, with the post-war Veterans' Act and then Open Admissions policies in the 1960s and 1970s being key to opening up higher education to non-traditional university students. Even before this, universities had taken the plunge in recognising that students need instruction in writing and composition. Indeed, the first such programme was set up at Harvard in the late nineteenth century as a response to perceived poor student writing for the Harvard entrance examination which was introduced in 1874 (Connors, 1997, p. 11; Bamberg, 2003, p. 109). It is striking that in the US the first such programme was established at the most elite of that nation's universities.

In the US, Freshman Writing soon spread from Harvard to most of the US campuses, and has contributed to an enormous writing industry with, on many campuses, hundreds of writing classes taking place each semester offering writing instruction for first-year students.

These Freshman Writing courses are a mystery for most UK academics. Typically, students might write five expository essays in each semester of their first year, often on general themes (though sometimes the classes might be associated with the complex and endlessly controversial "great books" courses or other similar introductory courses). During the course of writing these essays, writing instructors usually take students explicitly through the principles of good essay writing and effective argumentation, with particular emphasis on the thesis-driven essay in which students explicitly state the claim they are making in answering a particular question and then structure their essay to expound their claim effectively. More formal matters, such as logical argumentation and referencing correctly are also taught, and the comparatively generous nature of US university classroom time means that there may also be opportunities for expressive and more creative forms of writing.

Freshman Writing can be such an inspiring experience for students, which in part explains why so many subject experts in the US have become involved in the "Writing across the Curriculum" (WAC) movement that has become a familiar part of the US educational landscape over the last 30 years. WAC represents an attempt to bring the Freshman Writing emphasis on the importance of writing into students' other classes, and in particular to take advantage of the potential of writing for bringing about engagement, critical, and creative thinking (and it often cites as an intellectual influence James Britton and his colleagues' work in UK secondary education). Often WAC initiatives come into being through staff development work in co-operation with a university's Writing Program or Writing Center, and Young and Fulwiler (1986) provide an interesting account of staff workshops in this area in the pioneering days of WAC to reveal the energetic nature of this field. Subject experts also become involved in such work on their own initiative, and Bean (2001) offers a remarkably useful resource, the "WAC Bible", for anyone interested in embracing this aspect of student learning.[2]

WAC has been described by Mcleod and Maimon as "one of the most important educational reform movements of the twentieth century" (2000, p. 582). Given that, according to Russell and colleagues (2009, pp. 395–96), WAC has to date generated 2,400 articles and books, such a claim is probably not exaggerated and makes the fact that this work is relatively under-exploited in UK higher education surprising (see Bazerman et al., 2005 for an overview of WAC work).

More recently, WiD has emerged as an initiative related to WAC in the US. This discipline-based writing development has become popular amongst the same people who supported WAC in the US, namely rhetoric and composition experts interested in taking responsibility for their students' writing (Russell et al., 2009, p. 398). As Bean discusses in Chapter 12, one of the major rationales for the WiD movement is the mismatch between the expository writing required in the generic composition classes and the actual writing that students are required to do for the assignments in their major subjects.

WiD is an attempt to assist subject experts in helping their students meet these challenges, focusing on how academic writing shapes and is determined by disciplinary knowledge, and supporting students in coming to terms with disciplinary writing conventions. WAC insights can be retained in WiD, and, as Russell and colleagues have recently argued, there is inevitably overlap between them (2009, p. 395). WiD's emphasis on disciplinary specialisms rather than more generically focused instruction is an important development that is likely to appeal to the disciplinary focus of tertiary teaching in the UK.

In fact, discipline-based writing instruction would seem to have a particular potency in the UK context, where students specialise in a subject from the start of their university careers (Mullin, 2006). *Writing in the Disciplines* hopes to contribute to debate about what effectives models of disciplinary writing development in the UK might look like.

▶ WiD and "Academic Literacies" theorising

In the UK, the Academic Literacies (AcLits) movement has been a prominent voice in recent years, raising attention to student writing, not as a matter of student deficits or weaknesses, but rather as a consequence of the often mystifying epistemologies and practices of disciplines which may not be clear to students (Lea and Street, 1998; Lillis, 2006; Russell et al., 2008). AcLits also draws attention to the power aspects of academic writing and focuses on students, often nontraditional students, who may feel disempowered through expectations that they must write in particular ways, and whose identity may be compromised in the process (Lillis, 1997; Ivanic, 1998). Thus, AcLits has in large part a critical agenda. WiD work may, from this perspective, be critiqued as being *naïve*, or even as complicit in disciplinary power and dominance and in silencing alternative voices and ways of doing (Russell et al., 2009, p. 411).

Such concerns are understandable, but we argue that they may be misplaced. Often subject experts are themselves among the most aware of the politics of their own disciplines, and by teaching writing conventions explicitly to their students, they may take the lead in bringing about change. More pragmatically, attention to writing allows students to feel more confident at writing in a discipline and arguably makes them more inclined to challenge disciplinary conventions and retain a sense of themselves as individual, authentic writers and professionals. Certainly, keeping disciplinary know-how obscure seems of very little benefit to anyone. Potentially, students who are enabled to participate fully in a discipline are most likely to challenge the ways in which disciplines operate. Through its attention to particular needs and requirements, we believe that WiD also empowers rather than disempowers academics, encouraging them to decide for themselves what is right for them and their students rather than forcing solutions or agendas upon student writers.

A strength of WiD as a pedagogic approach is its flexibility. It would doubtless be *naïve* to believe that this way of teaching writing is ideologically uncompromised or neutral. Indeed, its pragmatic rather than ideological nature can in itself be seen as conforming to institutional and governmental agendas. However, we feel that teaching students explicitly about genres and writing cultures provides an opportunity for exploring issues that matter. Hopefully this will be an evolving process in which subject experts become increasingly proactive in attending to their students' learning through writing development.

Offering subject-based writing instruction certainly offers space for a critical or AcLits agenda, but equally it provides opportunities for the manifestation of the humanistic impulses that lie behind so much writing work. We believe that work of all kinds can take place within a WiD framework, and that this chameleonesque character is part of its appeal. Disciplinary writing development is not an area where any model need dominate, and we hope that this volume will be of interest to all academics no matter where they are based on their campuses. Whilst WiD lays stress on the role of discipline-based academics, the case studies in Part II of this book emphasise the fundamental role of writing developers and learning technologists in collaborating with subject experts to bring about pedagogic change.

▶ *Writing in the Disciplines*: The argument of the volume

Part I: Contexts

Part I of this book locates British discipline-based writing development in the context of international responses to this issue. In Chapter 1 Christiane Donahue, Director of the Institute for Writing and Rhetoric at Dartmouth College, surveys North American research on teaching disciplinary literacies. She provides a critical overview of traditional approaches to writing development, and through her analysis of findings from recent longitudinal research projects, Donahue makes the case for disciplinary rather than generic writing development.

In Chapter 2, Emily Purser from the University of Wollongong discusses recent trends in Australia, where learning developers have become increasingly alert to the effectiveness of embedding academic literacies instruction within disciplinary contexts. Purser's introduction to the Australian pedagogic approach "Developing Academic Literacy in Context" (DALiC) is important because this method of teaching writing alongside disciplinary knowledge influences a range of chapters in Parts II and III, including numbers 5, 6, 8, and 13.

These two international perspectives are followed by a UK view from Katherine Harrington, a writing specialist based at London Metropolitan University. Harrington points out that academics teaching in the UK are already inevitably involved in disciplinary writing development, not least through their attention to learning issues such as assessment. In Chapter 3, she shows how the work academics are already doing to design effective formative and summative assessments can be harnessed to support students in developing confidence and competence as writers in their fields.

Part II: Collaborating to support student writers

Part II reports on eight examples of discipline-based writing development in UK universities. These case studies of WiD work discuss re-designing curricula, giving feedback to writers, addressing widening participation through the creation of inclusive teaching strategies, and other issues of contemporary concern. The strategies for supporting student writers within their subject studies presented here are informative for all academics because they can be adapted and integrated into other disciplinary contexts. Each case study is influenced by the disciplinary culture from which it comes, and the varying formats reflect the flexibility that is integral to WiD work.

In Chapter 4, Ursula Wingate, lecturer in language in education at King's College London, reflects on her experiences of collaborating with academic staff, and she compares the effectiveness of "embedded" disciplinary writing development with "add on" approaches that supplement students' subject learning with a separated academic writing component. Wingate argues strongly for the former approach. In Chapter 5, Steve Foster, a Law expert, and Mary Deane, a writing developer from Coventry University, suggest strategies for enhancing students' legal writing. In Chapter 6, Dave Horne, a Geography specialist, and Kelly Peake, a writing developer from Queen Mary University of London, offer ideas for improving Geography students' writing. In Chapter 7, a team from the London Metropolitan University Business department, Myrtle Emmanuel, Debbie Holley, Linda Johnson, and Sandra Sinfield, describe their collaboration with the writing developer Peter O'Neill to support students' use of disciplinary discourse.

In Chapter 8, Peter Samuels, a mathematics education expert, and Deane suggest strategies for helping doctoral candidates in the field of Maths gain the confidence to produce journal articles before completion of their theses. In Chapter 9, Birgit Schippers, a Politics specialist, and Jonathan Worley, a writing developer from Saint Mary's University College Belfast, discuss ways of engaging students with subject-based genres. In Chapter 10, Dipti Bhagat, a design expert, and O'Neill share methods for enhancing Design students' writing. Finally, in Chapter 11 a group of colleagues from Nottingham Trent University, Rebecca Bell, Sarah Broadberry, and Julius Ayodeji, put WiD on trial to assess the usefulness of this approach in different disciplinary contexts.

Constraints of space mean that many innovative examples of disciplinary writing development cannot be represented here, but this cross-section of British higher education institutions gives an indication of the different pressures and opportunities facing academics working to foster students' disciplinary writing. These case studies show that WiD work is taking place at both research-intensive and more teaching-orientated institutions. The chapters also indicate that whilst most writing development takes place at the undergraduate level, the ever-expanding postgraduate population can also benefit from WiD work.

Part III: WiD and the institution

Part III widens the book's focus from examples of WiD work to discussion of the locations in which disciplinary writing development might be rooted in UK higher education institutions. In Chapter 12, John Bean, Professor of Writing and Assessment at Seattle University offers a North American perspective on the increasingly key issue of professional development for academics in the disciplines, focusing on effective use of staff workshops for promoting curricular and pedagogic change. He makes a powerful case for the need to promote time for thinking about these issues, not only within a single course, but also across degree programmes and departments. Bean shares practical and theoretical advice which will be useful to those in the UK who are responsible for organising professional development workshops for academics.

In Chapter 13, Celine Llewellyn-Jones, Martin Agombar, and Deane explore the role of learning technologists in disciplinary writing development. They examine the crucial question of what makes an effective collaboration, and argue that learning technologists should not be considered as mere service providers, but rather as full participants in the dialogue that is necessary to bring about change. Given the likelihood that blended learning will be viewed increasingly as a panacea for universities, particularly in resource-scarce times, it is clearly wise for writing developers and subject experts to consider involving learning technologists in creating sustainable WiD initiatives.

In Chapter 14, Lisa Ganobcsik-Williams, the Head of Coventry University's Centre for Academic Writing, discusses the potential of writing centres for WiD work. She suggests that a writing centre in the UK might not look like the traditional student-facing US writing center, but could also promote institutional agendas such as academic staff development, pedagogic research, and the implementation of effective technological enhancements for teaching writing in the disciplines.

In the Conclusion, Deane and O'Neill suggest that WiD not only attempts to solve practical problems associated with the contemporary university, but also has the potential to make connections with long-standing, yet perhaps neglected, traditions of rhetoric. Attention to writing means attention to the art of persuasion, and educators should remember their responsibility to help students develop this competency in ethical ways so student writers can become engaged citizens able to take part fully in the discourse of a modern democratic society.

▶ Notes

1 On influences of the Australian DALiC approach, see Chapters 2, 5, 6, 8, and 13.
2 See Chapter 12, on disciplinary writing and curricula review.

▶ References

Bamberg, B. (2003) "Revision" in I. Clark (ed.) *Concepts in Composition: Theory and Practice in the Teaching of Writing* (Mahwah: Lawrence Erlbaum Associates) pp. 107–129.

Bazerman, C. (1988) *Shaping Written Knowledge: The Genre and Activity of the Experimental Article in Science* (Madison: University of Wisconsin Press).

Bazerman, C., Little, J., Chavkin, T., Fouquette, D., Bethel, L., and Garufis, J. (2005) *Writing Across the Curriculum: Reference Guides to Rhetoric and Composition* (Parlor Press and WAC Clearing House) <<http://wac.colostate.edu/books/bazerman_wac>>. Date accessed 23/01/2011.

Bean, J.C. (2001) *Engaging Ideas: The Professor's Guide to Integrating Writing, Critical Thinking, and Active Learning in the Classroom* (San Francisco: Jossey Bass).

Burke, K. (1950) *A Rhetoric of Motives* (Berkeley and Los Angeles: University of California Press).

Connors, R.J. (1997) *Composition-Rhetoric: Backgrounds, Theory and Pedagogy* (Pittsburgh: Pittsburgh press).

Crowley, S. (2003) "Composition is Not Rhetoric" *Enculturation* 5 (1) <<http://enculturation.gmu.edu/5_1/crowley.html>>. Date accessed 25/02/2010

Habinek, T. (2005). *Ancient Rhetoric and Oratory* (Malden: Blackwell).

Halloran, S.M. (1975) "On the End of Rhetoric, Classical and Modern" *College English* 36 (6): 621–631.

Halloran, S.M. (1982) "Aristotle's concept of Ethos, or If Not His Somebody Else's" *Rhetoric Review* 1 (1): 58–63.

Ivanic, R. (1998) *Writing and Identity: The Discoursal Construction of Identity in Academic Writing* (Amsterdam: John Benjamins).

Lea, M. and Street, B. (1998) "Student Writing in Higher Education: An Academic Literacies Approach" *Studies in Higher Education* 23 (2): 157–172.

Lillis, T.M. (1997) "New Voices in Academia? The Regulative Nature of Academic Writing Conventions" *Language and Education* 11 (3): 182–199.

Lillis, T.M. (2001) *Student Writing: Access, Regulation, Desire* (London: Routledge).

Lillis, T.M. (2006) "Moving towards an 'Academic Literacies' Pedagogy: Dialogues of Participation" in L. Ganobcsik-Williams (ed.), *Teaching Academic Writing in UK Higher Education* (Houndmills: Palgrave Macmillan), pp. 30–48.

McLeod, S. and Maimon, E. (2000) "Clearing the Air: WAC Myths and Realities" *College English* 62: 573–583.

Mitchell, S. and Evison, A. (2006) "Exploiting the Potential of Writing for Educational Change at Queen Mary, University of London" in L. Ganobcsik-Williams (ed.), *Teaching Academic Writing in UK Higher Education* (Houndmills: Palgrave Macmillan), pp. 68–84.

Monroe, J. (ed.) (2002) *Writing and Revising in the Disciplines* (Ithaca: Cornell University Press).

Monroe, J. (ed.) (2003) *Local Knowledges, Local Practices: Writing in the Disciplines at Cornell* (Pittsburgh: University of Pittsburgh Press).

Mullin, J.A. (2006) "Learning From – Not Duplicating – US Composition Theory and Practice" in L. Ganobcsik-Williams (ed.), *Teaching Academic Writing in UK Higher Education* (Houndmills: Palgrave Macmillan), pp. 167–179.

O'Neill, P. (2008) Using peer writing fellows in British universities: Complexities and possibilities [Special issue on Writing Fellows]. *Across the Disciplines*, 5 <<http://wac.colostate.edu/atd/fellows/oneill.cfm>>. Date accessed 26/02/2010.

Purser, E., Skillen, J., Deane, M., Donahue, J., and Peake, K. (2008) "Developing Academic Literacy in Context." *Zeitschrift Schreiben* <<http://www.zeitschrift-schreiben.eu>> Date accessed 13/07/2009.

Russell, D.R., Parker, M.L.J., Street, B., and Donahue, T. (2009) "Exploring Notions of Genre in 'Academic Literacies' and 'Writing Across the Curriculum' *Approaches Across Countries and Contexts*" in C. Bazerman, A. Bonini and D. Figueiredo (eds) *Genre in a Changing World* (Fort Collins: The WAC Clearing House and Parlor Press), pp. 395–423.

Street, B.V. (1995) *Social Literacies: Critical Approaches to Literacy Development, Ethnography and Education* (London: Longman).

Skillen, J., Trivett, N., Merten, M., and Percy, A. (1999) "Integrating the Instruction of Generic and Discipline Specific Skills into the Curriculum: A Case Study" *Cornerstones: Proceedings of the 1999 HERDSA Conference* (Canberra: HERDSA).

Wingate, U. (2006) 'Doing away with 'study skills.' *Teaching in Higher Education* 11: 457–469.

Young, A. and Fulwiler, T. (eds) (1986) *Writing Across the Disciplines: Research into Practice* (Upper Montclair: Boynton/Cook).

1 Cross-Cultural Approaches to Writing and Disciplinarity

Christiane Donahue

▶ Introduction

Academic writing has been established by many writing scholars as a powerful mode of thinking and knowledge production in the disciplines. Scientists, humanists, and social scientists do not just "write up" what they have worked on (Monroe, 2002), but in fact produce knowledge and understanding, as they write what will be read informally or formally by others, or even what might be read only by themselves. The relationships between writing and disciplinary knowledge are complex, and for students making their way through higher education (HE) even more so.

Some existing models of university writing instruction in the US, including the generic "introduction to college writing" model, the "autonomous literacy" model, and the contrastive rhetoric "features/conventions" model have been shown to be insufficient responses to university students' needs as they move through their studies. A deeper understanding has, therefore, become necessary. This must focus on using writing as discovery and as an epistemological tool to develop with students a meta-awareness of how academic conventions come to shape a field, but also to consider the shaping of the students themselves, as they resist or adapt those conventions. This chapter considers existing and new models, the theories from which they build, and the role longitudinal studies have played in helping us to recognise the development of writing expertise in relation to disciplinary knowledge.

▶ Contexts for teaching writing

The rhetoric of crisis concerning student writing focuses on a perceived lack of "basic skills" and a rapidly changing terrain cited as responsible for dumbing down students' abilities and even their cognitive processing—this, in spite of substantial research that shows no decline, over as much as a century, in students' writing abilities, level of error, or processing capacity (see for example Crowley, 1998, Lunsford and Lunsford, 2008). Whilst the call for work on students' writing skills reappears frequently in public discourse around the globe, there is no widespread agreement as to how that work should be carried out. Approaches are context-tied in ways that offer deep insight into the very nature of writing and disciplinarity.

The traditional US response to this question of student writing ability has been, since as early as the 1700s at Harvard, in the form of first-year writing courses designed to bridge the secondary/tertiary gap and to initiate students into the new demands of university writing. A close examination of the resultant "industry" of first-year composition has evolved as well. Crowley has suggested that 160,000 classes of first-year composition are offered each year in the US. This industry's components say a lot about the generalised understanding of writing and its instruction; faculty are most often poorly paid adjuncts or trained graduate students, and initially these adjuncts were in fields like English or Creative Writing, although the evolution of the field of composition studies has produced many PhDs in "composition" or "composition and rhetoric" in the past 20 years.

The ubiquitous first-year writing/first-year composition course has, over the past 40 years, evolved in four broad models that are sometimes seen as historical stages but in fact currently co-exist: the expressivist, the current-traditional, the socio-constructivist, and the "critical consciousness" models, each with its beliefs about what students need, how students learn, what the purpose of HE is, and what writing does for and with knowledge.

Composition scholars and teachers have also explored and developed "Writing Across the Curriculum" (WAC) and "Writing in the Disciplines" (WiD). These strands have been focused on integrating students into specific discourse communities. WAC embeds writing as a mode of learning into every discipline, using low stakes and high stakes writing as support of learning. This "writing to learn" approach is thus ubiquitous in a different way, aiming to "improve students' learning and writing (or learning through writing) in all university courses and departments (with some attention to school and adult education as well)" (Russell et al., 2008, p. 395). Inspired from the start by the work of Britton and colleagues, further developed in the US by scholars like Emig (1977), the "writing to learn" movement has taken four main shapes over time, as summarised by Bangert and colleagues (2004): writing as in itself learning; writing as an educative approximation of personally expressive and thus appropriative speech; writing as having an impact on learning that is moderated by context; and writing as affecting learning because it fosters "rehearsal, elaboration, organization, and self-monitoring" (p. 48). The initial write-to-learn work has also been critiqued, however, for its lack of critical distance and its tendency to confirm intuitive understandings of the writing-learning relationship (see for example Bangert et al., 2004), rather than building understanding from research.

The term WiD is also used, somewhat synonymously, but suggests greater attention to the relation between writing and learning in a specific discipline (Russell et al., 2008). The WiD strand, however, has been most often focused on integrating students into the discourse communities of their disciplines. WiD supports developing courses in "writing in…X discipline", offering faculty training, and studying textual practices, epistemologies and conventions tied to disciplines.

In keeping with the model of expert genres and communities into which students must be introduced or progressively initiated, at first work in this domain assumed an acculturation model: the disciplinary knowledge and its related literate conventions exist, and students are brought into them—compositionists studied the ways of being and conventions of a community and then taught them. Frequently this was painted as a discourse community model, with students making progress from novice to expert, from outsider to insider—a view supported by most US assessment models. The perspective is always one of progressive integration, moving from (simple) reproduction to (complex) production. Many studies of disciplinary work assume the experts are "pure purveyors of their disciplines" (Prior, 1998, p. 13) and thus the relationship with students becoming disciplinary members is uncomplicated.

Until fairly recently in US research, however, there had not been much analysis of students' actual literate activities as they evolve in their appropriation of disciplinary discourses; most of the research had focused on students entering into the university's first year or students exiting from the university into the workplace. Occasionally the focus had been on graduate students (see, for example, Prior, 1998, Berkenkotter and Huckin, 1995). Now, however, longitudinal studies are beginning to offer insights into what goes on in between these two stages (see the reference list of pages 26–9 for a list of the most well-known published longitudinal studies in the US).

▶ Critiques of current US models

Recent US scholarship suggests that the generic first-year course may miss the mark in both theory and practice. These studies have also begun to show the cracks in the acculturation model. At the same time, UK-centred criticism suggests that WAC and WiD developments might also need to be framed differently. As Russell and his colleagues have recently pointed out, while the US focus has largely remained on integration and acculturation, other countries with different research agendas and different evolutions focus differently; the UK, for example, has since the 1990s developed deep attention to critical language awareness and to student resistance in disciplinary contexts, not just in the first year. UK Academic Literacies work has contributed to the critique of a model that does not account for the student's role, the student's resistances, and for some (particularly, Theresa Lillis, 2001) the student's desires (see also Russell et al., 2008).

Carter's 1990 review of the novice-to-expert literature and the interrelatedness of the cognitive and social models set the stage for closer examination of the relationship between discipline-specific contexts and generalised writing knowledge. While he presents fairly linear stages of development from novice to expert, his model can be read as recursive both within one particular trajectory and across multiple trajectories in any individual's life. Novice-to-expert work on students' writing by Nancy Sommers (2008) suggests that the degree to which a student is immersed in the knowledge of a discipline directly affects the student's facility with writing. She notes that even in a discipline, students who specialise (her example is history) fare better than those who follow eclectic interests. There is some analysis in broader discussions about the way professionals in disciplines consider expertise and literate activity, accepting diversity and heterogeneity more willingly for their own work than for the work they expect of their students (Thaiss and Zawacki, 2006). This is further complicated by the fact that disciplinary specialists teach, in US HE, both general education (non-specialist) and discipline-specific (specialist) versions of their material.

While the most frequent US theoretical model has thus been the "discourse community" and acculturation models, Prior offers an excellent critique of the structuralist underpinnings of "community" versions of disciplines and disciplinary writing and speaking. Prior suggests that the notion of "discourse community" shaped theory and research on writing in the disciplines for a couple of decades (1998). Usually disciplines are seen, in this frame, as "unified social territories" or "abstract systems of codified knowledge". The discourse community model uses spatial metaphors, terms of norming, and governance modes for regulating interaction. He suggests that the structuralist underpinnings function in a cycle: theorists create a research space that transcends the everyday, decontextualise and abstract out information, and then govern with rules that explain the workings of the space. In the US history of the frame, it arrived at a key point in our history, when we wanted to resist cognitivist frames (Prior, 1998). But as Russell (1990) has pointed out, academia as a whole could not be considered a discourse community with shared linguistic forms. Carter (1990) furthers this critique by pointing out that the US discourse community model was heavily influenced by the sociolinguistic concept of the speech community, as initially developed by Hymes (1974). His "profoundly cultural and contextual" local theory of linguistic practice was taken up by compositionists studying disciplinary discourses and memberships (Carter, 1990, p. 278). The discourse community model has been criticised by others in the US field, notably Harris (1996) and Donahue (2008), for the way "community" was imagined as relatively homogeneous and apolitical; both suggest that we need to better capture the heterogeneous, multilayered, conflicted nature of both universities in general and disciplines in particular in which literate activities are the currency of knowledge production. These model shifts would have direct impact on teaching.

▶ New models of expertise

More recently, studies suggest replacing discourse communities (academia or discipline) with Lave and Wenger's "communities of practice' model" (1991). Prior defines Lave and Wenger's communities of practice concept as not defined by a discrete shared core of abstract knowledge and language that people internalise to become expert members; instead, a community of practice is an open, dynamic body, a "set of relations among persons, activity, and world, over time and in relation with other tangential and overlapping communities of practice" (1997, p. 21).

Community of practice is more subtle as a concept, and depicts participation in practices; activity is partially improvised by participants, partially by collective context (p. 20). The emphasis on practice, rather than on discourse, shifts us towards the more complex interaction Carter suggested between the local and the general.

Prior (1998) "learning...[as] generated by a person's embodied, active, perspectival trajectory through multiple, interpenetrated and internally stratified communities of practice in the world, communities that are themselves dynamic, open, and evolving" (1998, p. 99). In this model, "disciplinary enculturation thus refers not to novices being initiated, but to the continual processes whereby an ambiguous cast of relative newcomers and relative oldtimers (re)produce themselves, their practices, and their communities" (Prior, 1998, p. xi). Prior offers, again citing Lave and Wenger (1991), the term "mature" practices as a way to understand developed expertise.

Note that the emphasis is on the practices rather than the person, contrary to much previous US scholarship. We see disciplines, in this framework, as conflicted, shifting, fluid, "open networks, forged through relational activity" (p. 25), and thus a process rather than a product. Disciplines are thus quite human rather than "just a unified anonymous structure of linguistic, rhetorical, and epistemic conventions" (Prior, 1998, p. 22).

Carter (1990) suggests that the two central frames in writing studies for understanding the nature of this kind of expertise are the cognitive rhetoric frame and the social rhetoric frame. For Carter, the first posits expertise as general (and generalisable) knowledge and the ability to bring well-developed general strategies to any writing task; the second posits expertise as the acquisition of specialised local knowledge, "domain-specific knowledge attained through much experience within that domain" that enables a writer to participate in a discourse community (p. 269). Each of these perspectives differently influences our understanding of the writing expertise we seek to develop in students as they move into the knowledge-producing writing of their disciplines. In an educational model that requires students to study simultaneously as novices in some domains and as specialists in others, this contrast is particularly interesting. It has been the subject of much attention in US composition work (Russell and Yanez, 2003) and much work focused on "the degree to which a writer's success depends upon knowledge of context-specific discourse conventions" (Faigley, 1985; Broadhead and Freed, 1986; Doheny-Farina, 1989; Anson and Forsberg, 1990; Odell, 1992).

Carter suggested as early as 1990, predicting interests that would develop 15 years later, that in fact educational research supports the interaction of cognitive and social rhetoric as a more effective model of how expertise develops. He called for a "pluralistic" theory of expertise that accounts for the application of global strategies that can be applied across contexts as a starting point in any new context in which a writer has not yet developed expertise. He also called for the replacement of those global strategies with "fluid performance that is seldom based on analytic, conscious deliberation" (p. 272) over time and experience. The general strategies support the initial experiences with specialised discourses; they also allow writers to be more flexible in their expertise, not relying only on local knowledge (p. 274). We are no longer, here, in the realm of expertise as the acquisition of discipline-specific conventions, but in the domain of rhetorical flexibility, the hallmark of advanced literacy, a flexibility that includes both versatile use and the ability to analyse rhetorical variation. How, then, might student writers develop their abilities into expert disciplinarity and appropriate the scientific writing of their fields? The model enables a different way of thinking about developing expertise, one that affords transfer of writing knowledge.

▶ Transfer of writing knowledge: Learning from longitudinal studies

As we have seen, the work on discourse community alternatives offers ways to insightfully critique the generic and compulsory first-year US writing course, as well as the models of writing-disciplinary knowledge connections (including Beaufort, 2007, Crowley, 1998, Downs and Wardle, 2007, Smit, 2004). Two recent parallel developments in US scholarship have furthered this questioning in useful ways: the growth of longitudinal studies of student writing in various forms, and the attention to work in the field of knowledge transfer.

Longitudinal studies tracking students' writing across their college experience offer new sources of data about writing and knowledge at the university. Results from work by Donahue and others on longitudinal studies in the US allow us to question the tradition of a generic Level 1 writing course and the modelling of both writing to learn and WiD models (e.g. Sommers and Saltz, 2004, Wardle, 2007). These studies (which are discussed in more detail below) are not all equal in breadth, depth, or methodological soundness, but they are laying the groundwork for broadly framed understandings about knowledge transfer. They reveal that writing is not perceived by students as a generalisable skill; that students' pre-existing conceptions of writing from other contexts can prevent transfer; that students who transfer writing ability successfully begin "seeing texts as accomplishing social actions" and develop a "complex of activities" rather than a set of generalisable skills; that students whose teachers help them deconstruct the genres of their field transfer writing knowledge/ability more effectively; and that the kinds of scaffoldings required to support transfer differs from student to student. In fact, Wardle's work in particular is beginning to emphasise the transformational nature of effective transfer (Wardle, 2007, p. 69).

A considerable body of recent scholarship includes new attention to studies of knowledge transfer in general and offers insight into the writing-disciplines relationship in a way that helps us to understand the complicated nature of HE writing instruction. We do not know in any detail how students "transfer" or generalise what they learn about writing from one context to another. In order to understand the development of complex, advanced writing ability, however, this happens to be **the** essential question. It matters in particular in the US context because the passages between generic and specialised coursework and knowledge are more frequent in this HE milieu. We know that any program that hopes to establish coherence across its sequence of courses must not only develop a strong sense of how learners transfer knowledge from task to task, but must also determine the reasons learners fail to demonstrate positive transfer in new learning contexts, as well as developing the necessary conditions for learners to transfer knowledge successfully (Bransford et al., 2000; Haskell, 2001). Research further suggests that the transfer of knowledge depends on specific instructional framing, that is, situations that emphasise meta-cognition, scaffolded learning, a motive for learning, and sufficient time for the learning to "take" (Dias et al., 1999; Bransford et al., 2000; Haskell, 2001).

Research suggests that students cannot transfer knowledge when classroom learning does not connect to the rest of the world and when abilities are associated only with the context in which they were learned (Bjork and Richardson-Klavhen, 1989; Eich, 1985). All of our questioning about writing, knowledge, disciplines, and connections across earlier learning and university learning rest on these questions of knowledge transfer.

Transfer is more likely to occur in particular contexts which we can encourage:

- When first and following tasks are similar (Bransford et al., 2000).
- When similarities between the situations are made explicit and "affordances" for transfer are present in the next situation (Tuomi-Gröhn and Engeström, 2003).
- When initial learning is not rushed.
- When learners can explicitly abstract principles from a situation (Gick and Holyoak, 1983).
- When material is taught through analogy or contrast.
- When learners engage in self-reflection and mindfulness (Langer, 1992, Bereiter, 1997, Bransford, 2000).
- When the learning of new material is scaffolded (Dias et al., 1999).
- When teachers provide work that is appropriately challenging to students' current ability levels, drawing on students' zones of proximal development (Alsup and Bernard-Donals, 2002; Jaxon, 2003).
- When learners are "supported to participate in an activity system that encourages collaboration, discussion, and some form of 'risk taking' " (Guile and Young, 2003, p. 74).
- When learners "have opportunities to share and be inspired by a common motive for undertaking a specific learning task" (Guile and Young, 2003, p. 74).

We know as well that in order to afford transfer, learning must take place in "real" contexts: "writing might be expected to influence learning to the degree that it is an authentic act of personal meaning-making" (Bangert et al., 2004, p. 31). The relationship to situated learning (Brown et al., 1989, p. 32) is equally clear; because learning is always situated, always in-use rather than autonomous, we cannot encourage transfer by focusing on a-contextual skills. Nor can we expect school-based learning to produce the same effects as "authentic" tasks (Brown et al., 1989, p. 34). What they describe as cognitive apprenticeship builds from principles of transfer: new tasks must be embedded in familiar ones, affirming existing knowledge; heuristics function differently in different tasks; and active engagement in developing tools and approaches shifts the focus to students' appropriation of the work and values in question (p. 38). And finally, the level of meta-cognition is cited as central to enabling "learners to deploy cognitive strategies flexibly" (Bangert et al., 2004, p. 32), which is one of the key features of learning for transfer. Many of these features exist in our writing courses, but often not intentionally; their effectiveness is thus not fully exploited.

In a longitudinal study that took place at Harvard University from 2000 to 2004, Sommers studied 90 students' writing across 4 years. Sommers has pointed out that in each new context a student faces, the student's expertise and knowledge are critical for the writing. This result fits larger patterns seen in other longitudinal studies. She has focused in particular recently on students in the field of history: in the first year, she established that students are challenged by the novelty of this new kind of writing, the difficulty, and the sheer number of tasks, while by the fourth year, she was able to show that student success in history writing could be attributed to a combination of factors: frequent opportunities to write; immersion in the subject; explicit frequent instruction in the discipline's methods; commitment to learning both method and content; and interest in pursuing the questions of the field.

These features were common across different disciplines. Among her results, Sommers points out that students "who prosper as writers...cultivate a desire to enter disciplinary debates, to find their place in an academic exchange, with something to gain and something to give; when students don't know the method in one discipline, they are less likely to look for disciplinary connections elsewhere" (2008, pp. 155–56).

This notion of disciplinary framing as tightly linked to writing is one of the major points in the broader move to understand writing as socially situated rather than generic. Wardle suggests, based on her 2-year longitudinal study of seven students moving from generic first-year writing to more specific second-year contexts, that the unified "academic discourse" (what is sometimes, in Europe, called "scientific discourse") so often posited as a first step in US universities does not exist (2007). The misconceptions of writing that her study uncovered include: that writing is independent of content; that "writing" is about syntax and mechanics; and that "writing" can be taught in a non-content-driven context and then unproblematically applied in new contexts—the very basis of many US first-year composition courses. In fact, Wardle suggests, academic discourse needs conceptualising based on which content, genre, activity, context, or audience is in play. But teachers of first-year college writing are in fact usually trained in literature, and fall back on those models of what "writing" might be. Wardle suggests, as do many of the authors of longitudinal studies, that students need to learn within the new discipline—to pay close attention to what "counts" in that discipline. What might be added to that is an understanding that it isn't just a question of replicating "what counts" but of affecting it and interacting with it (Bazerman, 1981; Russell, 1995; Prior, 1997).

Additional critique is offered by Beaufort, who indicts current composition teaching, in which "writing becomes writing for the sake of a writing class, rather than writing for the sake of intellectual pursuits" (2007, p. 12). Beaufort's stated goal is to improve the enterprise of college level writing instruction. What role can composition play in preparing a student, she asks, for the rest of his or her courses? Beaufort argues for "a writing curriculum that consistently, logically fosters developmental growth in writers" (p. 103). It seeks to inform both teaching and, indirectly, assessment, reminding us that "progress towards expertise may proceed slowly" (p. 102), thus detailing what many teachers know intuitively, but for which they have not always been able to provide evidence to colleagues or administrators.

Composition instruction is critiqued from several perspectives: it is too close to English or creative writing or cultural studies, cut off from intellectual substance, disconnected from the tasks of future university courses, and it fosters a sense of writing as generic skill. Composition may well introduce students to the writing of English discourse communities, Beaufort writes, but does not offer students ways to reflect on the specific contexts in which they are working (2007). Beaufort singles out in particular the lack of attention to subject matter or "content knowledge" in composition, a critique that echoes the concerns of decades of writing in the disciplines scholars and teachers working to convince their colleagues that students cannot learn writing apart from content. Subject matter, Beaufort reminds us, citing Kaufer and Young (1993), is wedded to writing constraints, skills used, and genres. But WiD approaches are equally subject to critique. Courses in this domain (including freshman seminar courses and writing intensive courses) tend towards writing to show learning or knowledge, Beaufort suggests, and academic faculty are unable to uncover and teach the tacit knowledge about writing that they have naturalised over time.

My own longitudinal study (Donahue, 2004–2008) suggests that linear development is certainly not the path students' writing takes but rather that the evolution of the writing is complex and complicated, and that content, assignment, reading, teacher emphasis, and student's disciplinary affiliation are interrelated. The study has collected all informal and formal writing from 20 students from a variety of disciplines for 4 years. We analysed their organisation strategies, their positioning, their macro-and micro-coherence strategies, including intertextuality, enunciative choices, number/type of error, forms of argument, influence of length and formatting, and so on. We also interviewed students twice, in year two and year four, and surveyed them at the end of each year.

While the data analysis is not yet complete, some preliminary trends are intriguing for the discussion here. In the first year, students describe writing criteria as arbitrary, associated with different faculty members and their requirements. By the fourth year, students articulate these criteria as related to the discipline of a course. Few students report usefulness of the first-year writing course; most point to formative pre-university periods, both positive and negative. In the texts we have studied, students' writing increases in its facility with handling sources and in its forms of intertextuality. Students, in this writing, do not integrate or acculturate so much as they negotiate with and in the knowledge and conventions they are working to appropriate.

Another promising initial result is related to students' meta-narratives. While the student writers in our study do not appear to evolve in their conscious understanding of literacy, knowledge, and disciplinarity, although certainly they acquire a certain facility and a set of ways of articulating experience, in their written texts their relationship to knowledge as represented in their source use and interactions changes substantially. These observations suggest that expertise is perhaps developed with less meta-awareness than is usually recognised.

▶ Conclusion: Learning from recent developments in France and the US

Recent non-US writing approaches have also shown how the generic approach can be bypassed. In France, where this issue is currently under debate in the context of reforms in HE, research from linguistics and education about writing is embedded in layers of disciplinary work. Extensive research has been carried out on voice, polyphony, intertextuality, research writing, and writing intersecting university and internship or professional programs at the undergraduate and graduate levels in different disciplines (see, for example, Boch, 1999, Boch and Grossman, 2001, Daunay, 2002, Donahue, 2007, Flottum, 2007, Guibert, 2001, Reuter, 2001, Reuter and Lahanier-Reuter, 2008). Additionally, the field that is evolving in France around HE writing is one in which writing and disciplinarity are symbiotic (*la didactique de l'écrit*). All research about writing in HE is thus connected to disciplinary construction.

What do these various points suggest about working with students? At least a few alternate models are available. I will describe just two, not as "the" models, but as possibilities that indicate potential future models for writing instruction embedded in HE, working from what we know from the research cited. Both models suggest a different understanding of writing, as essentially always disciplinary, always tightly entwined with knowledge in a field.

The first model is practiced at many US institutions where some version of a composition course and a "first-year seminar" course are required of students. I have experienced such a combination at two institutions, Dartmouth College and the University of Maine-Farmington (UMF). In each case, students take both a "writing" course and a writing-based first-year seminar, although at Dartmouth these are in sequence and at UMF they can be taken in either order. The key is that the "writing" course is generally taught by writing specialists and the seminar, by faculty from across the disciplines. When these two groups are in some communication, the likelihood of transferring the learning from one term to the other increases, and the faculty themselves see writing differently.

The second model, and a new development, is the first-year writing course or which the material is in the discipline of composition studies. The notion of discipline moves to the centre in quite a different way, as the course both studies and produces writing. Smit, in *The End of Composition Studies* (2004), has suggested that composition as an endeavour is always in a crisis of purpose, and that shifting our roles to facilitators and minimising our importance as writing teachers will be the most effective future path. In fact, while Smit was not dealing directly with writing in the disciplines, we see easily how a shift to disciplinary writing would encompass what he suggests.

These two models begin to respond to what the longitudinal studies are suggesting: that writing and disciplinary knowledge are embedded in each other, that expertise develops in multi-layered, overlapping recursive activities; and above all that instruction related to writing in HE should not be delivered outside the disciplines—which are themselves equally heterogeneous and constructed.

In practice, this means that courses and programs focused on writing in HE will need to attend to several key factors as they take shape, grow, and evolve:

- Faculty must work together, know each other's work, and know how to interact about that work.
- Students' meta-awareness must be the primary focus of instruction.
- Instruction must keep authentic meaning-making as its primary mode of work.
- Faculty must have opportunities to discuss and develop their own work as writers.
- Writing conventions must be taught as manifestations of deeper epistemological issues.

These features will enable courses to avoid a generic, autonomous model that delivers highly partial and relatively limited writing instruction to students whose writing lives are bound up in disciplinary ways of being.

▶ References

Alexander, P.A. and Murphy, P.K. (1999) "Nurturing the seeds of transfer: A domain-specific perspective" *International Journal of Educational Research* 31: 561–576.

Alsup, Janet and Michael Bernard-Donals (2002) "The Fantasy of the 'Seamless Transition.' " In T. Thompson (ed.), *Teaching Writing in High School and College.* Indiana: NCTE, pp. 115–135.

Anson, C. (1988) "Toward a multidimensional model of writing in the academic disciplines." In D. Jolliffe (ed.), *Writing in Academic Disciplines.* Norwood: Ablex, pp. 1–36.

Anson, C. and L. Forsberg (1990) "Moving beyond the academic community." *Written Communication* 7 (2), 200–231.

Bangert, R., M. Hurley, and B. Wilkinson. (2004) "The effects of school-based writing-to-learn interventions on academic achievement: A meta-analysis." *Educational Researcher* 74 (1): 29–58.

Bazerman, C. (1981) "What written knowledge does: Three examples of academic discourse." *Philosophy of the Social Sciences* 11: 361–388.

Beaufort, A. (2007) *College Writing and Beyond: A New Framework for University Writing Instruction.* Logan: Utah State University Press.

Bereiter, C. (1997) "Situated cognition and how to overcome it." In D. Kirshner and J.A. Whitson (eds), *Situated Cognition: Social, Semiotic, and Psychological Perspectives.* Hillsdale: Erlbaum, pp. 281–300.

Berkenkotter, C. and T. Huckin (1995) *Genre Knowledge in Disciplinary Communities: Cognition/Culture/Power.* Mahwah: Lawrence Erlbaum Associates.

Bjork, R.A. and A. Richardson-Klavhen (1989) "On the puzzling relationship between environment context and human memory." In C. Izawa (ed.), *Current Issues in Cognitive Processes* 19. Hillsdale: Erlbaum, pp. 313–344.

Boch, F. (1999) *La tâche d'écriture et de réécriture à l'université – La prise de notes, entre texte source et texte cible.* Villeneuve d'Ascq: Presses Universitaires du Septentrion.

Boch, F. and Grossmann, F. (eds) (2001) "De l'usage des citations dans le discours théorique: des constats aux propositions didactiques." *Lidil* 24: 91–112.

Bransford, J.D., Brown, A.L., and Cocking, R.R. (2000) "Committee on developments in the science of learning, commission on behavioral and social sciences and education, and national research council." In J.D. Bransford, A.L. Brown, and R.R. Cocking (eds), *How People Learn: Brain, Mind, Experience, and School.* Washington, DC: National Academy Press.

Broadhead, G. and R. Freed (1986) *The Variables of Composition: Process and Product in a Business Setting.* Urbana: CCCC.

Brown, J., A. Collins, and P. Duguid (1989) 'Situated cognition and the culture of learning.' *Educational Researcher* 18 (1): 32–42.

Carroll, L.A. (2002) *Rehearsing New Roles: How College Students Develop as Writers.* Carbondale: Southern Illinois UP.

Carter, M. (1990) 'The idea of expertise: An exploration of cognitive and social dimensions of writing.' *CCC* 41: 265–286.

Crowley, S. (1998) *Composition in the University.* Pittsburgh: University of Pittsburgh Press.

Daunay, B. (2002) *Eloge de la paraphrase,*coll. Essais et savoirs, Presses Universitaires de Vincennes.

Dias, P., Freedman, A., Medway, P., and Paré, A. (1999) "Virtual realities: Transitions from university to workplace writing." In Dias, P., Freedman, A., Medway, P., and Paré, A. (eds), *Worlds Apart: Acting and Writing in Academic and Workplace Contexts.* Mahwah: Lawrence Erlbaum Associates, pp. 201–221.

Doheny-Farina, S. (1989) "A case study of one adult writing in academic and nonacademic discourse communities." In Carolyn B. Matalene (ed.), *Worlds of Writing: Teaching and Learning in Discourse Communities of Work.* New York: Random, pp. 17–42.

Donahue, C. (2007) "Reformuler la reformulation: reprises-modification, négociation, et literate arts, vus dans des textes d'étudiants en première année universitaire." *Recherches Linguistiques* 29: 180–192.

Donahue, C. (2008) *Ecrire à l'Université: Analyse Comparée en France et aux Etats-Unis.* Villeneuve d'Ascq: Presses Universitaires du Septentrion.

Downs, D. and E. Wardle (2007) "Teaching about writing, righting misconceptions: (Re)Envisioning 'first-year composition' as 'introduction to writing studies'." *College Composition and Communication* 58 (4): 552–584.

Eich, E. (1985) 'Context, memory, and integrated item/context imagery.' *Journal of Experimental Psychology* 11: 764–770.

Emig, J. (1977) *The Composing Processes of Twelfth Graders.* Indiana: NCTE Press.

Faigley, L. (1985) 'Nonacademic writing: The social perspective.' In L. Odell and D. Goswami (eds), *Writing in Non-Academic Settings.* New York: Guilford, pp. 231–248.

Flottum, K. (2007) 'Argumentation through author presence and polyphony in the genre of the research article.' *Argumentation in (Con)text.* University of Bergen, 2007-01-04–2007-01-06. Full text: https://www.aic.uib.no/program.php

Gick, M. and Holyoak, K.J. (1983) "Schema induction and analogical transfer." *Cognitive Psychology* 15: 1–38.

Guibert, R. (2001) "Citer et se situer. L'apprentissage de l'écriture avec les discours d'autrui." *Lidil 24 Apprendre à citer le discours d'autrui.*

Guile, D. and Young, M. (2003) "Transfer and transition from vocational education: Some theoretical considerations." In Tuomi-Gröhn, T. and Engeström, Y. (2003) *Between School and Work: New Perspectives on Transfer and Boundary-Crossing.* New York: Pergamon, pp. 63–81.

Harris, J. (1996) *A Teaching Subject: Composition Since 1966.* Upper Saddle River: Prentice-Hall.

Haskell, R. (2001) *Transfer of Learning: Cognition, Instruction, and Reasoning.* San Diego: Academic Press.

Hymes, D. (1974) *Foundations in Sociolinguistics: An Ethnographic Approach.* Philadelphia: University of Pennsylvania Press.

Jaxon, K. (2003) "And now a word from the sponsors: The university, high school, and student identity." *CCCC* Presentation 2003.

Kaufer and Young (1993) 'Writing in the Content Areas: Some Theoretical Complexities.' In Odell, l. (ed.) *Theory and Practice in the Teaching of Writing: Rethinking the Discipline.* Carbondale: Southern Illinois University, pp. 71–108.

Langer, J.A. (1992) "Speaking of knowing: Conceptions of understanding in academic disciplines." In Herrington, A. and Moran, C. (eds), *Writing, Teaching, and Learning in the Disciplines.* New York: Modern Language Association, pp. 69–85.

Lave, J. and Wenger, E. (1991) *Situated Learning: Legitimate Peripheral Participation.* Cambridge, UK: Cambridge University Press.

Lillis, T. (2001) *Student Writing: Access, Regulation, Desire.* London: Routledge.

Lunsford, A. and Lunsford, K. (2008) "Mistakes are a fact of life: A national comparative study." *CCC* 59 (4): 781–806.

Monroe, J. (ed.) (2002) *Writing and Revising the Disciplines.* Ithaca: Cornell University Press

Odell, L. (1992) "Context-specific ways of knowing and the evaluation of writing." In A. Herrington and C. Moran (eds), *Writing, Teaching, and Learning in the Disciplines* . New York: MLA, 86–98.

Prior, P. (1997) "Literate activity and disciplinarity." *Mind, Culture, and Activity* 4: 275–295.

Prior, P. (1998) *Writing/Disciplinarity: A Sociohistoric Account of Literate Activity in the Academy.* Mahwah: Lawrence Erlbaum Associates.

Reuter, Y. (2001) "Je suis comme un autrui qui doute. Le discours des autres dans l'écrit de recherche en formation." *Lidil 24 Apprendre à citer le discours d'autrui* 24: pp. 13–27.

Reuter, Y. and Lahanier-Reuter, D. (2008) "Presentation of a few concepts for analyzing writing in relation to academic disciplines." *L1 Educational Studies in Language and Literature* 7950: 47–57.

Russell, D.R. (1995) "Activity theory and its implications for writing instruction." In J. Petraglia (ed.), *Reconceiving Writing, Rethinking Writing Instruction.* Hillsdale: Erlbaum, pp. 51–78.

Russell, D.R. and Yanez, A. (2003) " 'Big picture people rarely become historians": Genre systems and the contradictions of general education.' In C. Bazerman and D. Russell (eds), *Writing Selves/Writing Societies.* http://wac.colostate. edu/books/selves_societies/.

Russell, D. (1990) "Writing across the curriculum in historical perspective." *College English* 52: 52–73.

Russell, D., Lea, M., Street, B., J. Parker, and C. Donahue (2008) "Exploring notions of genre in 'academic literacies' and 'writing across the curriculum': Approaches across countries and contexts." In Charles Bazerman, Adair Bonini, and Débora Figueiredo (eds), *Genre in a Changing World.* Fort Collins: Parlor Press.

Smit, D. (2004) *The End of Composition Studies.* Carbondale: Southern Illinois University Press.

Sommers, N. (2008) 'The call of research: A longitudinal view of writing development.' *CCC* 60(1): 152–164.

Sommers, N. and Saltz, L. (2004) 'The novice as expert: Writing the freshman Year.' *CCC* 56 (1): 124–149.

Thaiss, C. and Zawacki, T. (2006) *Engaged Writers, Dynamic Disciplines.* Portsmouth: Boynton-Cook.

Tuomi-Gröhn, T. and Engeström, Y. (2003) "Conceptualizing transfer: From standard notions to developmental perspectives." In T. Tuomi-Gröhn, and Y. Engeström (eds), *Between School and Work: New Perspectives on Transfer and Boundary-Crossing.* New York: Pergamon, pp. 19–38.

Wardle, E. (2007) "Understanding 'transfer' from FYC: Preliminary results of a longitudinal study." *Writing Program Administration* 31 (1/2): 65–85.

2 Developing Academic Literacy in Context: Trends in Australia

Emily Purser

▶ Introduction

As the diversity of the student population grows in the tertiary education sector, and communications become more multi-modal, the nature of "literacy" in university curricula both changes and needs more explicit development. We cannot assume that students have, or can develop in the given time, an appropriate level of academic literacy without writing being given careful attention. Various models for the development of students' academic language, including their writing, are in play and under scrutiny, but the broad trend seems to be away from extra-curricular attempts to address students' literacy development, and towards seeing this as a responsibility best shared and addressed within the disciplines.

The term "Developing Academic Literacy in Context" was used to label a specific collaborative project (DALiC) through which a group of writing specialists from different countries (many of whom are represented in this volume) shared experience of improving students' academic learning in specific disciplines (see Purser et al., 2008, for an account of this project. The focus in this chapter is on the thinking behind the approach—what is, and what drives collaborative, curriculum-integrated literacy development, what difference it makes to student learning, and how opportunities for it can be created. After a general account of why we focus on contexts where language is experienced as a problem, the chapter reflects on specific challenges and successful practices at a university where a curriculum-integration approach to academic literacy development has been taken for over a decade.

▶ The Australian experience: background and directions

We all want to help students get the most out of their studies and ensure disciplinary knowledge is maintained, but what educational practice looks like on the ground is shaped by so many different perspectives, motivations, and voices that there never will be "one way" to teach academic writing. Trends in teaching practice respond to a range of contextual factors and Current conditions. These include what incoming students do and do not seem to know about academic learning and presentation in the forms expected in higher education (HE). The issues also include what educators know about language communication, the degree to which insights into language development influence educational practice and policy, the current goals, directives, and incentives of employing institutions around the management of diversity, language proficiency, and teaching innovation. Other issues are the policies, legislation, and funding arrangements of national governments in relation to the provision of educational services, the recruitment of students, and various other aspects of social welfare, employment, international trade, and "nation building".

Government in Australia, as in the UK, has pursued an agenda to significantly increase the number of socio-economically disadvantaged people participating in HE. Individual universities develop internal policy frameworks to manage the anticipated greater diversity, and to recognise and reward teachers who devise effective ways of supporting student learning. External agencies monitoring teaching quality (such as the Australian Universities Quality Agency or the Quality Assurance Agency for HE in the UK) look for evidence that institutions of HE are providing adequate support for students. The next round of teaching quality "audits" by AUQA/TEQSA (Tertiary Education Quality and Standards Agency) will include questions about "transition", in response to a recent review of HE (Department of Education, Employment and Workplace Relations, 2008). This theme focuses particularly on the experience of students in their first year of study at undergraduate level, and how well universities are or are not providing what students need in order to learn successfully and remain at university. The Bradley/DEEWR review brings significant implications for literacy development work in universities, as it recommends not only change in the student population, but also greater institutional accountability for recognising and adapting to their needs. It contributes significantly to the current policy framework to focus on students who, for whatever reason, find themselves in an educational environment for which they feel linguistically and culturally unprepared.

As well as the impact that social inclusion or widening participation agendas have on literacy development work, another important factor in the cultural and linguistic changes going on in HE is internationalisation. Very many students are entering the system with backgrounds in very different educational systems and only "intermediate" proficiency in English. This is a global trend in HE, but in Australia it also has variable and sometimes controversial links to the government's immigration agenda and the business case of the international education "industry" (recent policy changes made to redress the sorts of issues recounted succinctly in ABC radio's *Rear Vision* (2009) are finding a very mixed response). The view of how much, and how, literacy development support for international students should be provided by universities is influenced also by legislation relating specifically to "educational services to overseas students" (*ESOS Act*), and by the fact that postgraduate coursework programs (where most international students in Australian universities are enrolled) come under the same eye as undergraduate coursework programs (overseen by the Minister for "Jobs, Skills and Workplace Relations" rather than the Minister concerned with supporting research-oriented HE).

While teaching practice in HE is influenced by the political environment (articulated in various discourses on equity, internationalisation, student transition, retention, graduate qualities, and employability), the specific goals and directives at national and institutional levels may or may not themselves be strongly influenced by what experienced teachers and researchers of language actually know about its nature and development. The code of practice relating to the *ESOS Act* (2000), for example, recommends a "study skills" centre on every campus, as a basic standard for the provision of resources for international university students. However, on the ground, it has long been recognised that extra-curricular activities are neither the only nor the most key strategy needed to assist students in the transition into academic life and literacy practices to achieve general learning goals or satisfactory progress towards meeting the learning outcomes of particular courses (see for example Cargill, 1999).

Practice is sometimes far ahead of policy. Arguments about the need for a curriculum-integrated approach to academic language and learning development have, however, now reached national policy level in the form of a set of "good practice principles" (DEEWR, 2009), which has been developed through consultation with various providers of language education within universities and a review of the literature. As of 2011, the auditing of teaching quality in Australian universities is also including questions about how the English language proficiency development of students is being managed, based on the *Good Practice*

Principles, which strongly emphasise the need to integrate academic language and learning development work into the design and delivery of mainstream curricula in the disciplines. These *Principles* were conceived specifically with the language development needs of students from non-English speaking backgrounds in mind (who now make up a very high proportion of the student populations in most Australian universities), but are considered to apply broadly to the academic literacy development needs of all students.

The curriculum-integrated approach to learning development practice is also endorsed by the national campaign of a senior fellow at the Australian Learning and Teaching Council, promoting "transition pedagogy" (Kift, 2009). And, in an interesting sign of the *Zeitgeist* in tertiary literacy education, positions relating to literacy teaching in universities tend now to be advertised in terms of the applicant's ability to lead collaboration with colleagues in the disciplines in order to bring about improved learning outcomes for students, especially those in their first year (at university or in Australia).

Other factors influencing perceptions of, and responses to, educational problems include funding, the knowledge and ability of incoming students, established traditions, and what is known from experience in particular institutions and from theory. In terms of funding, a complex and ever-changing set of requirements frame any institution's direction in recruiting and supporting students. Fees charged for education are determined and regulated differently for domestic and international students, affecting the mix, and there is often no simple or transparent relationship between fees paid by international students and the development of appropriate academic support for their learning. Development and demonstration of quality teaching is increasingly funded indirectly, like research, by external adjudicators (e.g. the Australian Learning and Teaching Council, which is funded by DEEWR), through a competitive grants-for-projects basis.

Universities thus compete with one another for government funds via grants and annual "star ratings", which are based on evidence-based quality assessment of both research and teaching around specific performance criteria. In terms of students' ability to grasp and participate in the local institutional traditions of academic work, the less we can assume about what students already know, the more it becomes the teaching they experience that will help or hinder their rapid development. Institutions need to anticipate and prevent causes of disengagement and failure, and provide appropriate "support", but they also need to carefully consider what "support" is, because the word can be interpreted in various ways. It might be considered to be an additional aid, a kind of "crutch" for individuals in occasional times of crisis, or it might be considered as a synonym for normal teaching practice facilitating students' use of resources to complete intelligently designed tasks. How the word, and the educational problems it addresses, are initially defined have implications for the subsequent development of academic literacy. Providing literacy development support when and where students need it involves both helping students understand the nature of academic work, and helping teachers across the disciplines recognise the linguistic nature of academic learning and teaching, so they design tasks, resources, and strategies that enable substantial literacy development.

Overall, in this period of rapid change in student populations, all "seems" well in terms of general direction, sharing of knowledge and planning. Some areas of funding for HE are actually increasing (remarkably, given recent history in Australia). Universities are busy reviewing their practices in relation to literacy development, making strategic recommendations for stronger performance in this area, and encouraging collaborative curriculum design in response to the challenges of a diverse student population and unpredictable prior experience of English and academic learning.

Institutions employ staff to specialise in academic language and learning development, as well as in the professional development of teachers and in learning technologies and design. Academic language support staff are increasingly sharing a general goal of developing academic literacy within the specific contexts of disciplinary learning, in both their theoretical discussions and in practice; their work is increasingly organised to align with institutional goals, which themselves increasingly reflect the arguments that literacy educators promote. The professional Association for Academic Language and Learning (AALL) is discussing and showcasing, through its online forum, its biannual conference, and its journal, examples of how the *Good Practice Principles* are being implemented in curriculum-integrated, discipline-specific literacy development work across the country. There seems to be a healthy mix of approaches being taken, projects being funded, and reports being written in relation to a large range of literacy practices. Innovations and best practices in teaching work for improved literacy development are shared across institutions (as a condition of project funding), and internally funded projects are increasingly being designed with a subsequent stage of national level funding in mind. There is interest in tertiary level teaching practice generally, and quite intense theorisation of literacy, language, and the social construction of knowledge is taking place. The time has probably never been riper for teachers to collaborate and integrate good literacy development practice into mainstream curricula. What happens on the ground, though, depends on a complex mix of factors, including how willing or able individuals are to collaborate.

▶ Challenges

The future of literacy development may theoretically be within the disciplines, but achieving best practice across the broad range of contexts is challenging. First, the demand for academic language development work is rising, often without an increase in staffing. Secondly, academic literacy is dynamic, as is the knowledge base about it. Thirdly, interdisciplinary work around literacy development depends on dialogue, which can be impeded by various factors, including limited understanding of language and education. The demand for teaching to focus on academic language development is rising as more academics across the disciplines find that we can assume increasingly less about the prior knowledge and experience of increasingly more new students. As with fundamental knowledge of maths and statistics, many disciplines are feeling the need for more explicit attention to the fundamental structures and patterns of linguistic representation defining academic work, from text to word level. As demand rises, the responses devised to address gaps in linguistic knowledge and know-how need to be made sustainable, especially where staffing for literacy education is unlikely to be increased.

Sustainable development in education, as in any field, means engaging the majority in every discipline to be part of the solution. The solution cannot be only to have more students doing more courses that focus only on "language communications" because such a model has little, if any, effect on what happens in the mainstream classes where students spend most of their time. Students without the rich language repertoire needed in their chosen discipline will continue to struggle as long as most of their educational experiences ignore the medium of instruction.

Expanding students' linguistic repertoire requires some conscious focus on language, everywhere it is in play. The development of students' language proficiency in ways that make a difference to their learning of academic disciplines is arguably no more separable from daily discourse in the disciplines than is the reduction of carbon footprints from the normal domestic and industrial activities going on every day. We are beginning to see how possible it is to change perceptions about carbon emissions, and modify behaviour in individually simple ways that can collectively reduce the problem significantly. Similarly, to really make a significant difference to the learning of students coming into HE today, we need to focus on what goes on, language-wise, in their mainstream learning environments. This is where obstacles to learning can occur, and can be prevented.

Whether or not such an argument makes much sense depends on one's theory of language. Research and pedagogy in many fields have taken a "sociolinguistic turn" (Frankel, 2000, p. 82; Kress, 2001), and "literacy" is not defined, by educators in the twenty-first century, as a "basic skill". The current definition of "literacy" given by UNESCO, for example (Wikipedia 2010a), is the ability to interpret, use, and create written materials in specific and various contexts, and literacy is understood to develop through complex, goal-oriented processes through which people develop knowledge by participating in social activity. This is a very different view from the still commonly held one that language structures and "skills" can be taught and learned to a high level outside of any particular context in which they are authentically used. At every level of education, it is recognised, at least in theory, that becoming "literate" means learning to participate meaningfully in specific contexts, and that linguistic competence beyond an intermediate level is not separately teachable and subsequently transferable to the context where this is needed (McDonough, 2005, p. 59; Wingate, 2006).

Whatever the challenges of rising demand for help, and of moving targets around the need for and knowledge about literacy, the greatest obstacle to great literacy development practice in the disciplines is probably resistance to dialogue. Bringing the knowledge about language and effective literacy development know-how into the situations where it is most urgently needed depends on dialogue and collaboration, but that is not always easy to establish and maintain. Constructive dialogue across departmental divides can be hindered by a number of factors. It may not be widely known across an institution who has what kind of useful knowledge about language education, what the role of academic language and learning educators is, what "integration" might look like, and what collaboration might involve. There may be little structural support for interdisciplinary collaborations in teaching and educational research, or an unhelpful sense of competition between different providers of language education.

Most difficult to overcome, though, are default beliefs about teaching, learning, and language that can make teaching collaborations seem an unnecessary waste of precious research time. When the conventions of an academic discourse seem "self-evident and universal" to its practitioners (Kindelan-Echevarria, 2007, p. 73), any need for explanation and guidance tends to be read as evidence of the learners' deficiency, either in intelligence (in which case "they shouldn't be here") or in "basic skills" (which could presumably be developed outside the mainstream curriculum). Alternatively, disciplinary teachers may simply think that any form of collaboration would be adding to their workload pressure, rather than relieving it.

Many lecturers view themselves, naturally, as teachers of "content", not as teachers of "language". Yet, from a literacy point of view, they are selecting and providing the linguistic input that their students will experience of a subject (textbooks, journal articles, and other recommended reading texts, lectures), making the decisions about the nature of language communications that their students will perform in order to demonstrate learning, orchestrating classroom, and online dialogue (or failing to), and making judgements about the quality of learning based largely on the quality of writing and speaking.

Doing these things in a way that is uninformed about the nature of language learning may inadvertently disadvantage students who need to significantly develop their linguistic repertoire. When relevant knowledge about language is brought to both the teachers and the learners of disciplines, the textual incoherence of novice writers and insecure thinkers can be more systematically noted, and mainstream learning environments designed to anticipate areas of ignorance that students experience and *guide* them through the expected intellectual processes.

Students come to university to develop knowledge, and knowledge construction is socio-linguistic work that they tend not to yet know how to perform particularly well. It is the teaching they are exposed to on a daily basis that needs to help develop their ability to do academic work. To help provide some of the evidence needed to support these arguments, and persuade teachers across our institutions that it is not a waste of precious time to discuss and plan pedagogy with literacy specialists, the following section presents some examples of collaboration that are effectively meeting the academic literacy development needs of specific groups of students, identified by the institution as potentially at risk. The work described is carried out at a mid-sized university in Australia, and represents responses to literacy development needs in two typical scenarios: first-year undergraduates using English as their first language, and postgraduate coursework students with less proficiency in English, and less time to develop it.

▶ Balancing the priorities

The practices described below occur within the Faculty of Science at the University of Wollongong, and represent successful collaborations between subject specialists in the disciplines and writing developers from the language and learning development unit. There are important differences in the needs of the two cohorts targeted, and the corresponding pedagogical response, but the logic in common is that when it works well, the planning process begins with a focus on desired outcomes and literacy development needs, then moves through the discussion and collaborative design of tasks, resources, and teaching strategies (to support students' use of resources to complete the tasks that would lead to the learning outcomes stated). What differs is the complexity and intensity of teaching required in relation to language development between situations where English is and is not the first language of the students.

At first-year undergraduate level, two tasks within the *Climate Change* subject were designed to develop students' ability to argue and to explain, and to prevent some of the predictable risks of disengagement and failure that many first-year undergraduates face (Moss et al., 2006; Kift, 2008; James et al., 2010; Potter and Parkinson, 2010). Most first-year undergraduates in the Science Faculty at Wollongong tend to be school leavers, using English as their first language. They need to develop abilities to gather appropriate evidence, report, and argue in ways expected throughout the degree program. They also need to develop social networks and supportive study groups to get used to a range of interactions within the online learning environment, to learn to use online library databases efficiently, and they want to enjoy the general learning experience and get a sense of where their degree might lead. The abilities to act independently while solving problems collaboratively and to communicate effectively with different audience types were considered further learning outcomes worth focusing on in the first year, and these are further developed throughout students' curricula in whichever discipline they spend most of their time.

The *Climate Change* subject was targeted for literacy development work for reasons from two perspectives. From the faculty's point of view, scientific knowledge of global warming and climate change needs a larger audience, so to make this subject attract students from across the disciplines (not just those majoring in Science), the subject co-ordinators are particularly open to input from other educators, and have linked the development work with a cross-institutional, nationally funded project on climate change educational networking. From the writing developer's perspective, targeting a widely recognised cause that students want to be able to talk and write well about is a more effective way to achieve an educational agenda than making any particular "writing" or "reading" practice *per se* the focus of attention (in the students' perception of what is going on). People tend to learn what, and when, they feel the need to, and needs felt at a personal level of identification and agency are naturally responded to ahead of those felt to be imposed arbitrarily or dictatorially from "above".

To help students develop their ability to construct a persuasive, evidence-based argument, an inter-disciplinary role-play debating task was set up, whereby first-year students of the science subject worked for 5 weeks with third-year students of law to develop and present a petition to a moot court. The cohort of about 90 students was divided into small groups to defend the interests of either a caravan park operator (whose business premises regularly flood and who has applied to council to relocate to higher ground) or of an endangered species (found by environmentalists at the proposed new site). The amount, speed, and quality of reading and writing done to gather and present the evidence needed to support a collaboratively developed argument far exceeded what is normally achieved in other types of group work and oral presentation activity. The importance of task authenticity, peer mentoring, and of collaboration between teachers was convincingly demonstrated: in the first iteration of the subject, the oral presentation task began as a fairly rushed compromise, with instruction delegated to the writing specialist, who had little opportunity to discuss the science learning objectives with the Science teachers. In the next academic year, with more opportunity to plan collaboratively, alternative learning designs were shared, and the learning outcomes for students were significantly better (evidenced in their written reflections and informal feedback on their enjoyment of and satisfaction with the learning process, as much as in the quality of the science and the logic and coherence of arguments they presented).

Interestingly, the use of a debate format resulted in not only better preparation and presentation, but also in a reduced teaching load. Students became so engaged in the task and felt so acutely the need to get good material together for the more senior student from Law who was to present the case that they effectively mentored one another. Assessment was easy also, as it was shared between subject specialists and writing developers. Teachers had only to listen to the quality of evidence and logic of argumentation in eight cases, presented formally before mock judges with genuine, relevant professional experience[1] and to read brief follow-up reflections from individual students. Feedback for students was provided in the form of videos for each group of their own performance, and informal commentary.

The students' ability to quickly gather evidence, document sources, and collaborate on solving a problem was further enhanced by a subsequent group task, this time focusing on explanation rather than argument. Groups were assigned to one of five regions of the world, about which they had to produce a poster explaining food security issues to the general public. Instruction for this poster-making task was also easy yet effective, taking the form of a poster that took just a few hours to produce. Presented through the subject's eLearning site, an example and guide poster explained the poster development process and modelled how a template could be adapted. As a result of the modelling, template resources, and guidance given, students were able, within a week or two, to produce a very impressive set of posters which effectively communicated scientific knowledge to a general audience, demonstrating both their understanding of the issues and a learned ability to communicate in a multimedia format fundamental to the broad dissemination of science knowledge.

At postgraduate level, the subject *Fundamentals of Science Communication* was also the locus for collaboration between subject specialists and writing developers, this time for MSc students. The task aimed to prepare international students for literacy demands encountered within the specialties of Biotechnology, Chemistry, or Earth Sciences. Postgraduate coursework programs are typically populated by international students, using English at an intermediate level (IETLS score around 6.5), who are generally unfamiliar with the academic practices of an Australian university, particularly the "critical" stance expected.

The collaboration between subject and writing specialist had to be carefully designed. This collaboration has been extended into a cross-faculty project to develop and share learning designs for "Content and Language Integrated Learning", through which students can effectively develop language proficiency at every level as they develop disciplinary knowledge (for explanation of CLIL methodology; see, for example, Marsh and Wolff, 2007, Dalton-Puffer, 2007; Lyster 2007; Mephisto et al., 2008). Various areas of educational research have also been considered around the needs of international students (e.g. Arkoudis, 2006), literacy-focused "teaching learning cycle" pedagogy (Ellis, 2000; Hyland, 2007, p. 159), "ICT-based learning design" (see the UOW *Learning Designs* Web site), "universal design" (see Wikipedia 2010b on architectural accessibility in education), academic literacy, and literacies" and WAC.[2]

The subject is organised around three key tasks, each carefully scaffolded through a sequence of sub-tasks, and involving a great deal of dialogue. Students' understanding of the context they are in is built up through a series of lecture audits around the faculty, interviews with staff and more senior students, recorded reflective commentary and personal stories posted on an eLearning blog.

Disciplinary language is also sampled and analysed (simply) with the aid of "lexical" profiling' software (Cobb, 2010) and classroom discussion of typical features of academic discourse, such as nominalisation at the clause level and organisation at the text level, which is then further evidenced and discussed via the blog. The oral presentation that students are to make is carefully developed over several weeks through a process of modelling and joint negotiation, online discussion, and feedback in small, private groups. For this task, students select and present a journal article relevant to their discipline. They need to demonstrate not only comprehension (which is developed through some rigorous critical discussion in the small groups), but also to develop ability to translate a complex written text into a spoken, multimedia communication that works for a non-specialist audience (the class comprises students from various Science disciplines and from a Public Health program in another faculty, as well as the writing specialist, who does not have a Science background).

The literature review which students are to produce individually is explained and carefully modelled through a series of instructional sessions on the use of the library, use of the preferred referencing style, annotation of bibliographies, critical and comparative analysis of sources, and the development of questions and arguments to discuss issues arising in chosen topic areas.

Importantly, from a language learner's perspective, the overall design of the subject, and everything involved at each stage of the learning process relating to the major tasks, is communicated in various ways. The tasks, resources, and supports are visualised in single page, very simple and clear flowchart-type diagrams, which as well as laying out each step of the process, also indicate all the resources and all the pedagogical support available and required for successful completion of each sub-task. Even more than the first-year undergraduate students, new international students need to quickly develop social networks, form supportive study groups, get used to a range of interactions within the online learning environment, use online library databases, and enjoy the general learning experience they have come so far for. Positive benefits for students are observed (and are now being measured) in terms of greater confidence, language repertoire and fluency, improved performance in key aspects of "knowledge work", and, as noted in some unsolicited feedback recently, higher IELTS scores as well:

> "you covered all the aspects of English—speaking, writing, grammar and presentation"

> "now I can critique, I can analyse … this is the most important thing, I missed this point (before), I could read articles in medicine and analyse them, give treatment, everything, but I couldn't compare one study with another … now I compare naturally … because of that assignment, the critical annotated bibliography …."

> "I did an IELTS test 3 months ago, and again two weeks ago … I've improved by .5—that's good … it's only 7 weeks but I feel my skills have improved, through the eLearning, through your efforts."

▶ Conclusion: Projects to develop literacy in the disciplines

How we teach academic writing, and support student learning in other ways, depends on how we interpret the educational problems they experience. On the basis of a decade of experience, far more than the examples described above, the argument here is that fast and effective literacy development depends on collaboration and learning design, and the following strategies are recommended:

- Collaborate! Ensure teaching academics across the institution who are likely to have students struggling with English know who on campus has what expertise in language education, and what literacy specialists do (the relevant professional association in Australia, for example, gives a basic role statement on academic language and learning educators in HE: http://aall.org.au/sites/default/files/AALLpositionStatement2010Final.pdf).
- Consider predictable literacy development needs as the starting point for curriculum design, rather than a "problem", and seek opportunities for collaboration, considering published examples of curriculum-integrated literacy development practice across the disciplines.
- Openly discuss educational problems in specific contexts with a range of other educators, investigating whether problems are experienced by just a few students (who can be effectively helped individually) or whether students' capacity to perform the specific types of literacy practices is being hindered by a "hidden curriculum"—by subject design and delivery that makes it unnecessarily difficult for a large number of students to recognise and master what is actually being assessed when they submit written work.
- Discuss advantages and disadvantages of various models of language education in relation to the literacy development needs of specific cohorts in the disciplines (e.g. those in their first year at the institution and new to the local traditions): everything from consultations with individual students, to extra-curricular workshops and credit bearing courses on aspects of language communication (run by academic support units or other faculties), to curriculum-integrated literacy development (as separate writing or communications courses within a degree program taught by discipline outsiders, as separate courses within a program but co-designed and delivered by academics from the target discipline and colleagues specialising in language education, or as part and parcel of the normal teaching of disciplines, with or without co-delivery from colleagues outside the target discipline).

- Consider learning and assessment tasks from a language development perspective. For example, if students are not proficient in English and are new to the local literacy practices, avoid tasks which have students producing written language by reading written language. When linguistic repertoire is limited, learners literally cannot paraphrase and summarise well, so asking them to do it without instruction leads either to mindless copying or fairly incoherent text. Get them to talk about what they have read and submit a recorded review. Get them to write about material presented to them audio-visually, and stage the writing through concept mapping and discussion.

- Investigate multiple perspectives on literacy problems, including the learners', to help clarify main causes: whether, for example, students' struggles to comprehend and participate in disciplinary work are best described in terms of knowledge they "lack" before they commence tertiary level study, or in terms of how their legitimately limited initial capacity is being predicted and responded to in the preparation and teaching of courses across the disciplines.

- If possible, relate literacy development work to funded, interdisciplinary projects, so that there are career development benefits for all participants. The sense of support, the opportunities for dialogue and critical reflection, and for mutual professional development that this brings seems to be one of the greatest outcomes of team-based project work.

▶ Notes

1 See, http://media.uow.edu.au/news/UOW087735.html.
2 For instance, Bazerman and Prior (2004), Belcher and Braine (1995), Belcher (2006), Berkenkotter and Huckin (1995), Coffin *et al.* (2003), Coffin *et al.* (2004), Friedrich (2008), Ganobcsik-Williams (2006), Johns (1997), Johns and Swales (2002), Lea (2004), Lea and Street (2006), Lee (1997), Lillis (2001, 2003), Poe *et al.* (2010), Ravelli and Ellis (2004), Russell (2002), Street (2004), Taylor and Drury (2007).

▶ References

AALL (Association for Academic Language and Learning), accessed at http://www.aall.org.au/.

ALTC (Australian Learning and Teaching Council) *Funding*, accessed at http://www.altc.edu.au/funding-opportunities.

Arkoudis, S. (2006) *Teaching International Students: Strategies to Enhance Learning.* Report for the Centre for the Study of Higher Education,

University of Melbourne, accessed at http://www.cshe.unimelb.edu.au/pdfs/international.pdf.

AUQA (Australian Universities Quality Agency) and *TEQSA* (Tertiary Education Quality and Standards Agency), accessed at http://www.auqa.edu.au/aboutauqa/teqsa/.

Bazerman, C. and Prior, P. (eds) (2004) *What Writing Does and How It Does It: An Introduction to Analyzing Texts and Textual Practices* (Mahwah and London: Lawrence Erlbaum).

Belcher, D. (2006) "English for Specific Purposes: Teaching to Perceived Needs and Imagined Futures in Worlds of Work, Study and Everyday Life", *TESOL Quarterly*, 40:1, 133–152.

Belcher, D. and Braine, G. (eds) (1995) *Academic Writing in a Second Language: Essays on Research and Pedagogy* (Norwood: Ablex-Greenwood).

Berkenkotter, C. and Huckin, T. (1995) *Genre Knowledge in Disciplinary Communication* (New York: Lawrence Erlbaum).

Cargill, M. (1999) "Resisting generic-ness: a discipline-specific, integrated, collaborative and faculty-wide model of language and learning skill development", in G. Crosling, T. Moore and S. Vance (eds) *Language and Learning: The Learning Dimensions of our Work. Proceedings of the Third National Language and Academic Skills Conference.* Melbourne, Monash University.

Cargill, M. (2011) *An Integrated, Discipline-Specific Model of Communication Skills Development*, accessed at http://www.adelaide.edu.au/clpd/resources/leap/case_studies/cargill.html.

Cobb, T. (2010) *Compleat Lexical Tutor*, accessed at http://www.lextutor.ca/vp/eng/.

Coffin, C., Hewings, A. and O'Halloran, K. (eds) (2004) *Applying English Grammar: Functional and Corpus Approaches* (London: Arnold with Open University).

Coffin, C., Curry, M.-J., Goodman, S., Hewings, A., Lillis, T. and Swann, J. (2003) *Teaching Academic Writing: A Toolkit for Higher Education*, (London: Routledge).

Dalton-Puffer, C. (2007) *Discourse in Content and Language Integrated Learning (CLIL) Classrooms* (Amsterdam/Philadelphia: John Benjamins).

DEEWR (Department of Education, Employment and Workplace Relations) (2008), *Review of Australian Higher Education Report* [The Bradley Review], Commonwealth of Australia, accessed at http://www.deewr.gov.au/HigherEducation/Review/Pages/default.aspx.

DEEWR (Department of Education, Employment and Workplace Relations) (2009) *Good Practice Principles for English Language Proficiency for International Students in Australian Universities*, Commonwealth of Australia, accessed at http://www.deewr.gov.au/HigherEducation/Publications/Pages/GoodPracticePrinciples.aspx.

Ellis, R. (2000) "Flexibility in genre-based literacy pedagogy: Critical assessments of flexibility", in *Flexible Learning for a Flexible Society: Proceedings of the ASET/HERDSA 2000 Joint International Conference*, University of Southern Queensland, Toowoomba, accessed at http://www.ascilite.org.au/aset-archives/confs/aset-herdsa2000/procs/ellis-r.html.

ESOS Act (Education Services to Overseas Students) (2000, reviewed 2009), AEI (Australian Education International), accessed at http://www.aei.gov.au/AEI/ESOS/ESOSLegislation/default.htm.

ESOS National Code (2000, revision 2007) *Part D: Standards for Registered Providers*, AEI, accessed at http://aei.gov.au/AEI/ESOS/NationalCodeExplanatoryGuide/PartD/Default.

Frankel, R. (2000) "The sociolinguistic turn in physician-patient communication research", in J. Alatis, H. Hamilton and A.-H. Tan (eds) *GURT: Linguistics, Language and the Professions* (Washington: Georgetown UP), pp. 81–103.

Friedrich, P. (ed.) (2008) *Teaching Academic Writing* (New York and London: Continuum).

Ganobcsik-Williams, L. (ed.) (2006) *Teaching Academic Writing in UK Higher Education: Theories, Practices and Models* (Basingstoke: Palgrave Macmillan).

Hyland, K. (2007) "Genre pedagogy: language, literacy and L2 writing instruction", *Journal of Second Language Writing*, 16: 148–164.

ICRJ (*International CLIL Research Journal*) accessed at http://www.clilconsortium.jyu.fi/index.php?option=com_content&task=view&id=30&Itemid=50.

IELTS (International English Language Testing System), accessed at http://www.ielts.org/default.aspx.

James, R., Krause, K.-L. and Jennings, C. (2010) *The First Year Experience in Australian Universities: Findings from 1994 to 2009*. Centre for the Study of Higher Education, University of Melbourne, accessed at http://www.cshe.unimelb.edu.au/.

Johns, A. (1997) *Text, Role and Context: Developing Academic Literacies* (Cambridge: Cambridge University Press).

Johns, A. and Swales, J. (2002) "Literacy and disciplinary practices: Opening and closing perspectives", *Journal of English for Academic Purposes*, 1, 13–28.

Kift, S. (2008) "Articulating a Transition Pedagogy: The First Year Experience and Curriculum Design", accessed at www.altcexchange.edu.au/system/files/KiftWAForumKift021208_ppt.pdf.

Kift, S. (2009) "Articulating a transition pedagogy to scaffold and enhance the first year student learning experience in Australian higher education", accessed at http://www.altc.edu.au/resource-first-year-learning-experience-kift-2009.

Kindelan-Echevarria, M.-P. (2007) "The learning of genre: Are there any favourable conditions?", *Estudios Ingleses de la Universidad Complutense*, 15, 61–77.

Kress, G. (2001) "From Saussure to Critical Sociolinguistics: The Turn Towards a Social View of Language", in M. Wetherell, S. Taylor and S. Yates (eds) *Discourse Theory and Practice: A Reader* (London: Sage in association with the Open University).

Lea, M. (2004) "Academic literacies: a pedagogy for course design", *Studies in Higher Education*, 29:6, 739–756.

Lea, M. and Street, B. (2006) "The 'academic literacies' model: theory and applications", *Theory into Practice*, 45:4, 368–377.

Learning Designs: Products of the AUTC project on ICT-based learning designs (2003), accessed at http://www.learningdesigns.uow.edu.au/project/learn_design.htm.

Lee, A. (1997) "Working together? Academic literacies, co-production and professional partnerships", *Literacy and Numeracy Studies*, 7:2, 65–82.

Lillis, T. (2001) *Student Writing* (London: Routledge).

Lillis, T. (2003) "Student writing as 'academic literacies': drawing on Bakhtin to move from critique to design", *Language and Education*, 17:3, 192–207.

Lyster, R. (2007) *Learning and Teaching Languages Through Content: A Counter-balanced Approach* (Amsterdam/Philadelphia: John Benjamins).

Marsh, D. and Wolff, D. (eds) (2007) *Diverse Contexts—Converging Goals: CLIL in Europe* (Frankfurt: Peter Lang).

McDonough, J. (2005) "Perspectives on EAP: an interview with Ken Hyland", *ELT Journal*, 59:1, 57–64.

Mephisto, P., Marsh, D. and Frigols, M.J. (2008) *Uncovering CLIL: Content and Language Integrated Learning in Bilingual and Multilingual Education* (Oxford: Maxmillan)

Moss, T., Pittaway, S. and McCarthy, R. (2006) "The first year experience: Transition and integration into teacher education", in P. Jeffery (ed.) *Proceedings of AARE conference*, Adelaide, accessed at http://www.aare.edu.au/06pap/mos06557.pdf.

Poe, M., Lerner, N. and Craig, J. (2010) *Learning to Communicate in Science and Engineering: Case Studies form MIT* (Cambridge/London: MIT Press).

Potter, A. and Parkinson, A. (2010) "First year at risk intervention pilot project: an intervention to support first year students experiencing early assessment failure", in J. Thomas (ed.) *Proceeding of the 13th Pacific Rim First Year in Higher Education Conference*, Adelaide (Brisbane: QUT Publications), accessed at www.fyhe.com.au/past_papers/papers10/content/pdf/4B.pdf.

Purser, E., Skillen, J., Deane, M., Donohue, J. and Peake, K. (2008) "Developing academic literacy in context", *Zeitschrift Schreiben*, accessed at http://www.zeitschrift-schreiben.eu/Beitraege/purser_Academic_Literacy.pdf.

QAA (Quality Assurance Agency for Higher Education), *Outcomes*, accessed at http://www.qaa.ac.uk/reviews/institutionalAudit/outcomes/InstitutionsSupport.asp.

Ravelli, L. and Ellis, R. (eds) (2004) *Analysing Academic Writing: Contextualising Frameworks* (London: Continuum).

Rear Vision (2009) "Australia's education exports", podcast radio programme, ABC Radio National, 5 August, accessed at http://www.abc.net.au/rn/rearvision/stories/2009/2771756.htm on 17 December 2009.

Russell, D. (2002) *Writing in the Academic Disciplines: A Curricular History* (Carbondale and Edwardsville: Southern Illinois University Press).

Street, B. (2004) "Academic literacies and the 'new orders': implications for research and practice in student writing in higher education", *LATISS: Learning and Teaching in the Social Sciences*, 1:1, 9–20.

Taylor, C. and Drury, H. (2007) "An integrated approach to teaching writing in the sciences" in A. Brew and J. Sachs *Transforming a university: the scholarship of teaching and learning in practice*, accessed at http://ses.library.usyd.edu.au/bitstream/2123/2121/1/TransUniTaylor11.pdf

Wikipedia contributors (2010a) "Literacy", in *Wikipedia, the Free Encyclopedia*, accessed at http://en.wikipedia.org/w/index.php?title=Literacy&oldid=388012367.

Wikipedia contributors (2010b) "Universal Instructional Design", in *Wikipedia, the Free Encyclopedia*, accessed at http://en.wikipedia.org/wiki/Universal_Instructional_Design.

Wingate, U. (2006) "Doing away with study skills", *Teaching in Higher Education*, 11:4, 457–469.

3 The Role of Assessment in "Writing in the Disciplines"

Katherine Harrington

▶ Introduction

The fundamental aim of all Writing in the Disciplines (WiD) work is to facilitate students' learning and understanding and their ability to contribute to the dialogue and knowledge generation processes of their fields of study. This chapter looks at the important role assessment can play in any WiD approach to the development of students' learning and writing. It suggests that assessment is in a uniquely powerful position to promote student writing development where it is most effective—within students' academic disciplines—and argues that the success of any discipline-based approach to writing development depends on using assessment in the service of, rather than simply as a measurement of, students' learning, and more specifically, their learning through writing.

Focussing on the role of assessment also illustrates and reinforces one of the central tenets of WiD work, which is that all lecturers are in a position to help their students learn to write as part of the academic subjects they are studying. Assessment—designing, conducting, evaluating, and modifying it—is something lecturers already do as an integral part of their everyday teaching practice. With this starting point in view, the current chapter hopes to offer some new perspectives on assessment and argues for the value in stepping back from habitual practice in order to observe freshly, reflect, and develop a greater awareness of how assessment is and is not being used to support students' learning and writing development. Ultimately, the goal is to be able to make thoughtful and relevant decisions about our own practice in order to make best use of the potential of assessment to help students learn, and learn to write, within their disciplines.

It is now generally acknowledged, and continues to be supported by a growing body of evidence, that assessment is one of the most important influences on student learning in higher education (HE) (e.g. Biggs, 2003, Ramsden, 2003; Brown et al., 1997). Indeed, it has been argued that assessment shapes students' experiences even more than the teaching they receive (Gibbs and Simpson, 2004–5), and early difficulties with assessment have been associated with student attrition (Krause, 2001). However, it is much less widely acknowledged that assessment can be an important influence on students' development as academic writers. The argument for WiD is premised on a fundamental connection between writing and thinking—clear thinking produces clear writing (Bruffee, 1984)—from which follows an equally important connection between students' writing and their learning. Through writing, and opportunities to practice writing, students learn not only to recognise the conventions used in the disciplines they are studying, but also, more fundamentally, they learn how these conventions reveal and contribute to creating the epistemological orientation and knowledge-making practices at play in the disciplinary fields they are beginning to inhabit themselves.

It is helpful, therefore, to conceptualise writing as an essential part of the processes of thinking and learning, rather than, for example, as the translation of already-formed thought into the appropriate written forms of a certain discipline. The vast majority of assessment methods used in HE involve writing as a substantial component. If learning can be located in the act of writing, it follows that appropriately and thoughtfully designed assessment, which includes writing for both summative and formative purposes, can play a determining role in facilitating students' active engagement with the subject matter, concepts, and epistemologies relevant within their fields of study.

This aim of this chapter is to discuss ways in which assessment can be used to facilitate students' writing development and, more specifically, the powerful and crucial role assessment is able to play in cohering and extending any writing in the disciplines work. Building on literature on student assessment, learning and writing, the chapter presents a set of principles underlying WiD-supportive assessment practice and provides some illustrative examples from actual teaching contexts. Further examples of using assessment to support students' disciplinary writing development are explored in several of the case studies in subsequent chapters of this volume.

▶ Assessment for learning

There is now a substantial body of conceptual and empirical literature on student assessment, providing extensive and thoughtful debate as well as practical guidance relevant to lecturers across academic disciplines who wish to reflect on and improve their own teaching and assessment practice (in addition to the studies already mentioned, see, for example, Brown and Knight, 1994; Brown and Glasner, 1999; Falchikov, 2005; Bryan and Clegg, 2006; Bloxham and Boyd, 2007). This chapter focuses on a few key concepts and findings distilled from this larger field, in the interest of providing a convenient conceptual framework for helping lecturers to think specifically about how assessment can be used to support students' disciplinary writing development.

Those who work in the field of assessment, as researchers or theorists, academic developers or teachers, commonly distinguish between different purposes of assessment, and more specifically, between whether assessment is used for the purpose of measuring student learning—assessment *of* learning—or for the purpose of facilitating it—assessment *for* learning. This distinction is also conceptualised as assessment used for summative purposes, that is, in order to measure an amount of learning that has already taken place (such as through a final examination), contrasted with assessment used for formative purposes, or in other words to support students' learning development (e.g. through self-assessment or peer review exercises). In practice, these two aspects rarely occur independently. For example, a summatively assessed essay at the end of a module encourages formative, developmental activity over time through reading, note-making, and drafting; or an online discussion forum for which students receive marks for their written contributions can facilitate collaborative peer learning processes. However, it is still helpful to work with these broad conceptions as they can enable reflection on how different forms of assessment affect student learning within local teaching situations. And when used as a focus for thinking about one's own teaching practice, assessment can facilitate a process of professional development that parallels, and therefore can shed light on, the learning processes experienced by students.

Paul Ramsden (2003) summarises these three interrelated functions of assessment as: (a) a means of helping students learn, (b) a way of reporting on student progress, and (c) a way of making decisions about teaching (p. 205). When thinking about how assessment can be used to facilitate students' growth and development as academic writers in their disciplines, it is important to keep the first and third functions identified by Ramsden in the foreground. Using assessment as an aid to learning does not preclude the provision of marks. However, the benefit of doing so would be seen to lie less in the measurement of what has been achieved, than in the incentive to engage and devote time to the assessment task generated in students by the knowledge that their work will be graded. The understandings of assessment advocated in this chapter as compatible with a writing in the disciplines approach to helping students learn through writing are not essentially about marking, but about how assessment activity can be used to provide feedback to both students and lecturers for the purposes of evaluating progress and enabling further development.

The *Assessment for Learning* Centre for Excellence in Teaching and Learning (AfL CETL) based at Northumbria University describe the purpose of using assessment to facilitate students' learning as wanting "to foster student development in taking responsibility for evaluating, judging and improving their own performance by actively using a range of feedback", adding that "these capabilities are at the heart of autonomous learning and of the graduate qualities valued by employers and in professional practice" (AfL CETL Web site). Elsewhere, McDowell and Sambell (1999) argue for the value of using innovative, authentic forms of assessment, which in simulating the kinds of activities students are likely to confront outside HE, helps students to develop knowledge, skills, and abilities they will be able to take with them to these other contexts when they leave HE, such as employment—a perspective also shared up by MacAndrew and Edwards (2002) who discuss the benefits of moving beyond the traditional essay assessment format. The AfL CETL identifies six characteristics of assessment that is used to support the development of students' learning.

Assessment for learning:

1   Emphasises authenticity and complexity in the content and methods of assessment, rather than reproduction of knowledge and reductive measurement.
2   Uses high-stakes summative assessment rigorously but sparingly, rather than as the main driver for learning.
3   Offers students extensive opportunities to engage in the kinds of tasks that develop and demonstrate their learning, thus building their confidence and capabilities before they are summatively assessed.
4   Is rich in feedback derived from formal mechanisms, for example, tutor comments on assignments, student self-review logs.
5   Is rich in informal feedback, for example, peer review of draft writing, or collaborative project work, which provides students with a continuous flow of feedback on 'how they are doing'.
6   Develops students' abilities to direct their own learning, evaluate their own progress and attainments, and support the learning of others.

The last four of these characteristics refer to students receiving some form of information about their learning as they progress, whether the source of this feedback is the tutor, peers, or themselves, or comes in written or verbal form. It is not surprising to find such an emphasis on the importance of feedback in helping students learn: research has shown that when it comes to improving student attainment, feedback is the most significant aspect of the assessment process (Black and William, 1998). Because it is of such central importance to students' learning development, it is worth looking at the nature and role of feedback in more detail.

Nicol and Macfarlane-Dick (2006) argue that the importance of feedback is to be found in its potential to have an empowering influence on students, enabling them to develop a self-regulating approach to their learning. This view follows from a constructivist theory of learning, in which feedback is not seen as a one-way transmission of messages that are simply received and acted on by students. Rather, students are seen to inhabit a central, participative role in the feedback process, "monitoring and regulating their own performance, both in relation to desired goals and in terms of the strategies used to reach these goals" (p. 210). Looking at feedback in this way meaningfully connects students' learning with the substance of what they are studying in their disciplines: "students interact with subject content, transforming and discussing it with others, in order to internalise meaning and make connections with what is already known" (p. 200). Based on an extensive review of research on feedback in an educational context, the authors formulate seven principles of effective feedback practice.

Good feedback:

- Helps clarify what good performance is (goals, criteria, and expected standards).
- Facilitates the development of self-assessment (reflection) in learning.
- Delivers high-quality information to students about their learning.
- Encourages teacher and peer dialogue around learning.
- Encourages positive motivational beliefs and self-esteem.
- Provides opportunities to close the gap between current and desired performance.
- Provides information to teachers that can be used to help shape teaching.

Using assessment to support students' learning and writing development in a disciplinary context is to a large extent about putting the above feedback principles into practice by creating opportunities for students to receive information about their learning as an integral part of subject-based teaching on their courses of study. It is in this kind of formative assessment practice that the value and power of using assessment in the service of enabling students' development as academic writers—as participants in specific disciplinary field(s) of practice—lie.

As mentioned above, "feedback" as conceptualised in this chapter, and elsewhere in current literature on assessment, does not refer exclusively to that provided by a discipline specialist, in what might be regarded as the familiar, traditional process of a lecturer providing comments on students' written work either before or after it is submitted for marking. "Feedback" includes this kind of information provided by a lecturer, but it is also helpfully understood more broadly to include other sources of information on the progress of one's learning and writing development—namely, one's peers and, importantly, oneself. Examples of gaining feedback from these latter sources would include peer review and discussion of each other's work and keeping and regularly reviewing a learning journal or reflective log. Arguably, it is in enabling students to shift from a dependence on lecturers' judgements about their work (judgements which, in any case, may not be understood as intended (Hounsell, 1987; Lea and Street, 1998; Higgins et al., 2001; Harrington et al., 2006b)), to being able to assess their own performance in relation to internalised standards of the discipline—that is, to self-supervise their own learning—which is at the heart of all real and lasting learning and writing development.

▶ Using assessment criteria to facilitate dialogue and feedback

Facilitating students' internalisation of disciplinary standards and their ability to self-assess in relation to them—and also to see that this is the overall educational goal to be aiming for in the first place—is about much more than the provision of explicit assessment criteria and clear guidelines about what tutors want to see in students' written work. Some studies have demonstrated what many teachers already know from experience, namely that simply providing such criteria, perhaps especially when they are highly specified, does not result in any significant improvement in learning or achievement (O'Donovan et al., 2000) and can in fact lead to deleterious consequences, encouraging a mechanistic and instrumental understanding of the assessment task and the adoption of a surface approach to learning and writing (Norton, 2004; Mitchell, 2010). Instead, there is a need to create opportunities for students to engage with the criteria and guidelines, in dialogue with their tutors and each other—and themselves—in order to construct and internalise their own understandings of the criteria, and of what counts as achieving them at different standards of performance, within the context of their academic subjects. Providing model essays can have similar inhibiting effects on students' abilities to develop their own writing and meaning-making processes. The Evolving Essay Project, led by an undergraduate Psychology student at London Metropolitan University, Lynn Reynolds, sought to address this issue by using blog and wiki technology to write an essay online in a collaborative environment, with the aim of revealing the thinking and writing processes behind the finished product, and it vividly illustrates how valuable it can be for the development of students' understanding and confidence to create spaces in which they can receive ongoing feedback in dialogue with other students and with lecturers (Harrington et al., 2010). The finished project can be found online at <http://www.anessayevolves.com>.

Several studies have found that facilitating students' active engagement with the assessment criteria applied to their work can enable standards of achievement to be internalised and learning and performance to be demonstrably improved. Chris Rust, Margaret Price, and Barry O'Donovan at Oxford Brookes University (2003) embedded a programme of workshops in a first-year introductory business module with over 600 students, in which tutor-led discussion of assessment criteria combined with small-group marking exercises using the criteria and sample assignments resulted in significant improvements in module performance amongst those who attended the workshops compared with those who did not; and this improvement was still evident at a significant level when investigated 1 year later.

More recently, a similar intervention was embedded within a second-year cognitive psychology module at London Metropolitan University with the aim of improving students learning, writing, and assessment performance. The module was summatively assessed through one final examination and had been identified as having a consistently lower than average pass rate, and the university required the formulation of a response plan. For procedural and resource reasons, the form of the final assessment could not be altered within the workable short term. Instead, through a collaboration between writing and discipline specialists, a series of formative assessment activities focused on writing for cognitive psychology examinations was designed and embedded within regular module teaching. This involved designing a set of tailored resources using extracts from authentic examination answers annotated with the lecturer's comments on why the answers were regarded as strong or weak in relation to the assessment criteria. These resources were then used to facilitate discussion about what demonstrating assessment criteria at different levels of performance looks like in a second-year cognitive psychology module, and students were guided in small groups to adopt the role of the examiner and apply criteria to whole past examination answers. Peer Student Writing Mentors who had studied cognitive psychology in previous years, and who were currently working in the University Writing Centre, circulated amongst the small groups and contributed to the discussions. This study found that although the pass rate did not improve, students who participated in the workshops received statistically significantly higher grades on the examination. There was also a significant positive correlation between the number of workshops attended and higher grades, suggesting that the benefit of the workshops increased with the amount of participation. A number of minor changes to the content and delivery of the module in addition to the new workshops have meant that it is problematic to compare pass rates across years; however, the findings suggest that increasing attendance at the workshops could lead to better writing and improved performance for more students in future cohorts (Harrington et al., 2009). These findings are consistent with earlier work in psychology, in which similar formative assessment opportunities embedded within module teaching were linked to the adoption of a deeper approach to learning and improved grades on written assessments, as well as increased levels of student confidence and a greater sense of belonging at university (Harrington et al., 2006a; Lusher, 2007).

The above examples show how tutors can engage students in dialogue about criteria and standards as a way of providing feedback—from peers and the tutor—that aims to enable students' ability to self-assess, or supervise, their own development. The verbal aspect of this dialogue is perhaps most evident in these examples, in the instances of students' discussing and reviewing their own and others' work in relation to assessment criteria. However, there are also written elements of this dialogue, if less obvious at first glance, which also contribute to the development of students' capacity to self-assess, for example in the notes students make on handouts and other materials during discussion, as well as the final written assessment which can be seen as a more advanced response, building on many previous dialogic exchanges, to the ongoing discussion of standards and how to demonstrate them in written work.

"Dialogue" can therefore be thought of as including verbal exchange and debate, but also written expression, both of a formal and informal nature (work submitted for evaluation and grading as well as personal notes, freewriting, and drafts). As with the spoken word, all writing is both a response to previous utterances and an anticipation of new responses, from real or implied addressees (Bakhtin, 1986). In light of this concept of dialogue, writing can be seen as a participation in the discussions and debates taking place within, and helping to define, a particular field of knowledge and practice. It is through this process of dialogue, verbal and written, that meaning is constructed and challenged. With this broad understanding of dialogue in mind, it can be useful to think of our role as educators as that of helping students acquire their academic and disciplinary voices by enabling them to hear other voices in the fields they are attempting to inhabit (e.g. those voices establishing the meanings of assessment criteria and the standards of meeting them) and also by facilitating students' ability to engage with and respond to these voices, to make use of the specialist dialogue themselves, as participants in and contributors to their disciplinary arenas. In practice, and with respect to students' writing development in particular, this translates into designing our teaching to include formative assessment opportunities where students can, in collaboration with fellow students and tutors, practice hearing, playing with and discovering their own academic writing voices within the language of their disciplines.

▶ The problem of "academic writing"

"Academic writing" is not a homogenous, singular field of practice: there is not one form of academic writing that fits all disciplinary contexts where writing takes place. However, what is often shared across these different contexts are students' experiences of a gap between their own knowledge and understanding and that of those operating as professionals—whether as researchers, practitioners, or educators—within these specialist fields. Reading specialist writings is always to some degree, at least initially, an experience of incomplete understanding, and individual students will have different levels of tolerance for this defamiliarising and probably partly uncomfortable aspect of the learning process. Students can, and often do, respond to these experiences by focussing on what they perceive as the source of their confusion and by trying to imitate in their own writing the language they have found partly, or even completely, opaque and incomprehensible. Indeed, some students hold the belief that opacity and complexity beyond the reach of understanding are distinguishing characteristics of academic writing—characteristics that inhere in the writing itself, rather than in the process of trying to understand it. In attempting to model their own writing on this only partially understood language, students can end up inadvertently creating for their specialist readers a similar experience of incomprehensibility and discomfort.

The tendency to latch onto and try to imitate those features of specialist language that students find hard to grasp reveals an essentially surface approach to learning (i.e. the attempt to reproduce knowledge without having understood it), in contrast to a deep approach to learning, which is motivated by the wish to understand, forge connections with other areas of knowledge, and consider relationships between theory and practical contexts—all of which lead to changes in the way students experience the world and themselves within it (Marton and Säljö, 1976; Entwistle, 1988; Ramsden, 1992). For lecturers, an effective response to this situation involves trying to shift students' attention away from the language they are finding problematic and towards understanding the new thought processes, concepts, and ideas underlying it. To an extent this will involve engaging with a new and specialist vocabulary; however more fundamentally, and underlying successful use of these disciplinary terms and forms of expression, is the need for students to grapple with the ways of thinking and seeing and creating knowledge that pertain in their specific disciplinary fields. This emphasis on first and foremost helping students arrive at clear thinking and understanding is not to suggest that it can take place separately from the language used, specialist or otherwise; rather, it is to facilitate a re-focusing of students' attention away from imitating other people's at least partly incomprehensible voices, towards acquiring an appropriate and convincing academic voice of their own as part of the process of engaging with new ideas and developing one's own thought and understanding in response to them.

In his review of literature on the effectiveness of "study skills" training and advice, Graham Gibbs (2005), drawing on research by Säljö (1979), notes that adopting a surface approach to learning is often linked to a relatively unsophisticated conception of what learning is, for example learning as memorisation or as the acquisition of information and procedures for subsequent use. Regarding learning as memorisation can feel safe and reliable, though in practice it inhibits students' development. More sophisticated conceptions of learning—as understanding, or as changing the way the world is experienced—are connected to the specific knowledge creation practices within disciplines. Progression to these conceptions of learning, and to more sophisticated conceptions of knowledge itself, is neither easy nor inevitable; however, a learning environment where students feel safe to take risks and experiment with new ways of seeing and thinking is more likely to be conducive to their development. Discipline specialists are therefore in a particularly influential position to help create a learning environment where the development of new understandings and students' own authentic academic voices is encouraged and rewarded.

Gibbs (2005) also emphasises the importance of lecturers modelling the discourse of the discipline in action, for example through lectures and tutorials, for enabling students to learn how to use this discourse and become members of the disciplinary community themselves. This modelling of the language and practice of the discipline also applies to the way assessment and writing tasks are presented and written. In designing assessments and clarifying for students what is expected of them in their written assignments, doing so in the language of one's own discipline models the ways of seeing and understanding that operate in their specific area, and through this modelling—which can be seen as a form of mentoring—facilitates students' abilities to see and develop their own thinking and writing processes. In this, assessment, and the way assignments are constructed and presented, is effectively used as a means for bringing students into a dialogue with others who are already operating more securely within the disciplinary field, and of enabling them to begin to participate within that field.

▶ Principles of WiD-supportive assessment practice

Drawing on the research literature on student learning and assessment discussed above, and keeping in mind the overarching goal of WiD work to enable students develop their understanding and contribute to the meaning-making practices of their academic subjects through writing, it is possible to identify a set of general principles underlying assessment practice that is supportive of a WiD approach to students' learning and writing development.

Assessment that promotes student writing development within their disciplines:

- focuses on facilitating student learning, as contrasted with measuring it
- is used to model the language and meaning-making practices of the discipline, and in doing so encourages students to respond to assessment in ways that help them learn how to participate in disciplinary ways of thinking and writing
- enables students to develop their own capacity for self-assessment in relation to the criteria, standards, and conventions operating within their disciplinary fields
- is context-dependent in that it is designed and implemented with reference to the specific writing and learning goals relevant to particular, local teaching contexts
- is authentic, in that it is aligned with specific learning and writing goals, as well as provides writing opportunities that are similar to those students are likely to confront in contexts outside of academia, including employment

- provides a focus for one's own reflective practice and ongoing professional development as an educator operating within a WiD framework.

The hope is that these principles can act as a reference point to guide the development of assessment practice that helps students become confident academic and disciplinary writers through the internalisation of processes and approaches that will continue to be of value and relevance beyond their time in HE. Working towards this larger goal can helpfully start with a focus on local teaching contexts, where choices about types and methods of written assessment can be used to promote learning, and learning through writing, that enables the achievement of discipline-based educational goals.

▶ Conclusion

The institutional contexts in which we work undoubtedly influence the ways we attempt to facilitate students' writing development, including the degree to which we might feel disposed, encouraged, or hindered to adopt a WiD approach. Indeed, later in this volume, Ganobcsik-Williams discusses the importance of "creating a whole university culture of writing" for supporting all students along a "continuum of writing development". However, although there are indications that "a sense of possibility exists for writing development in UK higher education", the majority of institutions in the UK have yet to take seriously the benefits to be gained by establishing a culture of writing and a coherent strategic approach to providing effective and relevant writing development opportunities for both students and staff.

Nevertheless, whilst development is occurring at this macro level, at varying rates within different institutions, there remains much within the scope and power of the individual lecturer that can be achieved at the micro level of specific courses and modules, and within the physical and virtual classrooms, where our teaching takes place. I hope this chapter has succeeded in illustrating how all lecturers are in a position to reflect on and evaluate their own assessment practices in terms of how well-suited they are to enabling students to meet specific learning and writing goals, and to make informed changes to aspects of assessment design and delivery accordingly. A wealth of published literature and a growing and lively community of professional practice in the area of assessment in HE are available to the interested subject-based academic who wishes to gain inspiration and ideas for the development of local WiD-supportive assessment practice.

However, at least as important as being able to draw on the experiences of others is the process of discovering for oneself what works and what does not, and why. Often the end result of one's efforts looks very similar to the conclusions others have found, and also published. As with all forms of practice, however, it is not the end result in itself where all the value lies. The learning that takes place in the process of putting principles into action, and of beginning with experience and allowing understanding and insight to follow from that, is arguably what matters most in the development of one's own professional competence, and therefore arguably also what matters most to the quality of education we provide for our students.

▶ References

Assessment for Learning Centre for Excellence in Teaching and Learning. Northumbria University. http://www.northumbria.ac.uk/sd/central/ar/academy/cetl_afl/whatis/?view=Standard [Accessed 23 November 2010].

Bakhtin, M.M. (1986) *Speech Genres and Other Late Essays*. Austin: University of Texas Press.

Boud, D. and Falchikov, N. (2007) *Rethinking Assessment in Higher Education: Learning for the Longer Term*. Abingdon: Routledge.

Biggs, J.B. (2003) *Teaching for Quality Learning at University* (2nd edn). Buckingham: Open University Press.

Black, P. and William, D. (1998) "Assessment and classroom learning." *Assessment in Education*, 5(1): 7–74.

Bloxham, S. and Boyd, P. (2007) *Developing Effective Assessment in Higher Education: A Practical Guide*. Maidenhead, England: Open University Press.

Brown, G., Bull, J. and Pendlebury, M. (1997) *Assessing Student Learning in Higher Education*. London: Routledge.

Brown, S. and Glasner, A. (1999) *Assessment Matters in Higher Education: Choosing and Using Diverse Approaches*. Guildford: Society for Research in Higher Education and Open University Press.

Brown, S. and Knight, P. (1994) *Assessing Learners in Higher Education*. London: Kogan Page.

Bruffee, K.A. (1984) "Collaborative learning and the 'conversation of mankind'." *College English*, 46: 635–652.

Bryan, C. and Clegg, K. (eds) (2006) *Innovative Assessment in Higher Education*. London: Routledge.

Entwistle, N. (1988) *Styles of Learning and Teaching*. London: David Fulton.

Falchikov, N. (2005) *Improving Assessment Through Student Involvement: Practical Solutions for Aiding Learning in Higher Education*. London: RoutledgeFalmer.

Gibbs, G. (2005) "How students develop as learners." Institute for the Advancement of University Learning, Oxford University. Available at: http://www.learning.ox.ac.uk/files/studyskills.pdf. [Accessed 23 November 2010].

Gibbs, G. and Simpson, C. (2004–2005) "Conditions under which assessment supports student learning." *Learning and Teaching in Higher Education*, 1: 3–31.

Harrington, K., Elander, J., Lusher, J., Aiyegbayo, O., Pitt, E., Norton, L., Robinson, H. and Reddy, P. (2006a) "Using core assessment criteria to improve essay writing." In C. Bryan and K. Clegg (eds) *Innovative Assessment in Higher Education*. London: Routledge.

Harrington, K., Elander, J., Norton, L., Reddy, P., Aiyegbayo, O. and Pitt, E. (2006b) "A qualitative analysis of staff-student differences in understandings of assessment criteria." In C. Rust (ed.) *Improving Student Learning Through Assessment*. Oxford: Oxford Centre for Staff and Learning Development.

Harrington, K., Freedman, M., Bakhshi, S. and O'Neill, P. (2009) "Helping psychology undergraduates improve examination writing." Presentation given at the Promoting Psychology Student Learning Through Assessment symposium, London Metropolitan University, 27 March 2009. Available at: http://www.psychology.heacademy.ac.uk/docs/ppt/p20090518_Helping_psychology_undergraduates_improve_exam_writing.ppt. [Accessed 26 February 2010.]

Harrington, K., O'Neill, P. and Reynolds, L. (2010) "Using wikis and blogs to support writing development: the online evolving essay project." In S. Little (ed.) *Developing Staff-Student Partnerships in Higher Education*. London: Continuum.

Higgins, R. Hartley, P. and Skelton, A. (2001) "Getting the message across." *Teaching in Higher Education*, 6 (2): 269–274.

Hounsell, D. (1987) "Essay writing and the quality of feedback." In J.T.E. Richardson, M.W. Ezsenck and D. Warren-Piper (eds) *Student Learning: Research in Education and Cognitive Psychology*. Milton Keynes: Society for Research in Higher Education and Open University Press.

Krause, K.L. (2001) "The university essay writing experience: a pathway for academic integration during transition." *Higher Education Research and Development*, 20 (2): 147–168.

Lea, M. and Street, B. (1998) "Student writing in higher education: an academic literacies approach." *Studies in Higher Education*, 23 (2): 157–172.

Lusher, J. (2007) "How study groups can help examination performance." *Health Psychology Update*, 16 (1–2): 34–38.

MacAndrew, S.B.G. and Edwards, K. (2002) "Essays are not the only way: a case report on the benefits of authentic assessment." *Psychology Learning and Teaching*, 2 (2): 134–139.

Marton, F. and Säljö, R. (1976) "On qualitative differences in learning, 1: Outcome and Process." *British Journal of Educational Psychology*, 46: 4–11.

McDowell, L. and Sambell, K. (1999) "The experience of innovative assessment: student perspectives." In Brown, S. and Glasner, A. (eds) *Assessment Matters in Higher Education: Choosing and Using Diverse Approaches*. Guildford: Society for Research in Higher Education and Open University Press.

Mitchell, S. (2010) " 'Now you don't see it; now you do': writing made visible in the university." *Arts and Humanities in Higher Education*, 9 (2): 133–148.

Nicol, D. and Macfarlane-Dick, D. (2006) "Formative assessment and self-regulated learning: a model and seven principles of good feedback practice." *Studies in Higher Education*, 31 (2): 199–218.

Norton, L. (2004) "Using assessment criteria as learning criteria: a case study in psychology." *Assessment and Evaluation in Higher Education*, 29 (6): 687–702.

O'Donovan, B., Price, M. and Rust, C. (2000) "The student experience of criterion-referenced assessment through the use of a common criteria assessment grid." *Innovations in Learning and Teaching International*, 38 (1): 74–85.

Ramsden, P. (1992) *Learning to Teach in Higher Education*. London: Routledge.

Ramsden, P. (2003) *Learning to Teach in Higher Education* (2nd edn). London: Routledge Falmer.

Rust, C., Price, M. and O'Donovan, B. (2003) "Improving students' learning by developing their understanding of assessment criteria and processes." *Assessment and Evaluation in Higher Education*, 28 (2): 147–164.

Säljö, R. (1979) 'Learning in the learner's perspective. I. Some common-sense conceptions', *Reports from the Institute of Education, University of Gothenburg*, 76.

Part II

Collaborating to Support Student Writers

4 A Comparison of "Additional" and "Embedded" Approaches to Teaching Writing in the Disciplines

Ursula Wingate

▶ Introduction

This chapter presents case studies of two different approaches to discipline-specific writing instruction which were carried out at King's College London. The "additional" approach consisted of an online course with three modules that was developed by a writing expert with some input from subject lecturers. Although the evaluation showed that the materials were suitable and regarded as helpful by students, the uptake of the course was low. The lack of student participation seemed to be related to the lack of interest and involvement by subject teachers which distanced the learning of writing from the learning of subject knowledge. The "embedded" approach, by contrast, was driven by subject lecturers who integrated writing instruction into the teaching of a first-year module. Five instructional methods were used to develop students' writing in the first term of their programme. The evaluation is not yet completed; however, first results show positive effects of the instruction on students' awareness and progress. The methods in which teacher input was the highest were rated as the most useful by students. It is argued that the involvement of subject lecturers must be higher than is the case in some additional approaches in order to provide effective and inclusive writing support for students.

Discipline-specific writing instruction is underpinned by genre theory (Swales, 1990; Berkenkotter and Huckin, 1995), by social constructivist theory (Bizzell, 1982), and by academic literacies (Lea and Street, 1998). These theoretical models have in common that they regard academic writing as social practice which reflects the norms, values, and epistemological understandings of specific discourse communities, and as the core activity through which academic disciplines construct and debate knowledge (Bazerman, 1988). Based on these theories, there has been a growing recognition that academic writing cannot be learned in separation from disciplinary knowledge. As a result, various types of discipline-specific writing pedagogies emerged, such as Writing across the Curriculum and Writing in the Disciplines (WiD) in the US (Russell et al., 2008), and genre-based literacy pedagogy in Australia (Martin, 1999).

At universities in the UK, however, the teaching of academic writing is still predominantly generic. Support is mostly offered outside the discipline, in remedial, extra-curricular "study skills" courses to which "at-risk" students from all disciplines are referred (Lea and Street, 1998; Ivanic and Lea, 2006). The approach is based on a deficit view of writing as the problem of the student (Mitchell and Evison, 2006), a view that has been frequently expressed in media reports highlighting falling standards and students who "can't write" (e.g. Shephard, 2006). The deficit approach to teaching writing is a leftover from the previous elite system in which those students who made it to university were expected to have adequate literacy competence. In today's mass higher education system, many students are not fully prepared for the demands of academic study, and the need to support students from all backgrounds has been repeatedly stressed (e.g. Thomas, 2002). As writing remains the "key assessment tool" (Lillis, 2001), it is obvious that the current generic and remedial model is outdated.

There is now an increasing number of WiD initiatives in UK universities (e.g. Ganobcsik-Williams, 2006; Mitchell and Evison, 2006; Morley, 2008, see also Part II of this volume). They are often driven by writing experts based in Learning Development or Language Centres who consult with subject teachers in order to tailor the writing sessions to the discipline. The level of subject teachers' engagement in these initiatives ranges from just providing discipline-specific information (e.g. Etherington, 2008) to embedding writing activities into regular subject teaching (Mitchell and Evison, 2006). Whilst there has been much theoretical and pedagogical discussion about these approaches, there is to date little empirical evidence of their effectiveness.

The case studies discussed in this chapter represent the low and the high end of subject teacher engagement. In the first, discipline-specific online materials were developed by a writing expert and offered to students as an "additional" learning tool, in the other case, writing instruction was integrated into the teaching of a first-year module. The objective is to compare the two approaches critically and contribute further insights to the growing body of "good practice" examples of teaching writing in the disciplines. In the next section, the distinction that is made in this chapter between "additional" and "embedded" approaches is explained in more detail. This is followed by the report of the two case studies, and a critical comparison of their viability and effectiveness.

▶ Additional and embedded approaches

Additional approaches are different from generic writing pedagogy insofar as instruction is based on discipline-specific texts and tasks. Etherington (2008) describes three modes of teaching academic writing, all of which are classified as additional in this paper: (1) cooperation, when writing instructors receive subject-specific texts and further information for the preparation of writing sessions from subject experts, (2) collaboration, when writing instructors and subject experts plan writing activities together, and (3) team teaching, when subject specialists are present in writing sessions to offer advice (pp. 37–8). In all three modes it is the writing instructor who does the teaching whilst the subject specialist offers varying degrees of assistance. The relatively low involvement of subject lecturers is a key characteristic of additional writing support. A second characteristic, closely related to the first, is that additional activities are not compulsory and not credit-bearing. Morley (2008) provides a range of examples of non-compulsory discipline-specific writing activities, offered by the Language Centre of his university, including workshops, weekly lectures and online writing programmes.

Research evidence shows that non-compulsory provision is often not taken up by the students who need them most, but by those who are already successful and want to enhance their performance (Durkin and Main, 2002). There are a few examples of compulsory writing modules which are delivered by writing instructors (e.g. Ganobcsik-Williams, 2006, Morley, 2008). However, making academic writing a compulsory element of the study programme does not on its own constitute the "embedded" approach as understood in this chapter. The approach also requires subject lecturers to take on the responsibility of teaching writing so that writing becomes "an integral, ongoing part of disciplinary learning for all students" (Mitchell and Evison, 2006, p. 72). Monroe (2002, 2003) strongly supports this approach on the basis that writing cannot be divorced from disciplinary thinking and learning. There are several important arguments for embedded writing instruction. First, as compulsory part of the curriculum, the approach achieves inclusiveness. Furthermore, subject experts, as highly proficient members of their "community of practice" (Lave and Wenger, 1991), are in the best position to induct novice writers. If they, as assessors of their students' writing, explain the criteria and requirements, mismatches between teachers' and students' understanding of academic writing criteria (as reported by Lea and Street, 1998 and Hounsell, 1987) can be avoided. Lastly, if academic writing is taught by subject lecturers, its status and relevance is enhanced in the view of students.

Although theoretical and pedagogical considerations support embedded writing instruction, there are some obstacles to this provision. One is the reluctance of subject teachers to teach writing, because they fear that this may lead to the reduction of subject content on the one hand, and an increase in their workload on the other hand. In addition, many subject experts feel that they should not be responsible for this aspect of student learning, an attitude that stems from the previous elite system (North, 2005). Another big obstacle is that many subject experts would have difficulty in teaching academic writing. Having gone through a lengthy process of acculturation in their discipline, their knowledge of the discourse and conventions remains "tacit" and "unarticulated" (Jacobs, 2005, p. 477). Because of subject experts' "lack of conscious knowledge" of their discipline's writing conventions, Etherington (2008, p. 33) argues that writing instructors are better able to "help both subject specialists and students focus on the pertinent aspects of specific writing and to show students how to start to include these within their own writing". However, Etherington's argument raises the concern that this kind of writing instruction may be limited to the linguistic, rhetorical, and textual level, whilst epistemological aspects—which are the domain of subject experts—remain untouched.

An important objective of conducting a case study of embedded writing instruction was to try out various instructional methods and consider their suitability for use by teachers from other disciplines. The case studies of the two different approaches were conducted to gather evidence of their strengths and weaknesses, with the long-term objective to make a case for embedded writing instruction and convince subject lecturers of its benefits. In the next part, the rationale, instructional design, implementation, and evaluation of the two instructional approaches are discussed.

▶ Case Study 1: "Additional" writing support

As part of a funded learning development project, three online modules, "academic writing", "referencing", and "avoiding plagiarism", were developed for first-year students of Management at King's College London. The author, then a member of a learning development unit, had been approached by lecturers of the Management Department who looked for ways of supporting their students with academic writing. The department had recently widened their intake to 180 first-year students per year, and the lecturers had noticed that increasing numbers of students struggled with their assignments and exam papers. Because of work pressures and the large number of students, the lecturers found themselves unable teach writing, and requested materials with which the students could start working independently upon their arrival at university. The lecturers agreed to provide relevant texts and materials so that authentic and discipline-specific modules could be created. These modules would be offered as a supplementary element in addition to the core modules of the first-year curriculum.

▶ Design of the modules

In addition to discipline-specificity, the design of the modules was guided by constructive and situated learning theory. According to constructivist theory, methods in which knowledge is transmitted were avoided, and activities were designed in a way that enables students to find answers independently and to construct their own knowledge (e.g. Biggs, 2003). Whilst many Web sites on academic writing contain of long lists of instructions, the activities in the Management modules required students to discover criteria and principles by themselves. Situated learning theory promotes the understanding that knowledge is best acquired in contexts that reflect the use of this knowledge in real life (Brown, 1997). This understanding further supported the choice of discipline-specific texts and "authentic activities" (Herrington and Oliver, 2000). Another concept that influenced the design was Lave and Wenger's "legitimate peripheral participation" which describes how "apprentices" gradually learn the social and cultural practices of their community of practice through "broad access to arenas of mature practice" (1991, p. 110).

The materials gathered from Management lecturers therefore included a journal article as example of "mature practice", student essays annotated with teachers' comments and other types of teacher feedback on student writing. Furthermore, two Management lecturers were asked in interviews to comment on their expectations of "good" essays. The modules' activities include analysing case studies and tutor feedback on student essays, as well as practical tasks such as proofreading, writing references, and paraphrasing statements from the literature which resemble the "real life" writing experience at university.

The online presentation of the modules provided a flexible teaching and learning format, as it afforded non-linear access to a range of texts, audio files, and hyperlinks, as well as immediate feedback through pop-up windows. To illustrate the pedagogical principles, the components of the module "academic writing" are discussed next.

▶ The module "academic writing"

The module's sequence, as shown in Table 4.1, guides students from discovering the features and criteria of academic writing to applying

Table 4.1 Components of the academic writing module

1.	**Possible problems with essay writing**
1.1.	Case study 1
1.2.	Case study 2
2.	**Identifying features of academic writing**
2.1.	Reading a journal article
2.2.	Making a list of typical features
3.	**What do tutors expect?**
3.1.	What tutors say
3.2.	Tutor feedback on essays
3.3.	Making a list of criteria for successful academic writing
4.	**Applying the criteria**
4.1.	Making comments on student essays
4.2.	Comparing your comments with the tutor's comments
5.	**Practising some skills**
5.1.	Structure
5.2.	Paragraphs
5.3.	Grammar, spelling, and expression
5.4.	Shortening sentences
5.5.	**Using Tables and Figures**
5.5.1.	Why use tables and figures?
5.5.2.	Finding three golden rules for using tables and figures

them. The verbs in the headings, for example, *identifying, making a list, applying, practising, finding*, demonstrate the emphasis on student activity and construction of knowledge.

The case studies in Component 1 had the objective of raising awareness of difficulties typically experienced by novice writers and encouraging students to think of ways of dealing with these difficulties. They describe first-year students' struggles with time management and with the critical discussion of relevant literature.

In the second component, students are introduced to the academic discourse of their discipline, as they are asked to identify features in an article authored by two lecturers from their department.

Component 3 offers the opportunity to identify the criteria for successful writing from the most authentic and authoritative sources possible, that is the subject teachers. Lea and Street's (1998) finding that there is often a gap between tutors' and students' understanding of the requirements of writing has highlighted the need for students to hear from their teachers what their expectations are. A sound file with teacher interviews, a PowerPoint presentation with essay feedback, and a list with one lecturer's comments on 14 student essays provided this context-specific information. The list of comments is shown in Appendix 1; the comments are presented together with the essay grade, so that students can develop a sense for the importance of certain criteria. From these sources, students are required to draw up a list of criteria of successful writing.

The next step is to enable student to internalise the criteria by applying them. In Component 4, PDF files with essays from previous first-year students are presented, and students are invited to use their list of criteria to comment on these essays. They can then compare their comments with the lecturer's feedback which is accessible in separate files.

Component 5 consists of a number of practical tasks concerned with the development of technical writing skills, or what Lea and Street (1998) call "surface features" of academic texts. Students are asked to proofread an extract from a weak essay, insert paragraphs in an unstructured text, provide headings for sections, and split overlong sentences into shorter ones. Finally, examples are given where tables and figures are more concise than verbal explanations, and the students have to derive rules for presenting tables and figures from annotated student essays.

The development of the two other modules, "referencing" and "avoiding plagiarism", was guided by same principles. It should be noted here that the structure of the modules (as presented in Table 4.1 for academic writing) is generic and can be filled with specific content for most other disciplines. Since the Management modules were implemented, the generic structure has been applied to undergraduate programmes in Pharmacy (Wingate and Dreiss, 2009), Classics, Modern Languages, and to a postgraduate programme in Applied Linguistics. The same procedures of collecting subject-specific materials were used for these adaptations. The next sections consider the piloting, implementation, and evaluation of the Management modules.

▶ Piloting of the modules

Before the modules were first offered online to the first-year intake of 180 students, they were assessed by a Management lecturer and a writing expert for their content and instructional approach. Some amendments were made before the modules were piloted with four first-year students. The students worked through the modules in individual sessions with the author, and were asked to think aloud while carrying out the activities. Their comments were audio-recorded, while at the same time a video camera was directed at the computer screen to identify any navigation problems that might occur. The pilot study is described in more detail elsewhere (Wingate, 2008). The results were encouraging: the students found the materials and activities relevant and useful, and the activities helped them to develop substantial knowledge of the nature of academic writing in their discipline. To give one example, it was apparent that the case studies made the students aware of potential problems with writing and made them think of how to avoid these problems. This is apparent in the following extract of the think-aloud data:

> S1: I think I am facing this problem that Andrew has... that you are reading books and they keep on giving you lots of references to other books, and you want to read those books as well and when you start taking notes you find you are copying down chunks of text and by the time you get around to actually going back and revising, it is almost as if you have to read the book again.

The student went on to say that "it is important to stick to the question and not get carried away by reading too much stuff". The four participants in the pilot study were successful in identifying various strengths and weaknesses in students' essays (Component 4), which demonstrated that the previous activities had enabled them to understand the discipline's criteria of academic writing.

▶ Implementation and evaluation

The modules were grouped under the title "Study Skills" in a section of the Blackboard Learning System. They were first made available to the 2007 first-year cohort of Management students, and demonstrated by the author in a two-hour introductory session in the computer lab. During this session, the students started working independently and had the opportunity to ask for help in case they had questions or technical problems.

These introductory sessions were not continued in the following years. Instead, a Management lecturer would recommend the online modules during induction week and give the students a worksheet on how to access and use them. The implications of this approach will be discussed later. As all first-year students are automatically enrolled into the "Study Skills Course", to date the number of registered student users is 533. This number, however, says little about the actual use. As a way of evaluating the modules, at the end of the first term a questionnaire was handed out to all first-year students of Management in 2007 and 2008. The questions sought to investigate students' perceptions of the modules as well as their motivation for using them. The use of the modules was monitored through the facility in the Blackboard Learning System. The findings are briefly summarised here.

In 2007, 72 of 179 (40.2%) students returned the questionnaire. In 2008, although the same procedures were followed, the number of returned questionnaires was much smaller; that is 37 of 180 (20.6%). The low return rate of the second cohort suggests a lack of interest in the modules. However, the majority of those who did respond rated the various activities as useful or very useful.

The students were asked why they used the modules to the extent they did. Most respondents stated that they would have liked to make more use of the online materials, but did not manage to log on more than once or twice because they were too busy with their coursework. Other questions were whether and in which context the students were further encouraged by subject teachers to use the modules after the introductory session/induction. Only a few students stated that they had been referred to the course when they sought advice on academic writing from their personal tutor. It appears that the course was not mentioned in any of the first term's teaching sessions.

The monitoring facility confirmed the low usage of the online course. Of the 2007 cohort, all students logged in and worked with the modules at least once, due to the introductory session in the computer lab, with the rate of follow-up usage rapidly decreasing. Of the 2008 cohort, only 102 out of 180 students logged in once, and only 25 students went back to the course a second or more times. The low uptake will be further discussed in the comparison of the two approaches.

▶ Case Study 2: "Embedded" writing support

The second case study describes a writing intervention which was carried out in the first term of 2009–10 by three lecturers in an under-graduate programme in applied linguistics. The intervention methods were embedded in the first-year module "Language Learning", which consisted of 11 weekly two-hour sessions. There were 60 students in the first-year cohort. The rationale for carrying out the intervention at the very beginning of the programme was to accelerate the students' learning of writing, and to prevent them from a lengthy trial and error period by providing early explanations and practice.

After a pilot in the previous academic year (Wingate et al., 2011), funding was obtained to re-run and systematically record the intervention with the objective to disseminate it to academic staff across the university. Part of the funding could be used for employing a teaching assistant to help with the increased workload. Five instructional methods were integrated into the module's curriculum. The choice of these methods was guided by the literature on, and the lecturers' experience of, student needs.

▶ The five intervention methods

1   Reading and writing

The challenges that academic reading pose for novice writers are rarely discussed in the literature (for an example see Hendricks and Quinn, 2000). These challenges include identifying sources, extracting relevant information from these sources, summarising and paraphrasing information, and integrating it with one' own ideas. Rose and colleagues (2008) recommend supporting students by providing guidance and "scaffolding" with their first academic texts. Therefore, the intervention included three pre-session reading tasks. The students were given journal articles with topics related to the coming week's seminar. The articles were carefully selected to ensure that they did not contain too much jargon, or too many technical details on research methods. They were accompanied by tasks and questions that helped the students to identify main issues in the text, recognise discourse features, take notes, and summarise information. The students had to submit their notes and summaries to the online discussion forum two days before the classroom session, and would get an individual response either by a lecturer or teaching assistant.

In addition to developing academic reading, the objective of this method was to get the students used to writing from the very beginning of their studies, and provide them with formative feedback on their initially short, but increasingly longer pieces. This also meant that reading or writing problems of individual students could be identified and addressed early on.

2 Discussion and writing in class

Bean (2001) points out that in order to become proficient academic writers, students must be provided with opportunities to develop critical thinking. Among other activities, he proposes small-group tasks and the discussion of open-ended questions. Group discussions were integrated into two classroom sessions. The students were given the last 30 minutes to discuss questions related to the theories and concepts that were introduced earlier in the sessions. The groups had to write up a summary of their discussion and submit it online. Feedback was given in the same way as to the individual submissions.

3 Explicit teaching of argumentation

Genre theorists and academic literacies researchers (e.g. Martin, 1999, Lea and Street, 2006) have emphasised the importance of teaching the epistemological nature, as well as rhetorical features of academic texts explicitly. In the intervention, explicit teaching had these two foci: the argument as the building block of the debate and construction of knowledge on the one hand, and discourse features for expressing the argument on the other hand.

Argumentation was taught in three 30-minute units; the objective was to enable the students to identify arguments in texts and build their own. In the introductory unit, the Toulmin model of analysing arguments (Toulmin et al., 1984) in which the structure of arguments is described by claim, ground, and warrant was introduced. In the second unit, the students were asked to analyse arguments in the journal articles they were given for the reading and writing tasks (see first method). In the final unit on argumentation which took place in the last classroom session of the term, samples from the students own essays were discussed; the students worked in groups to analyse these arguments and improve them where necessary. The task and an example of a student analysis are shown in Appendix 2.

4 Explicit teaching of discourse features

In two sessions, text extracts from the literature related to the session topic were presented, and the lecturer pointed out features such as structure, signposting, discourse markers, hedging devices, and the linguistic means of referring to the work of other authors. Another session was devoted to explaining the assessment criteria for the assignment, discussing plagiarism, and teaching the techniques of writing references.

5   Formative feedback

As explained earlier, the students received feedback on their writing from the beginning of the course. To move on from the relatively short online submissions to gradually longer and more complex work, the students were required to complete an "exploratory essay" of 1500 words in Week 5. The essays were returned to the students individually and, in addition to detailed written comments, the lecturers spent about 10 minutes with each student to address individual questions and problems. The same formative assessment procedures were followed for an assignment that the students had submitted in Week 7 in another first-year module. After having received extensive formative feedback twice, the students were encouraged to make good use of it for their final assignment that had to be submitted at the end of term.

Table 4.2 provides an overview of the methods and timing of the intervention.

Table 4.2 Overview of intervention methods

Method	Details	Timing
1. Reading and writing	Students read journal articles, take notes, and write summaries Online submission of notes and summaries	Reading article in preparation for Week 1/ Week 2/Week 4
2. Discussion and writing in class	Group discussions, writing up of summary of discussion Online submission of summary	Last 30 minutes of classroom sessions in Week 2/Week 4
3. Explicit teaching of argumentation	1. Introduction of Toulmin model 2. Students analyse arguments in journal articles 3. Group discussion and analysis samples from student writing	1. 30-minute lecture in Induction Week 2. Week 3/30 minutes of classroom session 3. Week 11/30 minutes of classroom session

4. Explicit teaching of discourse features	Lecturer pointing out discourse features in literature as part of lecture	Week 3 Week 4
5. Formative feedback	Individual and group feedback increasingly longer pieces of writing; Feedback to be used for final assignment Final assignment due in Week 12	1. Feedback on online submissions: Weeks 1, 2, and 4 2. Feedback on group submissions: Weeks 2 and 4 3. Feedback on exploratory essay provided in Week 7 4. Feedback on essay in parallel module, provided in Week 10

The overview shows that the bulk of reading and classroom activities happen in Weeks 1–4, to prepare students—and leave them time—for the larger writing tasks which are carried out from Week 4 onwards. By contrast, formative feedback is provided throughout the term. The integration of writing development activities into the regular subject teaching and the frequency of the feedback naturally raise a few questions about feasibility, for instance how time could be spared in a content-based curriculum, and how lecturers could spare the time to provide the feedback. These questions are addressed in the evaluation of the intervention.

▶ Evaluation

To evaluate feasibility and impact of the intervention, the following questions were asked:

1 Feasibility

    1.1 Could the subject content be covered despite the time that was spent on classroom writing activities?

    1.2 Was the workload increase for subject teachers manageable?

2 Impact

    2.1 Did the students perceive the intervention as useful?

    2.2 Was there evidence of progress in student texts?

2.3 In particular, was there evidence of the impact of the formative feedback?

2.4 Was there any other evidence of students' enhanced understanding of, and competence in, academic writing?

Not all questions can be answered comprehensively here. At the time of writing, the results of the final assignment were not yet available, and a number of student interviews had still to be conducted. The evaluation data were therefore limited to the notes and discussions of the three subject teachers involved in the intervention (to answer questions 1.1. and 1.2), a student questionnaire (2.1), the comparison of a sample of student assignments (2.2.), and the analysis of diaries that five student volunteers wrote while writing the exploratory essay and the assignments due in Weeks 7 and 12 (2.3). The findings from these data are reported next.

▶ Covering subject content

The subject teachers found that the subject content could be fully covered, because the classroom time devoted to writing activities was compensated for by enhanced student preparation and activity. In comparison to previous years, more content was shifted into preparatory reading, and as a result of the reading tasks and the requirement to submit the associated writing online, students came to the sessions better prepared. The teachers also noticed that the integration of writing activities, particularly the in-class discussions and the analysis of arguments in journal articles, had the positive effect of a more student-centred approach and heightened student interaction, while the delivery of content became more condensed and concise. These changes in the teaching/learning format allowed the teachers to interact with individuals and groups of students and monitor their understanding of the sessions' key concepts.

▶ Teacher workload

Providing frequent feedback for 60 students—which is not even a particularly large undergraduate cohort—within one term is extremely labour-intensive. In this intervention it was possible through the fact that three lecturers and a teaching assistant shared the work. At the same time, the formative feedback was in the teachers' and students' view (see questionnaire results below) the most effective method of the intervention. According to the questionnaire, a high percentage of the students made good use of the feedback comments. As explained later, in the pilot study improvements in students' writing could often be traced back to earlier feedback comments. Furthermore, the individual feedback meetings enabled teachers to understand individual students' difficulties and provide specific help. Despite its benefits, formative feedback can probably not be provided to the same extent in a normal undergraduate programme because of the work increase for teachers.

▶ Student perceptions of the intervention

At the end of the term, the students were given a questionnaire to evaluate the different instructional methods on a five-point Likert scale (including the option "did not do the task"). Table 4.3 shows the methods ranked according to the students' perception of their usefulness. The number of responses varied slightly (between 39 and 42), as a few students failed to answer all questions. Therefore, the answers are presented in percentages.

The fact that 7 out of 9 activities were rated as useful or very useful by between 70% and 90% of the respondents is encouraging. It is obvious that in the students' view, formative feedback—particularly the opportunity to write a formative essay—as well as explicit teaching of writing (positions 2 and 6 in the ranking, but with little difference in the percentage) are useful. It is particularly interesting that five out of the six most highly rated activities (with the exception of three) depend on high teacher involvement, ranging from commenting on the exploratory essay and online submissions to the explicit teaching of

Table 4.3 Rank list of instructional methods

Method/Activities	Very useful or useful (%)
1. Exploratory essay	90
2. Session on referencing and plagiarism	88.1
3. Analysing students' argument	88.1
4. Feedback on online submissions	88.1
5. Feedback on exploratory essay	87.5
6. Explicit teaching of features of academic writing	83.4
7. Submitting summaries/notes online	76.1
8. Discussions and writing in class	55
9. Presentations on argumentation	28.6

writing in class. The teaching of argumentation was considered least useful. This may be explained the early introduction of the Toulmin model (Induction Week). Some students scribbled comments such as "too early" and "too challenging" in the margin of the questionnaire. By contrast, using the Toulmin model to analyse arguments from students' writing ranked highly (position 3); the timing (Week 11) and the focus on the students' own writing may explain why this activity was preferred by the students. In the second part of the questionnaire, there were further questions about the impact of the intervention. The answers to these questions will be discussed below.

▶ Improvements in student texts and the impact of formative feedback

A systematic analysis of all the texts written in this intervention could not be carried out in time for this chapter. However, a thorough analysis had been done in the pilot intervention of 2007–8. The grade development from an earlier assignment (A1), on which the students received formative feedback, and the final assignment (A2) is shown in Table 4.4.

Whilst it is encouraging that 56% of students had made improvements as opposed to 24.5% who made none or deteriorated slightly, an important question was whether these improvements could be to some extent attributed to the formative feedback. Evidence for the impact of the formative feedback was seen as crucial to show the value of this work-intensive method.

The text analysis of those students who had made progress showed that weaknesses commented upon in the earlier assignment did not reappear in the final assignment. In follow-up interviews, the impact of the feedback on the successful students was apparent: they could recollect precisely which comments they had received and describe

Table 4.4 Grade development between A1 and A2 (2007–8 cohort)

Category	Number (N = 62)	%
Improvement by at least 10% (grade range in A1: 40–55)	18	29
Improvement between 5–9% (grade range in A1: 51–67)	17	27
Consistently high achievers (grade range in A1 and A2: 68–75)	12	19
No improvement (+/– 5%) (grade range in A1: 38–50)	9	14.5
Small deterioration (between 1–5%) (grade range in A1: 51–67)	6	10

accurately how they had taken action and devised strategies for improving weak aspects in their writing (Wingate, 2010).

The first impact question of the evaluation questionnaire asked about the extent to which the students of the 2009–10 cohort had used the formative feedback. Eighty-two per cent of the respondents (N = 39) agreed or strongly agreed with the statement "I used the feedback of the exploratory a lot for the next assignment." Evidence of the uptake and effect of the feedback could also be found in the diaries which five students kept during the process of writing their assignments, for example:

Diary 09/10–4; Extract 5

> Reading the essay back I feel I could really have improved the parts he had commented on however and realised the feedback really helped me. I realised my paragraphs needed to link together more, which I have now done for my new essay. I feel this makes it much easier to read.

▶ Other evidence of enhanced understanding and competence

Another "impact" item in the questionnaire was the statement: "The writing intervention has helped me to understand the requirements of academic writing." Seventy seven per cent of the respondents (N = 39) strongly agreed or agreed.

Further evidence of the impact of the intervention methods was found in the student diaries. The following example shows that the student had benefited from Method 4 (Explicit teaching of discourse features):

Diary 09/10–1; Extract 3

> My introduction should be outlining my essay plan and what I am going to be discussing as she explained to us the other day. I feel my introduction is lacking this so I will be working on it tonight.

Overall, the preliminary evaluation results of the 2009–10 intervention as well as the results of the pilot intervention are encouraging in terms of teacher and student perceptions and impact. Both dimensions will be further investigated through student interviews and the analysis of student writing. At present, it can be said that embedding writing into the regular teaching of the discipline has certainly positive effects on the students, and no negative effect on the teaching of subject content.

▶ A critical comparison of the two approaches

The evaluation of both approaches has provided some evidence of the suitability of the materials and methods, of positive student perceptions, and, although only to a limited extent, of the impact of the embedded approach. The comparison will consider some issues raised in the earlier discussion, namely inclusiveness, the involvement of subject teachers, and finally, the suitability of the instructional methods for use by teachers from other disciplines.

The additional approach presented in Case Study 1 was clearly not inclusive. The monitoring of uptake showed that online activity decreased rapidly in the first cohort after an introductory session which was offered by the author (who was not a subject teacher of Management) and attended by all students. The reason for the initial full participation was that the induction event was a timetabled compulsory activity. In the following year, when the introductory session did not take place, initial uptake decreased to 56% of the first-year cohort, and only 13.9% used the course again afterwards. The lack of participation seriously limits the impact of the online course, and it is likely that more successful and ambitious students took advantage of the provision (Durkin and Main, 2002) whilst weaker students did not.

The lack of student participation was in this case obviously linked to the low involvement of subject teachers. The teaching mode was that of "co-operation" (Etherington, 2008) where materials and other information for the development of the online course were provided by subject tutors. Their involvement did not go further, however. As the online course was not even introduced or recommended by subject lecturers, it was completely detached from the teaching of the subject. The lack of tutors' interest certainly lowered the relevance of the provision in the students' view and diminished participation. It shows that this provision offers the opportunity for subject teachers to shift the responsibility of writing development to the computer, in the same way as others would refer students to study skills courses to "fix" their writing problems. In this case, the writing instruction was a real "add-on" and only a slight improvement to the generic provision in the sense that the materials were discipline-specific.

In comparison, the embedded approach included all first-year students and helped them to understand the requirements of writing early on in their studies. The students participated well in the various activities and found the writing intervention relevant. This is shown by their evaluation of the instructional methods, and their use of the feedback comments. Interestingly, the methods with the highest teacher input (feedback and explicit teaching of writing) were rated as most useful by the students. Their commitment was certainly enhanced by the fact that the subject lecturers taught writing as part of the subject, thus attributing the same relevance to writing and the subject content.

The case study also demonstrated that the integration of writing instruction into subject lessons does not mean that subject content has to be reduced. On the contrary, the intervention led to improvements in the teaching format, as it involved more student-centred methods and independent learning.

Although the evaluation is not yet completed, the findings so far are convincing enough to recommend this approach to other first-year subject teachers. This raises the question of how easily the approach can be adopted, and a note of caution is in place here. The subject lecturers in this case study had a specific interest in academic literacy and therefore more than "tacit knowledge" (Jacobs, 2005, p. 477) of writing conventions, which made the teaching of writing easier for them. They also had obtained funding to pay for extra resources required in the intervention. This helped particularly with the provision of formative feedback. However, subject teachers who do not have these advantages can still embed writing instruction to an extent that is appropriate and manageable. They can begin by adopting one method, for instance the explicit teaching of features of academic writing, and this way gradually build up their own conscious knowledge of these features. They can also offer formative feedback less frequently than it was provided in this case study. However, considering the benefits of this method, universities should provide extra resources to offer some formative feedback in the first year.

▶ Conclusion

In this chapter, two approaches of teaching writing in the discipline have been presented and compared. The additional approach, an online tool, was less effective as students made only limited use of it. The low participation was explained with a lack of teacher involvement and interest. The observations from this case study suggest that the additional provision of writing instruction might work better if there were stronger links to the subject teaching. The embedded approach was clearly effective in involving and engaging all students and developing their understanding of academic writing. Further research will be needed to evaluate the long-term effect of the embedded approach on students' writing. If results show that embedded instruction leads to improvements in student writing early on in the programme, an even stronger case can be made for this approach.

One problem that was mentioned earlier is subject experts' reluctance to teach academic writing. This may be gradually reduced through dialogue and staff development measures, as described by Mitchell and Evison (2006). On the one hand, the awareness must be raised that subject teachers should take responsibility for students' writing; on the other hand, effective methods of supporting students must be developed and proven. For this purpose, case studies as presented in this chapter and this book are much needed for building a strong pedagogical argument.

This argument must be used to convince university leaders and policy makers to invest in staff development and resources that enable academics to embed writing instruction into subject teaching. Changing the mindset at the leadership level is necessary to move away from the predominant remedial provision towards inclusive methods which integrate the learning of writing with the learning of subject knowledge.

▶ Appendix 1: Screenshot of list of tutor comments

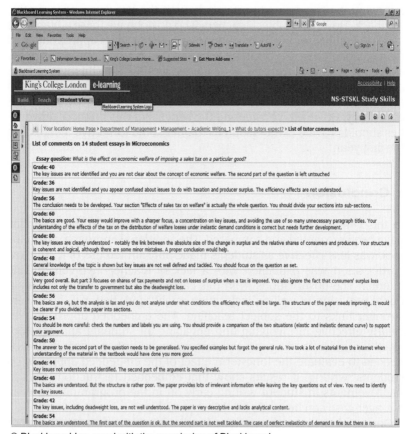

© Blackboard Inc, used with the permission of Blackboard.

▶ Appendix 2: Analysis of an argument from a student essay

Task:

Please analyse the following three examples from student texts. First, identify where the claim and grounds are in these arguments. Second, identify possible weaknesses (this is not saying that all examples are weak), for instance:

- Unsubstantiated claims (missing grounds).
- Lack of clarity/vague, imprecise language.
- One-sidedness.
- Factual inaccuracy.

Example:

| The opposite could be true (one-sidedness) | The majority of regional dialects come with a social prejudice attached, whether positive or negative. The Standard English dialect has connotations attached but these are prestigious and are associated with a higher social class, wealth, and higher educative standards. Unfortunately many regional dialects come with negative connotations; some dialects, especially from the north, are associated with a working social class and more poverty than wealth in a lot of cases. These sociological deductions from language happen whether conscious or subconscious and often affect the way people are treated. Therefore I believe if each region in the UK was to have its regional vernacular as its own individual official language used in education and in government, then these prejudices would creep deeper into further society and create bigger class divisions and social segregations between linguistically different areas. | Ground 1 Ground 2 Ground 3 Claim/conclusion |

▶ References

Bazerman, C. (1988) *Shaping Written Knowledge: the Genre and Activity of the Experimental Article in Science* (Madison: University of Wisconsin Press).

Bean, John C. (2001) *Engaging Ideas: The Professor's Guide to Integrating Writing, Critical Thinking and Active Learning in the Classroom* (San Francisco: Jossey Bass).

Berkenkotter, C. and Huckin, T. (1995) *Genre Knowledge in Disciplinary Communication* (Mahwah, NJ: Lawrence Erlbaum).

Biggs, J. (2003) *Teaching for Quality Learning at University* (2nd ed.) (Buckingham: Open University Press).

Bizzell, P. (1982) "Cognition, convention, and certainty: what we need to know about writing", *PRE/TEXT*, 3:3, pp. 213–244.

Brown, A. L. (1997) "Transforming schools into communities of thinking and learning about serious matters", *American Psychologist*, 52:4, pp. 399–413.

Durkin, K. and Main, A. (2002) "Discipline-based study skills support for first-year undergraduate students", *Active Learning in Higher Education*, 3:1, pp. 24–39.

Etherington, S. (2008) "Academic writing and the disciplines", in P. Friedrich (ed.), *Teaching Academic Writing* (London, New York: Continuum), pp. 26–58.

Ganobcsik-Williams, A. (2006) "Building an academic writing programme", in L. Ganobcsik-Williams (ed.), *Teaching Academic Writing in UK Higher Education: Theories, Practice and Models* (London: Palgrave Macmillan), pp. 98–109.

Hendricks, M. and Quinn, L. (2000) "Teaching referencing as an introduction to epistemological empowerment", *Teaching in Higher Education*, 5:4, pp. 447–457.

Herrington, J. and Oliver, M. (2000) "An instructional design framework for authentic learning environments", *Educational Technology Research and Development*, 48:3, pp. 23–48.

Hounsell, D. (1987) "Towards an anatomy of academic discourse: meaning and context in the undergraduate essay", in R. Säljö (ed.), *The Written World: Studies in Literate Thought and Action* (Berlin: Springer-Verlag), pp. 161–177.

Ivanic, R. and Lea, M. R. (2006) "New contexts, new challenges: the teaching of writing in UK higher education", in L. Ganobcsik-Williams (ed.), *Teaching Academic Writing in UK Higher Education: Theories, Practice and Models* (London: Palgrave Macmillan), pp. 6–15.

Jacobs, C. (2005) "On being an insider on the outside: new spaces for integrating academic literacies", *Teaching in Higher Education*, 10:4, pp. 475–487.

Lave, J. and Wenger, E. (1991) *Situated Learning: Legitimate Peripheral Participation* (Cambridge: Cambridge University Press).

Lea, M. R. and Street, B. V. (1998) "Student writing in higher education: an academic literacies approach", *Studies in Higher Education*, 23:2, pp. 157–172.

Lea, M. R. and Street, B. V. (2006) "The 'academic literacies' model: theory and applications", *Theory into Practice*, 45:4, pp. 368–377.

Lillis, T. M. (2001) *Student Writing: Access, Regulation, Desire* (London: Routledge).

Martin, J. R. (1999) "Mentoring semogenesis: 'Genre-based' literacy pedagogy", in F. Christie (ed.), *Pedagogy and the Shaping of Consciousness: Linguistic and Social Processes* (London: Cassell), pp. 123–155.

Mitchell, S. and Evison, A. (2006) "Exploiting the potential of writing for educational change at Queen Mary, University of London", in L. Ganobcsik-Williams (ed.), *Teaching Academic Writing in UK Higher Education: Theories, Practice and Models* (London: Palgrave MacMillan), pp. 68–84.

Monroe, J. (2002) *Writing and Revising the Disciplines* (Ithaca: Cornell University Press).

Monroe, J. (2003) *Local Knowledges, Local Practices: Writing in the Disciplines at Cornell* (Pittsburgh: University of Pittsburgh Press).

Morley, J. (2008) "Writing support in British higher education: an institutional case study", in P. Friedrich (ed.), *Teaching Academic Writing* (London: Continuum), pp. 125–146.

North, S. (2005) "Different values, different skills? a comparison of essay writing by students from arts and science backgrounds", *Studies in Higher Education*, 30:5, pp. 517–533.

Rose, D., Rose, M., Farrington, S. and S. Page (2008) "Scaffolding academic literacy with indigenous health sciences students: an evaluative study", *Journal of English for Academic Purposes*, 7:3, pp. 165–179.

Russell, D., Lea, M. and Street, B. (2008) "Exploring notions of genre in 'academic literacies' and 'writing in the disciplines': approaches across countries and contexts", Panel at SIGET IV International Symposium on Genre Studies, Brazil, August 2007.

Shephard, J. (2006) "Students today can't write, spell or count!" *Times Higher Education*, 10. February 2006.

Swales, J. (1990) *Genre Analysis: English in Academic and Research Settings* (Cambridge: Cambridge University Press).

Thomas, L. (2002) "Student retention in higher education: the role of institutional habitus", *Journal of Educational Policy*, 17:4, pp. 423–432.

Toulmin, S., Rieke, R. and Janik, A. (1984) *An Introduction to Reasoning* (New York, London: Macmillan).

Wingate, U. (2008) " 'Enhancing students' transition to university through online pre-induction courses", in Donnelly, R. and F. McSweeney (eds), *Applied eLearning and eTeaching in Higher Education* (Hershey, London: Information Science Reference, IGI Global), pp. 178–200.

Wingate, U. (2010) 'The impact of formative feedback on the development of academic writing', *Assessment and Evaluation in Higher Education*, 35:5, pp. 519–533.

Wingate, U. and Dreiss, C. (2009) " 'Developing students' academic literacy: an online approach", *Journal of Academic Language and Learning*, 3:1, pp. 14–25.

Wingate, U., Andon, N. and Cogo, A. (2011) "Embedding academic writing instruction into subject teaching: a case study", *Active Learning in Higher Education*, 12:1, pp. 1–13.

5 Enhancing Students' Legal Writing

Steve Foster and Mary Deane

▶ Introduction

This chapter reports on a collaboration at Coventry University between Steve Foster, a law specialist, and Mary Deane, a writing developer. They worked together to support students' transition to university and adoption of legal writing conventions, including referencing, analysis of cases, and formal expression. Foster and Deane also sought to address the relatively high proportion of students failing the first year of a law degree at their Institution. In this chapter, they explain the principles of their intervention and reflect upon the impact of widening participation for students of law, which is a discipline that makes particular academic demands. They conclude by suggesting a range of strategies to increase first-year students' confidence and competence as writers in their field to help smooth their transition to tertiary-level study.

Foster and Deane taught legal writing to 150 students on Coventry's LLB Law Degree in their first term at university. They designed an intervention that lasted for 5 weeks of the 10-week long autumn term, and this involved working together to create a range of teaching materials that explicitly taught legal writing. They shared their methods with colleagues in the Law department, and as the subject specialist, Foster extended these resources the following academic year to address issues which they felt they had not fully resolved. Their work began in 2008 and has continued to grow.

▶ Expectations of law lecturers about students' writing

An impetus for this initiative was concern within the Law School at Coventry University about the relatively high drop-out rate for students during the first year. Approximately 20% of law students either withdraw or fail to progress to the second year of the course. As writing is a substantial part of the assessment students undertake in law degrees, Foster and Deane felt that enhancing students' understanding of how to tackle assignments might help to reduce the drop-out rate. They chose to target the first-year course "Law Study" because this module is designed to equip students with the study and writing skills necessary to research, evaluate, and reference legal sources. As the Law Study course also teaches critical thinking, argumentation, and communication it was an appropriate context for teaching the culture and conventions of legal writing.

Students embarking on undergraduate law degrees discover early on that their tutors require them to employ a variety of writing and academic skills in both their general studies and in their written assessments. Often there is a gap between the expectations of academic staff and the skills students possess, and this often leads to frustration on the students' part when assessment grades reflect the gap. In the past, some academics have met with limited success in their efforts to promote sound legal writing. During the course of an undergraduate law degree, most students acquire good referencing and citation skills (mainly by the latter stages of their programmes) and become more comfortable with using legal materials in their assignments (again, usually towards the end of their programmes). Many students become more adept at understanding assessment tasks and identifying the issues raised in problem questions. However, despite dedicated instruction, it is not always the case that all students succeed, and in the past too many have failed to acquire sufficient legal writing skills, which has affected pass rates in the first year as well as latter years of degree programmes.

For some students the main barrier to effective legal writing is that English is a second language. For others the key challenge is that they are unused to demonstrating the critical thinking skills required of a law degree. For others the main issues are that they are unsure how to structure their ideas clearly or express them in an academic style. The formality required of legal writing often presents a hurdle, and too often students persist in using inappropriate sources (mainly from populist Internet sources) or a casual written style.

The traditional approach to assessment in law is simply to provide students with the assessment task and require them to produce a structured and properly referenced piece of work. This is based on the assumption that students starting a law degree have already acquired the basic skills of essay writing, which is not necessarily the case, particularly at institutions that pursue a proactive approach to widening participation in higher education (HE). Foster and Deane took a different approach by setting out to teach legal writing explicitly to all law students, thus ensuring that when students begin their formal assessments they are armed with the necessary writing competencies to succeed.

In summary, Law departments often have the following expectations of undergraduate law students' legal writing and use of sources:

Legal writing

- Students should be able to employ accurate **grammar** in their assessments; both in providing descriptive legal information and in offering analysis, criticism, and legal advice.
- Given the complex and flexible nature of legal material, it is expected that students make careful use of English and apply **appropriate legal English**.
- Students should construct clear legal **arguments** and evince sound legal reasoning.

Use of sources

- Students should make effective use of primary and secondary legal **sources** in support of their answers, and should learn to avoid plagiarism.
- Students should display a clear and lucid **application** of sources to the question or the facts of problem scenarios.
- Students must practise appropriate citation and **referencing** skills including the construction of accurate bibliographies.

Although these capabilities are required of all undergraduate students, the nature of law and legal study often requires students to employ enhanced, or specialised writing and referencing skills and related competencies (Foster, 2009, p. 3). For example, lawyers, and law students, are expected to research and utilise a wide variety and large volume of legal materials, to make clear use of complex legal data and arguments, to employ a clear and succinct written style, and to adopt the referencing style particular to law (Strong, 2006, p. 8). In particular, law students need to employ a certain level of "legalese" when writing their answers, showing familiarity with legal terms and institutions. For example, a non-lawyer may write, "The judge in the case said that the claimant should win his case in contract and that he should get money for that." In contrast, a law student would write: "Delivering judgment, Lindley J. held that the claimant had established that the contract had been breached and that he was entitled to substantial damages for loss of profits." Foster and Deane sought to help students recognise the features of legal writing and develop their ability to produce these features in their own work.

▶ Teaching legal writing to first-year students at Coventry University

Since 2000, Coventry Law School has made specific provision for the teaching of legal writing in addition to general law and legal skills courses. This focus on writing is partly due to local experience as Foster is the author of the popular book, *How to Write Better Law Essays* (2009). First-year students at Coventry University are offered the Law Study course, which helps them identify good (and bad) practice in research, essay writing, and referencing and citation of legal authorities. This course is delivered in a series of interactive lectures to assist students in acquiring sound research skills as well as helping them to avoid plagiarism by using primary and secondary sources appropriately. The module was formerly delivered in the first 4 weeks of the first term via three lectures and a short series of workshops covering the basics of research and essay writing. However, since 2007 it has been delivered via approximately 20 lectures throughout the academic year, allowing the module leader to give more intense and continuous tuition on essential research, writing and referencing skills and enabling the students to gradually acquire and enhance these skills. To supplement this course, students are recommended to research other study guides and purchase one of number of available texts on legal skills, such as Foster's volume (2009). Students are also given course materials and exercises via the University's Virtual Learning Environment to help them develop academically.

According to Bean, it is vital to embed writing instruction within disciplinary teaching because integrating "writing and other critical thinking activities into a course increases students' learning while teaching them thinking skills for posing questions, proposing hypotheses, gathering and analyzing data, and making arguments" (Bean, 2006, p. 1). Foster and Deane were informed by this insight, as well as by the premise that academic study involves learning about genres as well as developing disciplinary knowledge (Monroe, 2003). In addition they drew upon the Australian "Developing Academic Literacies in Context" (DALiC) approach to embedding the teaching of academic genres into subject courses (Skillen et al., 1999; Purser et al., 2008). They combined these North American and Australian traditions for the British university context in order to expose first-year students to the style, conventions, and legal content they would be expected to produce in undergraduate assessments.

Foster and Deane chose to work with a cohort of 150 students in order to maximise the reach of their work, and although the size of this group presented a challenge they wanted to develop strategies for teaching writing in a disciplinary context to a large group of students. They taught weekly sessions lasting 1 hour in a lecture hall during the first 5 weeks of the 20-week Law Study course. The student body comprised a mixture of international and home students, including many British students whose first language was not English. The gender mix was balanced, and the majority had recently come from school or college, although some were mature students. Foster and Deane invited the students to submit a formative writing task early in the course so they could get a sense of the issues that needed to be addressed. Despite working with a large cohort, they wanted the students to feel that their individual needs were met by giving them early and personal feedback. Foster and Deane introduced intensive teaching that ranged from tips on writing an introduction, to the concept of writing as a process and the technique of peer review, as shown in Table 5.1.

The students were given an opportunity to practice legal writing in the formative task, which was the essay question, "Should human rights thrive in times of terrorism?" They were given extensive feedback on their individual performance and on the characteristics and content their essays should contain. The students were then set a summative coursework assignment that required them to apply their knowledge of how to answer a legal problem essay appropriately (see Figure 5.1 below for a sample answer).

The rationale for organising the course in this way was to give students the maximum amount of time to practice legal writing before the summative coursework was due. Foster and Deane hoped that students who had tried to write a legal problem essay (in many cases for the first time) would be more receptive to guidance on how this could be done most effectively. The topics covered on this course thus moved from an introduction to legal writing as a process, to analysis of strengths and weaknesses in sample answers, and then to detailed guidance on the features of effective legal argumentation for an assignment of this type.

As Table 5.1 below demonstrates, the pace of the course was ambitious because students were required to produce the initial piece of coursework by the fourth week of term, although being a formative task the grade was not logged on their university records. However, the process of producing this work was staged by requiring students to write a plan and start drafting by the third week. Based on the principle that students need timely and targeted feedback, the formative task was marked and returned to students in week 5 before their summative coursework was due in week 8. This placed pressure on Foster and Deane, but they planned for this commitment and the advantage of allocating time to assess and discuss their feedback quickly was that they were not burdened with marking during the Christmas vacation period. As a legal expert, Foster paid particular attention to the content

Table 5.1 Law Study course

Week	Topic
1	Introduction to module: expectations of law academics regarding research and writing. Distribution of formative assessment task (due in week 4: a legal problem essay).
2	Tips on conceptualising legal writing as a process and advice on devising academic/legal arguments. Free writing exercise to gather ideas for formative task. Students asked to bring plan of the formative task and draft introduction of formative task in week 3.
3	Tips on essay planning and construction of paragraphs. Students critique each other's plans prior to submission in week 4.
4	Students submit formative task. Distribution of sample answers to this task, which students critique.
5	Feedback on formative task and guidance for (similar) summative task (due in week 8: a legal problem essay).
6	Advice on using legal sources as authority and on avoiding plagiarism.
7	Tips on legal referencing and using primary sources.
8	Submission of summative task. Further advice on legal referencing and using secondary sources.
9	Feedback on answering legal problem essays 1 (writing/referencing).
10	Feedback on answering legal problem essays 2 (interpretation of task).
CHRISTMAS VACATION	
11	Feedback on law assignment in European law (from relevant module leader).
12	Feedback on law assignment in Contract law.
13	Feedback on law assignment in Property law.
14	Feedback on law assignment in Constitutional law.
15	Feedback on law assignment in English Legal System.
16	Guidance on presentation of second summative task.
17	Advice on revising for examinations.
18	Tips on writing law answers in examinations.
19	Feedback on second summative task.
20	Overview of course.

Formative and summative coursework tasks

Every healthy democratic state prides itself on its human rights record and its willingness to uphold principles of equality, human dignity, liberty and due process. These principles are invariably contained in domestic law and form part of the state's international obligations, and a breach of them gives rise to possible breaches of the law and national and international criticism. However, these rights cannot be enjoyed absolutely and in times of emergency they may need to be compromised for the sake of the state and the rights of its citizens.

> The writer has explained the general context of the paper successfully.

> The writer is answering the question clearly with a one-sentence 'thesis statement' early in the paper.

Events such as 9/11 and the bombings in London in 2005 have resulted in the passing of a number of legislative provisions which were intended to restrict individual liberty and human rights in the name of public safety and national security. Recently, for example, legislation has been passed extending the period of police questioning of those suspected of terrorist offences to 42 days. This begs the question whether the enjoyment of human rights can survive emergency situations such as the imminent threat of terrorism and whether those suspected or found guilty of acts of terrorism should be able to rely on human rights law.

> This information makes the topic relevant and interesting for the reader.

International law provides some guidance in this respect, accepting that states may further restrict some human rights during times of war and other public emergency, and stating clearly that such measures cannot infringe on the most fundamental rights such as the right to life and freedom form torture In other cases, however, the exceptional measures must be reasonable and proportionate; but who decides where the balance lies between protecting basic rights and safeguarding national security and public safety?

> The writer establishes a sense of balance and examines both sides of the issue.

Figure 5.1 An annotated sample law essay.

of the assignments, and as a writing developer, Deane concentrated on the organisation of ideas, and they both found this a fruitful partnership.

Alongside the opportunity to practice legal writing and obtain feedback from peers and tutors, the students were exposed to sample answers to the formative problem essay they were set. Foster and Deane devised a strong sample answer and a weak response, and they annotated these, pointing out features of the legal content and the written style, as demonstrated in Figure 5.1 above.

▶ Breakdown of legal writing course components

Week 1
The first week of the course was the first experience of university study for many students, so Foster and Deane sought to channel students'

enthusiasm for this early engagement with academia. They began by discussing the finding from the National Student Satisfaction Survey that feedback is the key to a positive learning experience (NSS, 2008). They explained that during the coming weeks students would be invited to undertake a formative assignment and gain feedback from academics and their peers to improve their performance in the summative assignment. As the summative assignment was structured in a similar manner to the formative assignment, they suggested that lessons learned from the formative piece would be invaluable for the formally assessed written task (O'Donovan et al., 2008).

When giving writing guidance during the first week of the module, Foster and Deane introduced a process approach to writing with the aim of helping students to systematise and improve their approach to assignment writing (Pritchard and Honeycutt, 2006). Although it is potentially problematic to conceptualise writing as a process, they believed that this group of students would benefit from exploring a framework for managing their time and legal writing; partly because for past cohorts of students, poor personal organisation was a major factor that threatened their academic performance. As these students had not previously been exposed to a process approach to writing, on the whole they appreciated the option of using a process to organise their composition. However, a limitation of focusing on the process was that this concentrated attention on how to write rather than what students are required to learn about in terms of legal problems and approaches. In the future, Foster and Deane will interrogate the appropriateness of this approach for teaching legal writing, and will aim to employ a more subject-specific framework by using a greater range of texts containing substantive legal material.

Week 2

In the second week, Foster and Deane invited the students to reflect upon the components of a legal argument (Foster, 2009, p. 65). The students were asked to work in pairs to define an "academic argument", which the group as a whole then defined as the written communication of a reasoning process leading to a convincing conclusion. Despite their efforts to contextualise the topic of argumentation, Foster and Deane feel that in the future it would be valuable to link even more closely to the practice of argumentation in law. Nevertheless, students were directed to the course text book for further guidance, Foster's *How to Write Better Law Essays* (2009). This book and the accompanying Web site cover essential topics such as how to research sources, organise a legal paper, and present texts appropriately.

During this second lecture, they concentrated on how to organise an academic argument and students were asked to spend a few minutes free writing to generate ideas for their formative assignments. Their prompt for this short exercise was to think about the formative assignment question, "Should human rights thrive in times of terrorism?" Following this, time was allocated to sharing ideas and students were given key terms and suggestions before being given time to construct a preliminary plan for their formative assignments. Hence, Foster and Deane began the module by introducing the concept of writing as a process, then they involved students in modelling the writing process by short activities based around the formative and summative coursework tasks.

Week 3

Students were asked to bring assignment plans to the third lecture, and contrary to the academics' expectations a high proportion carried out this task. In fact, approximately 90% took advantage of this opportunity, and Foster and Deane were struck by the level of commitment shown by the vast majority of students. Despite being a group of approximately 150, the students also managed to give each other comments on this formative task in a large lecture theatre using the prompts for peer review and advice on being constructive in their feedback to peers. They discussed the importance of seeking feedback at an early stage in the composition process, and demonstrated how submissions for academic journals undergo a rigorous process of peer review. Students were not only given instruction on how to undertake peer review, but also informed that by critiquing colleagues' plans they would probably gain insight into how to improve their own assignments.

As peer review can be a challenging exercise and this group had not been required to undertake such an activity before, Foster and Deane hoped that the students would not be too intimidated by sharing their plans, whereas they may have felt awkward showing fellow students complete drafts. For the peer review session, Foster and Deane introduced the following ground rules:

- Give constructive, encouraging comments.
- Identify up to three features of the plan you appreciate.
- Identify up to three aspects of the plan which could be improved.
- Give examples so the writer has a clear idea of what you mean.

Week 4

In the fourth week students were required to submit the 500-word formative assignments, which were marked by Foster and Deane and returned the following week. This lecture was devoted to giving recommendations on the content of the assignment, and the rationale behind timing this detailed guidance was that having grappled with the assignment, students would be most receptive at this stage in the course. Although Foster and Deane had given instruction during the preceding weeks, they felt that it would have been counterproductive to tell students in too much detail what they might write. At this point, they also dedicated time to issues of composition such as effective research to locate appropriate sources, clear argumentation, and strong paragraph structure.

Emphasis was also placed on the required legal content, which for this assignment included reference to the European Convention of Human Rights and the Human Rights Act as well as discussion of the legal and constitutional doctrines of the separation of powers and the rule of law. The goal of offering these tips was to help guide students towards the types of arguments they might adopt in their future work. Students were not expected to cite legislation and other legal sources in their formative assignments because referencing was yet to be covered in detail (see Table 5.1), but they were informed that this would be essential for the forthcoming summative assignment. Building on the advice they received at this point, students were provided with online access to two chapters from key textbooks when they progressed to tackle the summative coursework assignment.

Week 5

In the last week of these intensive legal writing activities, students received both general feedback and specific comments on the formative work they had submitted the previous week. They were expected to think for themselves based on this teaching, for instance, they were asked to list the points markers had made about their work with the aim of avoiding those errors in future. They were again directed to Foster's *How to Write Better Law Essays* (2009). In addition, Deane responded to the frequency of grammatical errors in the draft texts by recommending a range of Web sites where students could learn more about English grammar, punctuation, and register and practice via quizzes or other activities (BBC Skillswise, 2008). The single most important piece of advice students received was to put serious time into revising and editing their assignments before submitting, and they were reminded of the utility of peer review in this regard.

Deane returned to the topic of argumentation to conceptualise the "DODJE" approach to remind the students of key ways in which they could avoid producing what she termed "dodgy" work that was unlikely to pass. She hoped this formula would be more suitable for this particular cohort than conventional process approaches to composition:

* **D**ECIDE upon your argument
* **O**RGANISE it

- **D**EVELOP it
- **J**UNK irrelevant material
- **E**DIT it

In order to illustrate how to write an effective legal argument, Foster and Deane selected two of the most successful formative assignments and obtained permission to distribute anonymous extracts during the lecture. They identified the strengths of these texts and invited students to reflect upon ways of enhancing the arguments further. Important characteristics of these samples included originality of approach, clarity of argument, and scholarly use of legal sources. In addition, these well-written pieces were characterised by formal language, which was significant because the majority of the formative assignments were not sufficient in this regard. Students engaged with these authentic examples because they had made their own attempts, and were therefore ready to learn how to gain the grades they desired but had not necessarily received for their own efforts. Students also appeared to be more willing to emulate successful peers than to take advice from academics at this stage in the course.

▶ Findings

This discipline-based approach to writing development resulted in three observations with implications for teaching first-year legal writing. The first insight Foster and Deane gained is that, unsurprisingly, five weeks of legal writing activities were insufficient to bring about major changes in students' performance, although they felt that they had improved the culture of writing, research, and referencing amongst this cohort. Indeed, the wider 20-week course is also inadequate to turn around students' academic writing. Whilst this seems a platitude, it is often believed that students' writing can be "fixed" in a matter of weeks, whereas this initiative demonstrated that the development of cognitive skills and discipline-based academic literacy is a long-term endeavour. Further, as proposed in the conclusions below, there may be other reasons for student failure in the first year apart from a lack of basic academic skills. Time management capabilities are essential for scholarly success, and engagement in the subject of study is also crucial. These are not necessarily helped by the intensive nature of assessment on law degrees and the tendency towards ever-shorter academic years.

Secondly, the schema of setting a formative task, employing peer review, giving prompt feedback about both the content and form of assignments enjoyed success. Compared to the previous year's cohort the majority of students who participated in this writing intensive teaching produced more structured assignments with more appropri-ate paragraphing, whilst many showed an improved ability to cite and evaluate legal sources. For example, between the formative and the summative stages there was strong evidence that students were adopt-ing a clearer logic in their paragraphing, and were able to provide reasonably coherent introductions and conclusions.

Further, there was evidence that the students were more capable of addressing and answering the set question than previous cohorts; although students obviously benefited from the sessions where key points of the question were identified in advance of submission—a facility that is not generally made available to students on their other courses. Nevertheless, the initiative did not resolve the intractable issue of students' written style, and despite modelling the kind of written expression expected of lawyers, too many formative and sum-mative assignments were written in an inappropriately informal style. It appeared, therefore, that although students were pointed to poor practice and could identify such, many of the cohort found it difficult to rectify errors or emulate the high quality writing samples provided (see Figure 5.1 above). This problem was compounded by the lack of intensive proof-reading adopted by most students before submission; a problem which can only be resolved by the students themselves by improving their time-management.

Linked to this point, this cohort of students suffered from a lack of exposure to academic texts and other sources, which meant that they struggled to reproduce scholarly language in their assignments. Thus, reading material made available online to the students appeared to be largely ignored; the students preferring to base their research on briefer and less formal Internet sources. It is widely recognised that students' limited reading, and their increasing reliance upon online sources, reduces their ability to produce appropriately clear and aca-demic language. However, Foster and Deane contend that this issue goes hand in hand with low levels of scholarly confidence in certain undergraduates. In the lecture that focused on academic argumen-tation, some students commented that they did not feel "academic" and revealed that they were confused about demands exerted by the academy.

Thirdly, and also linked to students' style of expression, it became clear during this intervention that students desired explicit examples, not only of common errors, but also of how to fix them. Foster and Deane hope that by sharing their learning from disciplinary writing development it will become increasingly practical to show students not only what is unacceptable in terms of register and style, but also how weak writing can be re-worked into appropriately academic texts. Thus, in the following academic year both law and writing developers produced exercises to help law students identify stylistic errors which were distributed in class and via the University's Virtual Learning Environment.

It is hoped that exposure to legal writing errors and continual practice at revising and editing will increase student confidence and ability in this area. In the light of changing literacy practices and a tangible reduction in sustained reading in some cases, academics can respond proactively through discipline-based collaborations by bringing together subject expertise and writing pedagogies to target the issues facing specific cohorts of students. Yet on reflection, the students in this group may have responded better to writing advice that was more integrally related to legal issues and contexts, and this initiative was only a starting point in developing a syllabus and resources to fit the profile of this group.

Contrary to Foster and Deane's hopes for this cohort, student performance, pass rates, and average marks on the Law Study course initially appeared to be slightly down on previous years. There were, however, a number of reasons for this early outcome that do not necessarily undermine the positive results that the intervention achieved. First, unlike previous years, students were not given an opportunity to present an optional piece of work to rectify failures during the currency of the course. Instead, students had to re-sit assignments during the summer period. When the pass rates were equalised, it was evident that the vast majority of students who re-sat the module displayed the necessary legal writing competencies and passed the first year.

Nevertheless, some students failed to submit one of the summative coursework assignments and thus achieved a fail mark overall, despite performing soundly in the other assessment. Happily, in contrast to previous years there were very few students who produced wholly inadequate or inappropriate work, and the vast majority of the failures were marginal. This suggests that most of the students improved their basic legal essay writing as a result of this targeted instruction, and encouraged by this, Foster and Deane's discipline-based intervention is ongoing, and as the legal specialist, Foster has taken full responsibility for extending and developing their work.

▶ Conclusion

This WiD initiative identified that students' ability to construct effective paragraphs improved through explicit guidance and feedback opportunities. In general, students' structure in assignments, including their ability to answer the set question, also improved. However, students' academic style and use of English grammar and punctuation was not necessarily improved by the teaching interventions and use of peer review.

Based on the use of samples of good and bad legal writing, it was evident that students were able to identify bad practice, but then failed to rectify the errors and write in an appropriate fashion. For instance, students appreciated where the language used in the samples they examined was too colloquial, but they could not suggest more formal alternative phrasing. To address this issue, they could be given small-scale exercises requiring them to re-write sentences. For instance, in the next academic year, students were given an inappropriately written essay containing grammatical, spelling, and referencing errors, which they needed to revise after identifying the mistakes.

In summary, the points Foster and Deane propose as foci for colleagues' explorations of discipline-based writing development include:

- Students benefit from intense tuition and guidance on essay structure and paragraphing, so it can be fruitful to offer legal writing development in the early part of the first undergraduate year.
- Students benefit from exposure to peer review and completing formative assessments, so this can usefully be built into curricula.
- Students benefited less from exposure to examples of good (and bad) writing practice, being unable fully to adapt to a more appropriate academic style. Therefore, it may be helpful to devise exercises to test students' ability to identify bad practice and to re-draft, in the expectation that intense practice of this skill will gradually enhance their legal writing style.
- The above measure could be supplemented by encouraging students to further their academic reading. In particular, throughout the academic year academics might provide access to a range of scholarly papers that students are expected to read and appraise.

Foster and Deane are continuing to collaborate and try different approaches to supporting the first-year law students. For instance, they are in the process of tracking the performance of this cohort during the students' second year. Their future research includes error analysis of students' draft assignments in comparison with their revised work in order to identify specific grammatical and stylistic issues to inform their next teaching interventions (Borg and Deane, 2011).

As a leading author on legal writing, Foster took the lead from the start of this initiative, and in the spirit of WiD initiatives he ran the writing intensive interventions within his Law Study course for the second iteration. Overall, this collaboration emphasised the importance of narrowing the focus of writing development and drawing firmly and consistently on subject expertise. This collaboration confirmed that writing development is a wider process than the timeframe of an undergraduate course, and whilst students can be encouraged to take responsibility for their intellectual development, no single course can address all the capabilities of advanced level legal writing. Foster's production of a text book on legal writing addresses the fact that students require time and space as well as intensive writing support. With a range of resources and opportunities for guided practice and feedback, this WiD initiative suggests that students can improve in certain aspects of legal writing, and can be usefully encouraged to equip themselves to progress.

▶ References

BBC Skillswise (2008) *Improve Your English*. Available from <http://www.bbc.co.uk/skillswise/> [20th April 2011].

Bean, J. C. (2006) *Engaging Ideas: The Professor's Guide to Integrating Writing, Critical Thinking, and Active Learning in the Classroom*. San Francisco: Jossey-Bass Publishers.

Borg, E. and Deane, M. (2011) "Measuring the Outcomes of Individualised Writing Instruction: A Multilayered Approach to Capturing Changes in Students' Texts." *Teaching in Higher Education* (forthcoming).

Foster, S. (2009) *How to Write Better Law Essays: Tools and Techniques for Success in Exams and Assignments*. 2nd edition. Harlow: Longman.

Monroe, J. (2003) *Local Knowledges, Local Practices: Writing in the Disciplines at Cornell*. Pittsburgh: University of Pittsburgh Press.

NSS (2008) *National Student Survey*. Available from <http://www.guardian.co.uk/education/table/2008/sep/11/students.highereducation> [20th April 2011].

O'Donovan, B., Price, M. and Rust, C. (2008) "Developing Student Understanding of Assessment Standards: A Nested Hierarchy of Approaches." *Teaching in Higher Education* 13 (2): 205–217.

Pritchard, R. J. and Honeycutt, R. L. (2006) "The Process Approach to Writing Instruction." In *Handbook of Writing Research*. ed. by MacArthur, C. A., Graham, S., and Fitzgerald, J. New York: Guilford: 275–290.

Purser, E., Skillen, J., Deane, M., Donahue, J., and Peake, K., (2008) "Developing Academic literacy in Context." *Zeitschrift Schreiben*. Available from http://www.zeitschrift-schreiben.eu [13th July 2009].

Skillen, J., Trivett N., Merten M., and Percy, A. (1999) "Integrating the Instruction of Generic and Discipline Specific Skills into the Curriculum: A Case Study" in *Cornerstones: Proceedings of the 1999 HERDSA Conference* (Canberra: HERDSA).

Strong, S. I. (2006) *How to Write Law Essays and Exams*. Oxford: Open University Press.

6 Writing *Hazards*

Dave Horne and Kelly Peake

▶ Introduction

In a sense, we are telling two stories here: the first is of an intervention into a Geography course, *Hazards*, to improve the quality of students' writing, while the second is of our attempt to write that situation, and in the process coming to question whether we had understood our first story at all. We must confess to having had a degree of revelation through the drafting of this chapter, an experience that, interestingly, mirrors the process of discovery underpinning the work we describe. In this work, as we will discuss below, it was mapping texts, deconstructing genre, and trying to make explicit our criteria for judgement that led us to a much greater awareness of what we valued in writing.

We set out to develop assessment criteria as a teaching tool, hoping to use the criteria to convey this awareness to students whose work we were marking. This collaborative model of immersing ourselves in the language of a subject and the form of a text in order to explain, define, and typify for students pushed us both to greater understandings of our practices than we had previously possessed, despite working successfully with them for years. Ironically, however, using this same process of reflective enquiry and intensive debate to review our work for this chapter has led us to another understanding—a critique of the criteria we worked so hard to develop—and now, when trying to explain why our collaboration was successful, we feel that the value lies in a very different location from that which we imagined originally.

▶ Thinking Writing

The starting point for both stories is the connection between Thinking Writing (TW) and the Department of Geography at Queen Mary University of London (QMUL). Thinking Writing is a collegiate staff and curriculum development initiative at QMUL that focuses on the role of writing in disciplinary learning and communication. The origins of Thinking Writing lie in the Writing in the Disciplines (WiD) program at Cornell University, where QMUL was the first UK university to participate in their summer consortium in 2001. The impetus for this connection was an intellectual and theoretical dissatisfaction with the deficit model of traditional study skills teaching (Lea and Street, 1998; Haggis, 2006) and the marginalising discourse that surrounded this. In adapting the WiD approach to the UK context, the staff of TW (initially one, now four) have aimed to develop writing awareness and enrich writing practices for learning and assessment across the university (Mitchell and Evison, 2006). Our approach has been to collaborate with departments and individual teachers in a deliberately decentralised, non-prescriptive way to, as Monroe puts it, "encourage faculty from these disciplines to speak of writing and the teaching of writing in their own terms and with their own voices" (Monroe, 2003, p. 10). A lot of our work was initially around reimagining the kinds of writing students were doing, moving away from the constraints of generic essayist literature (see Lillis, 2001) to shorter texts more closely aligned to authentic purposes (following the ideas of Pope, 1995, Booth et al., 1995, Bean, 1996, Biggs, 1999, among others) and examining how writing was positioned in particular courses. This was a deliberate attempt to move writing from being seen largely as a medium for assessment to also being used as a tool for teaching and learning.

The Department of Geography has been engaged with TW work for a number of years, focusing on the need to help students develop the critical reading skills needed for academic writing. Although TW had aided the department in a 2004–5 project to develop teaching materials for the CLEAR project (Critical Literature Evaluation and Review) which focused on third-year students' literacy skills, there had been little formal partnership; furthermore, prior to 2006, writing development work was not systematically embedded in the Department of Geography curricula. Since then, however, there have been significant changes in the way TW has supported and worked with the department with an increase in explicit attention given to writing within the disciplinary programme, and a system of ongoing collaboration in both the preparation and delivery of teaching materials across multiple modules.

▶ "Developing Academic Literacy in Context"

The catalyst for these changes was the invitation to participate in the "Developing Academic Literacies in Context" (DALiC) project at the University of Wollongong, in December 2006. The aim of our participation was twofold: to adopt and adapt methodologies and materials developed in collaboration with Wollongong Learning Development staff;

to evaluate the strengths of this work in different institutional and educational contexts; and to consider the impact that our collaboration had on writing in our wider context at QMUL. The Wollongong approach involves creating an integrated curriculum where reading, writing, and study skills are systemically embedded into a disciplinary course of study (as outlined in Skillen et al., 1999, James et al., 2004, among others). It is targeted at the successful production of specific genres. While TW's work had also involved integrating writing into courses/modules, the integration was more to do with writing in order to learn about a subject rather than learning to write a particular type of text (drawing on Britton et al., 1975); we had also rarely framed writing overtly as a set of skills. The DALiC collaboration offered an opportunity to focus more closely on the production of texts, and to trial elements of a genre-based approach to writing. In addition, it provided us with guidance in developing and using explicit assessment criteria, and a chance to explore how these approaches fitted with existing beliefs and practices at QMUL. The sites for the DALiC work were two well-established Geography courses that had already been running for several years, at two different levels. The first was one tutorial group of 5 Environmental Science students taking a module entitled *Introduction to Environmental Ideas and Practice* (essentially similar to the *Introduction to Geographical Ideas and Practice* module taken by the entire first-year cohort of Physical Geography students); the second intervention occurred in *Hazards*, a second-year module which was run with a new writing focus. Here we present the latter as an example of our collaboration.

Hazards—the context

The *Hazards* course is a second-year elective module taught mainly by one lecturer, Horne, with contributions by other lecturers, and taken by approximately 35–40 students. The aim of the module is to teach students about causes and consequences of environmental hazards, such as earthquakes or floods, as well as their associated mitigation policies and practices. A typical outline schedule for the module, with indicative content, is shown in Figure 6.1. Assessment is by coursework (30%) and an unseen examination paper (70%). We considered it an interesting module for writing development work due to the atypical nature of the assessed coursework: the single piece of written coursework is a largely unfamiliar kind of text, a briefing paper, and students are expected to write in groups rather than individually. These two features, a new genre and group writing, offered a unique situation for trialling a new approach.

In this context, a briefing paper is—and is described to the students as being—"a report such as might be given to a government official

---

Week 1. Introduction to Hazards
  Allocation of groups and topics for coursework Briefing Papers
Week 2. Thematic geoscience mapping for planning and development
  Group advising meetings
Week 3. Volcanic hazards
Week 4. Flood hazards
Week 5. Climate change hazards
Week 6. One-day field trip
Week 7. *READING WEEK – NO CLASS*
Week 8. *Coursework draft peer review workshop; group work*
Week 9. Earthquake and Tsunami hazards
  Submission of draft coursework
Week 10. Diseases and pandemics
  Return of drafts; feedback session
Week 11. *Group Presentations on Briefing Paper topics*
Week 12. Revision Session
  Final submission of coursework

Figure 6.1 Typical outline schedule for the *Hazards* module; main lecture topics in bold, coursework-related sessions in italics. Actual timing and delivery of elements has varied from year to year.

to read in preparation for a meeting to discuss how to deal with a potential hazard or respond to a recent disaster, or perhaps for a visit to the scene of a recent disaster…it is not an essay". In definitively not being an essay, or a laboratory or field report (the other text types that students have encountered frequently in their degree courses to this point), the task is asking students to do something new in both the way they approach the information in the subject and how they write about it. Even prior to their involvement in the DALiC project, the lecturers were aware of how challenging the writing task was to students, and issued very detailed guidelines at the start of the module on style, formatting, and content. Previous experience showed that simply issuing these guidelines to students was not enough. Alternative approaches were clearly needed to maintain, throughout the module, students' focus on the style and structure as well as the content of their briefing papers.

Experience also suggested that the mechanics of group writing contributed significantly to the typical successes and problems identified in briefing papers. Weaker briefing papers were characterised by fragmented tone and structure, and failed to draw together diverse types of information effectively. Much of this was connected with the process of jointly drafting and editing work, and, we felt, under-standing and acting on the assessment criteria. The most successful groups were often those that integrated and edited individually writ-ten sections into a well-balanced treatment of the topic, credit being given for clarity and concise style as well as the depth and detail of coverage of the subject matter. We suspected that the majority of groups producing mediocre or simply "acceptable" results may have achieved higher grades through the review and revision of a draft before final submission, paying particular attention to the quality of their writing—not simply a proof reading exercise to correct gram-matical and spelling errors but a critical appraisal of layout, language, integration, balance, and style. Hazard assessment, mitigation, and relief are multidisciplinary undertakings, and groups composed of stu-dents from different degree programmes (the course being taken mainly by Physical Geography, Human Geography, and Environmental Sci-ence students) benefited from the diversity of knowledge and approach that they were able to bring to the task; on the other hand, such groups did not always find it as easy to work together as, say, a group composed entirely of Physical Geographers. While the levelling effect of group work meant that there was a small spread of marks with few very weak papers, it had become apparent that the ability to express knowledge and ideas clearly in writing was as much a hurdle for the students as acquiring the specialist knowledge related to the discipline.

Indeed, the relationships between these two aspects—that good understanding of new specialist knowledge is a prerequisite for good written communication of that knowledge to non-specialists—were not appreciated fully by the students and possibly not by their lecturers either. Understandably, integrating the different fields of knowledge and their associated discourses is a challenge—our goal with this inter-vention was to support students in doing this, and to see if we could improve their writing in this new genre.

Materials development

Following the methods outlined by Skillen and colleagues at Wollongong (1999, James et al., 2004) for their intervention in a Biology course, we set out to build a rich picture of how knowledge in the sub-ject area is written: to look at what was asked for, what was produced in the broader field, and what was valued by staff marking students' work, and finally to identify features that would characterise strong student writing. It was an attempt to make explicit to ourselves what we were looking for and thence to assess whether this was reflected adequately in what was presented to the students.

Disciplinary immersion

As a first step this involved a detailed reading of all the types of texts students might encounter in the *Hazards* module, and a consideration of how students might use these different texts. To assess if the requirements published in or suggested by these documents matched what the staff felt they were asking students to do, we looked at all the module documentation, including rubrics and standardised departmental marking criteria. We also considered a selection of the kinds of texts that the lecturers expected students to read in the course, such as extracts from textbooks, various journal articles, recommended Web sites, and a selection of actual briefing papers (aimed at educating the lay public) published by United States Geological Survey, again to get an idea of the types of writing that students were exposed to, although the extent to which students actively use these texts as models was unclear. Most interestingly, we analysed a set of past student briefing papers together with written feedback comments and marks, attempting to verify that the published criteria were actually satisfied by high-graded briefing papers and to understand, with reference to the feedback, the relative importance assigned to the various criteria in the process of marking. In addition to our focus on texts and conversation, Peake attended several of the lectures as well as the one-day field trip (see Figure 6.1) to attempt to see what the subject was like in action, to share, slightly, the students' point of view in encountering much of this material for the first time, and gain a sense of how knowledge in this course might seem to the students.

This process of immersing ourselves in the material of the module and talking through it in detail, although a simple, frequently used, and unsurprising method of mapping a learning area, offered us a valuable experience of trying both to glean and to unpack tacit knowledge around the experiencing/learning of a subject (Smith 2003 discussing Polanyi, 2005). It enabled Peake, as a writing developer, to obtain a more textured sense of what was valued by the Geography staff and perceived by Geography students, evoking a more intuitive understanding than could be gleaned from simply reading the course guidance and marking criteria. In a complementary way the same process enabled Horne, as the originator and assessor of the coursework, to develop a more articulate and critical understanding of the challenges he was placing before his students. Although much of the initial consideration of the texts was done by Peake, the writing specialist, we realised that it was through looking at the texts together, with Peake offering her interpretations and thoughts as a starting point for discussion, that we really derived a sense of what was valued in the texts; it was not merely a case of Horne confirming a set of textual features. While this shared awareness may not have had a direct effect on the development of materials for assisting students with their writing in this course, it certainly contributed to an important understanding of how knowledge is built and can be written about in Geography. This in turn has had a significant impact on other writing development work in the department, which we discuss in more detail below.

▶ Developing assessment criteria

The aim of improving student writing linked our work inextricably to feedback and assessment, and we needed to consider both how we were to mark students' work and how we were to encourage them to understand our judgements, as well as critique their own and their peers' work. In the hope that increased awareness of the assessment criteria would help them shape their writing (Elander et al., 2006), and again following the approach taken at Wollongong, we adapted the "Measuring Academic Skills of University Students" (MASUS) criteria originally developed for considering university students' literacy and broken into macro- and micro-level skills (Bonanno and Jones, 1997). Our adapted criteria combined the features that we found through our immersion to be valued with existing module-specific criteria from instructions issued to students in week 1, the latter being listed as:

- depth of research, careful and critical use of a variety of sources
- demonstration of understanding of the subject matter
- clarity and concise style
- logical order
- citation of all sources
- good use of good diagrams
- originality
- conformance to specifications
- evidence of individual contribution to group work.

We decided on five categories which identified macro-level skills, a combination of Bonanno and Jones's original criteria and elements that emerged as central to this particular text. These were:

- use of information
- structure and development of the briefing paper
- control of writing style
- grammatical correctness
- maps and/or other illustrations.

B	Structure and development of briefing paper	4	3	2	1	N/A

	1. generic structure appropriate to task
	
	  – introduction giving details of the situation in question
	  – description of hazards and threat that they pose
	  – description of existing mitigation strategies
	  – conclusion summarising main issues and/or identifying problems with the information or situation and/or making recommendations
	
	2. legitimate paragraphing with clear focused topic sentences
	
	3. accuracy and completeness of answer
	
	4. appropriate length and formatting					

Figure 6.2 Category B of *Hazards* MASUS assessment criteria.

Each category was further broken down into more specific criteria like "accuracy and completeness of answer" and "relevant material selected", each of which can be marked on a scale of 1 (poor) to 4 (excellent) as shown (see Figure 6.2). In some cases, features from the original list of criteria, such as "logical order" or "critical use of a variety of sources" were elaborated as a subset of a new category, in this case "structure and development of briefing paper". Together these were presented as a feedback assessment sheet which both staff and students used.

Following the DALiC project, these criteria had multiple functions. Firstly, there was the research goal of attempting to standardise marking to facilitate comparison of an earlier and the final draft (as well as to help the lecturers be certain that they were making similar judgement to each other). Secondly, there were the pedagogical goals of attempting to clarify to students what was expected and valued in this task and providing a mechanism for feedback.

To operationalise the criteria, we used examples to focus students' attention on discrete elements of writing in the target genre. Within the categories, we selected extracts from past briefing papers which we identified as good or poor, and gathered these in pairs, annotated with explanations of why they were judged in this way. For each weak example there was a rewritten stronger corollary of the same text (or vice versa) so students were exposed to an exemplification of what might constitute a higher or lower mark for a particular aspect of writing, as well as one indication of how the writing could be changed to improve it (see Figure 6.3).

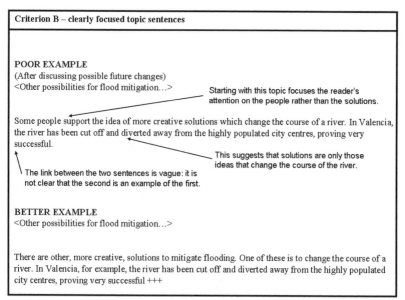

Figure 6.3 Annotated example of student writing to illustrate category B of assessment criteria.

Together this set of examples was given to the students in a booklet as a reference for reviewing both their own work and that of their peers, and was also used in teaching.

These materials were used in three main sessions with the class, as outlined (Figure 6.4): an initial brief introduction to the *Hazards* module, including the description of what a briefing paper is, and what the general assessment criteria for the module were, and two later, longer workshop sessions of approximately an hour each. In the initial session, Horne also told the students about the TW research project, partly to get consent to use their work, and partly in the hope of raising interest and engagement in the research and in writing.

Having formed groups, decided on their topics, and agreed on working titles and outlines with Horne, the students brought drafts of their briefing papers to the second session, which occurred in week 8 of the module. This was co-taught by Horne and Peake and had the goal of presenting the assessment criteria to the class. It was done in a plenary style and the class as a whole worked through each criterion using the annotated examples as illustrations, with students contributing their interpretations of what might be wrong with the weaker examples and suggesting ways to improve them. Working in their smaller groups, students then used the criteria on a standardised assessment criteria sheet

112

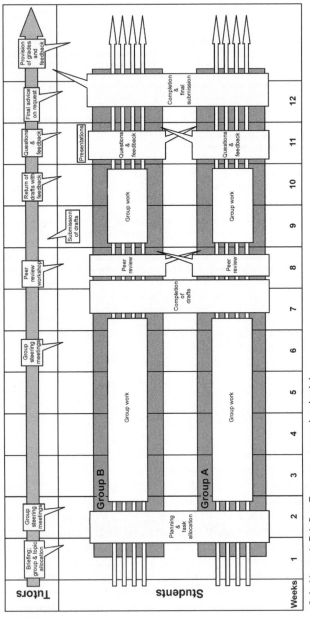

Figure 6.4 *Hazards* Briefing Paper coursework schedule

to assess and give feedback on another group's briefing paper, and had the opportunity to explain this feedback to the writers. After students had received feedback on their writing they had a few days to revise their briefing papers before submitting them for formative assessment by the staff.

These were marked by both Horne and Peake separately using the standardised assessment criteria sheet, and then discussed; this process revealed various idiosyncrasies in how we applied our own interpretation of the criteria and how we weighted different criteria too, making us, we feel in retrospect, somewhat more sympathetic to the students. Our discussions around this fed into the third session, in week 10, which started with whole class feedback (McCune and Hounsell, 2004; Hounsell, 2008). Here we focused on the criteria that had been difficult for significant numbers of students and using, with permission, examples from the students' papers to illustrate typical problems, as well as some examples of very good writing. Again, students were invited to reflect and comment on why these examples did or did not conform to good or excellent instantiations of particular criteria, and what could be done to improve them. Students were then given another chance to work on their briefing papers before the final deadline, two weeks away. This constant revisiting of both students' writing and the assessment criteria would, we hoped, encourage the students to actively use the criteria and the examples when they were writing. Oral presentations by the groups in week 11 (formally assessed as a component of the final coursework grade) provided a further opportunity for feedback on content and focus. The final briefing papers, submitted in week 12, were marked by both by the Geography lecturers, the students subsequently being provided with grades and summary written feedback.

▶ Outcomes and reflections

The first story—evaluation of the project at the time
Like most work on writing conducted within a post-positivist context, it is very difficult to assess effectiveness in any fixed way, and many of our judgements about this process have been formed through our impression and experience. Our evaluation of the work in the *Hazards* module focuses on a range of indicators, from the apparently quantifiable to the distinctly intangible: the students' ratings on the assessment criteria feedback forms, their success in writing a briefing paper, our feelings about the process, the aspects that we felt had an effect on our work as educators, and the impact this collaboration has had on writing development work in the rest of the department and college more

broadly. The measures for evaluation were the difference between the first and final scores on the MASUS feedback instrument, the difference between the initial and final grades that students received, a feedback survey questionnaire given to all the course students, and semi-structured interviews with the Geography department staff who worked on the module.

In terms of our initial goal, to use assessment criteria to improve students' writing, indications from all the measures suggest that this was a successful intervention. Feedback from students was very positive; they expressed enthusiasm for having the marking criteria in advance, and overwhelming support for the chance to draft and redraft and for receiving lots of feedback. All the groups' marks improved between the first draft and the final draft of the briefing paper, and the feedback comments from lecturers indicate that there was significant improvement in some of the areas that had previously been the source of much frustration, such as lack of attention to referencing or absence of good quality maps and illustrations. This correlated with the positive change in those areas on the MASUS feedback instrument.

It seems reasonable therefore to conclude there was a change in students' writing. As their marks for the briefing papers did increase, it would suggest that we had at least in part met our pedagogical goal of using assessment criteria to improve their writing. Of course attributing this achievement solely to our intervention would be unwise, as some change between two drafts of a text is to be expected regardless of the feedback given or criteria shared. It did, though, appear that, with regard to certain discrete assessment criteria, students had made a distinct and clear change to their work in response to the examples we had given. This would suggest that the combination of criteria and criteria-focused teaching and feedback affected their writing. The Geography staff in particular felt there was an improvement in students' ability to convey Geographical knowledge and for most students there was a small but not insignificant change in their marks on the MASUS criteria from second to final draft. Taking a closer look, both at what had changed and at comments on the process of change, raised a series of questions for us around using explicit assessment criteria in this way as a tool for writing development.

The majority of the improved scores for students' essays were seen to be effected in categories where they could make technical, often "surface level" changes to the text to meet the criteria for higher marks. It was particularly evident in correcting spelling, improving the image quality of a map, changing the form of the references, and using a larger number of references. In some cases, the new references were well-incorporated into the fibre of the text, and for these there was a substantive improvement to that section; in others, however, there was a sense that extra references were padding, used to add an extra entry to the bibliography rather than to refine or advance a point. This type of response corresponds to the distinction between "visible" and "invisible" criteria (described in Rust et al., 2003, p. 159) where students involved in evaluation of their peers' writing tended to provide feedback on those features of a text that were easy and clear to identify as problematic—like referencing, presentation, and macrostructure—and to avoid commenting on those that were harder to define, like use of analysis and evaluation.

Considering this behaviour, we wondered, at the time of our initial evaluation (see Purser et al., 2008), whether making the categories for marking so discrete and so explicit encourages students to adopt a very pragmatic approach to their writing; do they change primarily those elements that are immediately and apparently wrong rather than addressing more complex areas like restructuring the text. In such a pragmatic approach, it is possible that the peer review process is more akin to quality control than to the critical review we desired; we wondered, somewhat disappointed, if it encouraged an atomised, checkbox approach by placing an apparently quantifiable value on meeting discrete criteria, so moving students away from developing and attempting to show an understanding of *Hazards* Geography and the contexts in which this learned knowledge might be used. At the same time, we felt that as an element of quality control, "fixing" these problems should not be undervalued; the areas had been identified by the Geographers involved in the course as contributing to successful work, and so are important for successful writing in Geography. In this context at least getting these correct required little effort for the staff, which was not the case for all students, and there was significance to an activity that encouraged students to notice problems with their writing at any level or in any form. Additionally, it could be argued that ignoring features like incorrect spelling or grammar, or referencing formats is equivalent to accepting—and possibly even setting—lower standards. As Hill (2009) notes, acceptance of such features hides from students the fact that writing that is non-standard, whether through choice, error, identity, or all three, can at times be the stimulus for negative judgement both in higher education (HE) and beyond; drawing students' attention to these to change them if they wish is important.

As we discuss below, there is the additional concern that the use of explicit criteria does not truly reflect the complexity of what is valued by staff and this is compounded by the very focused, selective use of examples to illustrate discrete points. Although the principle of teaching through showing worked examples is sound and can have a positive impact on writing (Skillen et al., 1999), it is unclear whether using examples here really enabled the students to develop even some ability to make accurate judgements about what makes good writing in Geography (Sadler et al., 2008). In our methodology, through the necessities of time and design, examples are isolated from the larger (con)text of the briefing paper they come from, and students did not feel they were enabled to change their own writing on the basis of this—one student commented that they were disappointed that they hadn't been shown how to fix their writing. This is an honest criticism of our pedagogy and also a reflection, perhaps, of the expectations that this approach sets up as it may suggest to the students that there is a "right answer" or a "right technique" that will be given to them.

▶ Subsequent developments

James and colleagues (2004, p. 2) argue for the transformative quality of collaboration between disciplinary and writing specialists around curriculum development, and although we question the suitability of some of the elements of this approach in our situation, the collaboration has been influential on our practice within each of our professional contexts. Indeed, one of the key features of the work at Wollongong is to push for change on writing at a departmental and institutional level, rather than only at module or assignment level, and it is at this level that our trialling of this approach has been most successful.

At module level, the *Hazards* module has continued to run as described above, using the same materials but with increasingly less involvement from the TW team as Horne, the subject specialist, has felt more confident in discussing language, and the effect of language on communicating disciplinary content, with students. Working again in partnership with TW, he has also extended opportunities for multiple drafting, editing, and feedback chances into another module that he teaches, *Palaeoecology* (available to second- and third-year students), for which students write an individual essay-style literature review. At departmental level, the Department of Geography, with TW support, extensively restructured their first-year tutorial courses on core Geographical/Environmental ideas and practice, adapting many of the activities and approaches used in the *Introduction to Environmental Ideas and Practice* module, mentioned in the introduction, that was part of the larger writing intervention. This growth from a single tutorial group to a whole year module has extended across years too, to the second-year tutorial module on research methodologies and practice— these now have a differently structured focus on language, resulting from seeing what had been implemented in first-year tutorials and then adopting and adapting similar ideas, including the continuation of collaboration with TW.

Although the type of writing development work that has emerged differs somewhat from the approaches trialled in the intervention, it was largely participation in this international collaboration that raised the profile of developing students' writing in the department and put it on the agenda for future curriculum reviews as well as teaching and learning staff development. Following a recent curriculum review, the *Hazards* module will reappear in a new guise as a third-year option, *Environmental Hazards* which will allow us to review our approaches and materials at a different level. As the new package of modules is rolled out, the department proposes to map the second-year curriculum and consider the role of writing and feedback within and across all of the modules at that level, hoping to extend existing opportunities for students both to continue to develop their writing and to use writing to explore ideas in the discipline in creative and interesting ways.

The second story—re-viewing assessment criteria

While describing the work to integrate writing and language teaching into the *Hazards* module—our first story—we have returned frequently to the value of collaboration, particularly the insights into our thinking and teaching we gained through discussion. This has been true too for many of the students who have reported the group work and peer review to be unique and useful aspects of the course, and it is a key feature of the DALiC approach. In reviewing our work to present it here, however, we have repeated this process of collaborative reflection, and it has led us to some surprising observations—our second story.

In the chapter so far we have talked a great deal about assessment criteria; here and elsewhere (Purser et al., 2008) we have commented on and questioned the uses and usefulness of these criteria, and how accurately they represent what markers really value. In revisiting these questions, in particular the question of how accurately students' writing and marks can be plotted against the criteria we give them, we have come to suspect that, in this project, what we have been calling "assessment criteria"—and have presented to the students as such—are not actually assessment criteria at all. What we actually produced and employed, we realise, was a combination of the minimum standards students are expected to reach through drafting and editing their briefing papers and general guidance on the content and approach needed for a briefing paper. But if these are not the assessment criteria, despite our intention to make them so, and our belief for a great deal of our teaching that they were so, what happened? What does it say about the process of trying to make the tacit knowledge we use in assessment more explicit for students? And how does this change how we view our work on *Hazards*?

The DALiC model is based on the premise of making assessment criteria clearer, more detailed, so that students can understand what is expected of them—a well-intended attempt to clarify what Lillis refers to as "the institutional practices of mystery" (2001, p. 58). Indeed, it was exactly this that we sought to do, to devise a list of criteria encoding our knowledge of what makes a good briefing paper. Our approach was to take existing, simply stated assessment criteria and turn them into a finer-grained, more detailed set of criteria with the aim of clarifying them for students, and then to consider if they were effective in improving student writing. In that process, however, we were not questioning whether producing detailed assessment criteria *per se* was valid. It has only been through long discussions that it has emerged, here, that they may not be valid in this form. Disciplinary staff, by their own admission, rarely use such explicit criteria to arrive at their final marks; they rely on the much broader sense of what is appropriate, the sense that allowed them to construct assessment criteria in the first place. On reflection it seems that we have not been able to locate this knowledge in the criteria; it is by necessity located in the embodied experience of the teacher (Burwood, 2007). To call these criteria *assessment* criteria is therefore potentially misleading to the students and, as we have seen, to the people who devised them as well. By suggesting that our judgements are based entirely on these criteria we are also hiding and to some extent devaluing the knowledge and experience of the teachers, the very things that this collaboration nurtured and developed.

Although we have reservations about the naming—and framing—of assessment criteria, this is not to say that we reject the work we have done; having these criteria as a minimum standard and a guide is valuable for us and for the students. They have been valuable too as a fixed point in the course which has forced us to be increasingly reflective and reflexive about our judgements and expectations, and our constructions of these for students. Interestingly MASUS was initially used by Bonanno and Jones (1997) not as a set of assessment criteria but as a diagnostic tool; we conclude, in the *Hazards* context, that it is as a kind of diagnostic tool that they work best, not only for the students but for the staff too.

We are working towards a greater awareness of how we understand the guidance around writing in the course, and a need to communicate this far more overtly to the students. This is a dialogic process—it is not, as we first thought, an establishing and finalising of assessment criteria but rather a route to change and improve both students' and lecturers' knowledge of and engagement with their subject. For students the criteria produced are both a list of standards that staff feel should be correct or present in their paper, and a device to help them give each other feedback. For staff, they are a useful measure to gauge whether students are aware of these standards and able to meet them. More importantly, however, for both groups they act as a fixed point of reference for all the other activities around learning in *Hazards*—as a guide in the drafting and editing process, as examples in the class discussions about language and style, as statements against which to check internal understandings, and as a measure to be questioned. They are not, however, final and complete embodiments of how judgements are made, and to represent them to students as such can be detrimental.

As Mitchell (2010) argues just this in her discussion of the risks of codifying and commodifying thinking and writing in the university: if we say that assessment criteria really do capture expert knowledge of what is good writing and (therefore) represent it accurately to students, the criteria slowly come to stand in for that knowledge itself; they *become* the standard rather than indicating the standard. Assessment criteria become the point of reference towards which students work, and against which they are judged, in an ever-tightening circle where deeper understanding, appreciation, and craft are diminished, what Torrance (2007) refers to as "assessment as learning" where the criteria encapsulate the sum of learning. It is not, in fact, the assessment criteria themselves that allow the lecturers and students to share and construct knowledge, but all the activities surrounding these criteria; it is through these activities that students develop an understanding of how assessments are made, and learn to write like Geographers.

▶ Acknowledgements

We wish to thank the University of Wollongong Learning Development team, particularly Jan Skillen and Emily Purser (DALiC project). We would also like to thank the QMUL Dept of Geography: Ray Hall (CLEAR project and involvement in the *Hazards* module), Kate Heppell (*Ideas and Practice* trialling), Beth Greenhough (*Ideas and Practice* revision), Becky Briant, Geraldene Wharton, and Teresa McConlogue (involvement in *Hazards* module). Jeff Blackford (now at the School of Environment and development, University of Manchester) was the originator of the *Hazards* module and its briefing paper coursework.

▶ References

Bean, J. C. (1996) *Engaging Ideas* (San Francisco: Jossey-Bass).

Biggs, J. (1999) *Teaching for Quality Learning at University* (Buckingham: Open University Press).

Bonanno, H. and Jones, J. (1997) *The MASUS procedure, Measuring the Academic Skills of University Students: A Diagnostic Assessment* (University of Sydney: Learning Development Centre Publications).

Booth, W., Williams, J. M., and Colomb, G. G. (1995) *The Craft of Research* (Chicago: University of Chicago Press).

Britton, J., Burgess, T., Martin, N., McCleod, A., and Rosen, H. (1975) *The Development of Writing Abilities (11-18)* (London: Macmillan Education).

Burwood, S. (2007) "Imitation, Indwelling and the Embodied Self", *Educational Philosophy and Theory*, 51:2, 118-134.

Elander, J., Harrington, K., Norton, L., Robinson, H., and Reddy, P. (2006) "Complex skills and academic writing: a review of evidence about the types of learning required to meet core assessment criteria", *Assessment and Evaluation in Higher Education*, 31:1, 71-90.

Haggis, T. (2006) "Pedagogies for diversity: retaining critical challenge amidst fears of 'dumbing down'", *Studies in Higher Education.* 31:5, 521-535.

Hill, P. (2009) *Invisible Writing.* Paper presented at the European Association of Teachers of Academic Writing conference, Coventry, UK.

Hounsell (2008) "The trouble with feedback: new challenges, emerging strategies". *Interchange* 2, 1-10. www.tla.ed.ac.uk/interchange.

James, B., Skillen, J., Percy, A., Tootell, H., and Irvine, H. (2004) "From integration to transformation". In K. Deller-Evans and P. Zeegers (eds) *Language and Academic Skills in Higher Education 2003 Conference*, pp. 37-47.

Lea, M. and Street, B. (1998) "Student writing in Higher Education: an academic literacies approach", *Studies in Higher Education*, 23:2, 157-172.

Lillis, T. (2001) *Student Writing: Access, Regulation, Desire* (London: Routledge).

McCune, V. and Hounsell, D. (2004) "Development of first-year students' conceptions of essay writing", *Higher Education*, 47:3, 257-282.

Mitchell, S. E. (2010) "Now you don't see it; now you do: writing made visible in the university", *Arts and Humanities in Higher Education*, 9:2, 113-148.

Mitchell, S. E. and Evison, A. (2006) "Exploiting the potential of writing for educational change at Queen Mary, University of London". In L. Ganobcsik-Williams (ed.) *Teaching Academic Writing in UK Higher Education* (Basingstoke and New York: Palgrave MacMillan).

Monroe, J. (2003) *Local Knowledges, Local Practices: Writing in the Disciplines at Cornell* (Pittsburgh: University of Pittsburgh Press).

Pope, R. (1995) *Textual Intervention* (London: Routledge).

Purser, E., Skillen, J., Deane, M., Donahue, J., and Peake, K., (2008) "Developing academic literacy in context". *Zeitschrift Schreiben.* Available from http://www.zeitschrift-schreiben.eu [13th July 2009].

Rust, C., Margaret P., and O'Donovan, B. (2003) "Improving students' learning by developing their understanding of assessment criteria and processes", *Assessment and Evaluation in Higher Education*, 28:2, 147-164.

Sadler, D. R. (2009) "Indeterminacy in the use of preset criteria for assessment and grading", *Assessment and Evaluation in Higher Education*, 34:2, 159-179.

Skillen, J., Trivett N., Merten M., and Percy, A. (1999) "Integrating the instruction of generic and discipline specific skills into the curriculum: a case study" in *Cornerstones: Proceedings of the 1999 HERDSA Conference* (Canberra: HERDSA).

Smith, M. K. (2003) "Michael Polanyi and tacit knowledge", *The Encyclopedia of Informal Education*, www.infed.org/thinkers/polanyi.htm.

Torrance, H. (2007) "Assessment *as* Learning? How the use of explicit learning objectives, assessment criteria and feedback in post-secondary education and training can come to dominate learning", *Assessment in Education*, 14:3, 281–294.

7 Taking Action in Business

Myrtle Emmanuel, Peter O'Neill, Debbie Holley,
Linda Johnson and Sandra Sinfield

▶ Introduction

This chapter contributes to the emerging discussion around student writing through its focus on writing for Business for first-year students at the London Metropolitan University Business School. We focus on the student writing experience in one compulsory Management module, which was introduced as part of a broader revision of the first-year Business syllabus designed to make transparent to students the discourse of Business studies and of Higher Education more generally. The London Met student body is remarkably diverse in nature and the university has a long history of welcoming non-traditional and more recently widening participation students. The academic literacies approach pioneered by Lea and Street (1998) and others (e.g. Lillis, 2001 and 2003) has reminded us that writing cannot be detached from the social contexts in which it takes place. Therefore, integral to our approach has been the examination of the student voice in order to gain a wider understanding of the strengths and weaknesses associated with students' academic writing and how any weaknesses might be resolved.

One of the key findings of the chapter is that academic writing cannot be divorced from the reading that is required for academic writing assignments, as we have discovered that it is often at this early stage in the writing process that some students stumble. We argue that, for first-year students especially, in particular for students from widening participation or non-traditional backgrounds, encouraging motivation for both reading and writing is the key and that attention to these issues can bring positive results. Hence, one of our priorities in this project has been to learn from students about their reading experiences. Lecturers who may be unwilling to assume responsibility for student writing—perhaps seeing this as a skill which students should bring with them to a degree programme rather than something to be taught or developed—may be even less willing to take on responsibility for student reading. However, we suggest that attention to reading, like attention to writing, is something that does not need be taught or emphasised apart from disciplinary content, and that a few modifications to what we ask our students to do can lead to tasks which are more do-able for less prepared students and hopefully at the same time more stimulating for better prepared students. We also argue that academic writing (and the reading that this involves) offers a powerful lens through which broader issues of student motivation can be addressed. While there is no quick fix for deeply engrained concerns, attention to writing does potentially offer a long-term solution for helping lecturers do what they can to contribute to increased student success.

▶ Redesigning the first-year experience

In the academic year 2005–6, almost one in seven of all students in the UK were studying business and management. This represents nearly 300,000 students at all levels of higher education (HE): from foundation degree, through traditional three- and four-year undergraduate courses, specialist Masters, MBAs, and Doctorates. During the last 11 years, the number of undergraduate students studying for a degree in the UK has increased by 28% while the number of those studying business and management has grown by 59% (ABS, 2008, p. 19). Given this increase, it is not surprising to find that broader concerns across the academy concerning retention, progression, and achievement (RPA) have also occupied the attention of UK Business Schools as students enter HE with increasingly diverse biographies, expectations, and constraints (Holley and Oliver, 2009).

Against such a background, many Business Schools have recently embarked on re-designing large parts of the curriculum (Parrott, 2010). New approaches that have emerged often challenge traditional tutor-led lecture/seminar delivery and highlight the development of "key skills" in accordance with a government-driven skills and employability agenda (Leitch, 2006). The increase in introductory academic skills modules is testimony to such an approach. At London Metropolitan University, for example, all undergraduate courses are required to incorporate a higher education orientation (HEO) module to prepare students for the demands of HE. This model has been much debated across the University as these HEO modules are often expected to develop all the skills students require at University and as such can legitimate the inclinations of many lecturers to disclaim responsibility for their students' academic reading and writing. Dissatisfaction with this one-module-fix-all approach in part led to the decision by the new Business School to embed attention to all aspects of student learning within the discipline and across the curriculum in order to more effectively empower all students to profit from their studies.

The London Metropolitan Business School is a large business school with around 4500 students from a diverse range of backgrounds and as such a coordinated approach to curriculum design was needed. In 2007–8 LMBS embarked (with the support of the Learn Higher, RLO, and Write Now Centres for Excellence in Teaching and Learning) on a redesign of the Business and Management curriculum to include a specific focus on pedagogies for diversity, retaining critical challenge without "dumbing down" (Haggis, 2006), improving formative feedback and offering more personalised modes of delivery. The redesign was informed by a discussion regarding the purpose of the first year (for the importance of the first-year experience of students, see for example Parmar and Trotter, 2005; Yorke and Longden, 2008). The new common core first-year co-ordinates and "joins up" the curriculum and attempts to engage students in their studies, provide ongoing feedback, raise their aspirations and motivation to study, and develop their abilities and confidence to prepare them for success in HE and beyond. Skills are no longer relegated to a single module. Instead, attention to reading, writing, referencing, and other aspects of student learning are embedded within the subject matter across the curriculum (see Figure 7.1) and all lecturers are expected to focus on these as a fundamental aspect of their disciplinary teaching.

Analysis of the first cohort has provided a useful basis for further discussion and development. There is some evidence that our strategy has impacted positively on RPA but we will obviously need to carry out further analysis of future cohorts and to monitor the progress of students now on the second year of their studies.

▶ People Management: Challenges and Choices

The module leader for one of the new LMBS year-one modules had earlier worked together with the Write Now CETL Writing Specialist on an intermediate (year two and three) module. This initial collaboration flowed naturally into and has become embedded in the new first-year module, "People Management: Challenges and Choices" (PMCC). In general terms, we saw this new collaboration as informed by action research. In common with most action research, it grows out of real issues faced in teaching and determined by the practitioners;

Semester	Semester 1	Semester 1	Semester 1	Semester 1	Semester 2	Semester 2	Semester 2	Semester 2
Module	Creative and reflective Bus. Practice	Global Challenges for Business Management and Leadership	Understanding Information	People Management: Challenges and Choices	Introduction to Business Law	Economics for Business	Business Accounting	Principles of Marketing
1. Academic Reading								
Textbooks	IPA	IPA	IPA	IPA	IPA	IPA	IPA	
Newspapers	IPA	IPA	IP	IP	IP	IPA		
Journal articles		IPA		IPA	IP		IPA	
Internet sites	IPA	IP	IP	IP		IPA		
2. Researching								
Identifying sources	IPA	IPA	IPA	IPA	IPA	IPA	IPA	
Evaluating sources	IPA	IPA	IPA	IPA	IPA	P	IPA	
Research methodologies	IPA	IP	IP	IPA	IPA	P	IPA	
3. Analysing Data	IPA		IPA			IPA	IPA	PA

Figure 7.1 "Academic skills". Business and Management suite certificate level: Introduced (I) Practised (P) Assessed (A).

4. Presenting data	IPA		IPA		IPA		PA
5. Academic writing							
Reports	IP		IPA		A	IPA	
Essay			IPA	IPA (exam)	PA		IPA (exam)
Short tasks	IPA	IP		IPA	PA		
Referencing	IPA	IPA	IPA	IPA	A	PA	
6. Note-making	IPA	IP	IP		P		
7. Oral presentation	IPA	IPA			IPA		IPA
8. Written presentation style, grammar and spelling	IPA	IPA	IPA	IPA	PA	IPA	PA
9. Problem solving			IPA	IPA	PA	IPA	
10. Memorising strategies	IPA			IPA			PA
11. Self-assessment/reflection	IPA	IPA	IP	P	P	P	

Figure 7.1 (Continued)

interventions implemented grow out of reflective practice and listening to students rather than focusing on results alone; the aim is improvement—in terms of student learning, the curriculum, the department, the institution, and the wider sector; interventions are evaluated and followed by further reflective practice; and the process is repeated in the light of previous experiences (see Norton, 2009, pp. 54–56 for the features of action research). As Norton writes (building on Smith):

> What we have to be aware of is that action research is interpretative and needs to be thought of in terms of further refinements in following studies. I think this is an important point, as it is by carrying out further cycles of research that we begin to form a holistic view of our practice and the elements that need progressive refinement.   (Norton, 2009, p. 55)

Certainly, we do not view our project as complete, but we hope that others will be interested in what we have learned so far and our plans for the future.

The main aim of PMCC is to support a cross-curricular introduction to people management in contemporary organisations and to focus on empowering students to succeed in academic writing as a key aspect of their learning. The module runs at both the university campuses in the autumn and spring semesters. It is a very large module with several hundred students from diverse backgrounds and is ring fenced for all Business and Management students within the Business School. PMCC adopts the traditional one-hour lecture followed by a two-hour seminar format supported by independent study.

The module was designed to include two assessment strategies, a summary of which is shown (Figure 7.2). The assessments were designed to evaluate students' knowledge and understanding of people management as well as assessing their research, reading, analytical, evaluative, and written communication skills.

In thinking about how writing could be approached developmentally in this module, we were somewhat constrained by module specifications designed by others which had already been approved. The specifications required of students were two separate writing assignments of 1500 and 2000 words. One of the main outcomes of our initial

Assessment Type	Description of Component	% Weighting	Due in Week
Coursework	Individual written assignment	40	8
Coursework	Individual paper and personal reflection	60	14

Figure 7.2 Assessment of module.

discussions was that we decided that these two independent assignments might be perhaps unnecessarily onerous for first-year students. Rather than require less of them, we wanted to find a way to use the first writing assignment as a way to help new university students learn about the requirements of academic writing and to have a chance to explicitly put into practice the elements that this involves. We then wanted the opportunity to give students feedback that would be useful for students' writing development and which they could benefit from in writing the second assignment.

Therefore, rather than setting two separate writing assignments, we decided that the first assignment should be a briefing paper in which students are asked to give an overview of the key elements which will make up the final paper. This seemed appropriate for business students as it would have relevance to the types of writing that might be expected from them in a professional business requirement (see MacAndrew and Edwards, 2002, on the benefits of "authentic" writing). For the briefing paper, students were asked to be explicit about the elements where confusion sometimes is apparent. For example:

- the reasons for choosing the question they have selected
- an exposition of exactly what the final essay is asking students to do
- what they already know about their chosen topic
- what their particular focus might be
- their chosen title for the final paper
- what their preliminary argument/thesis will be
- an overview of the proposed structure of the final paper and how this will support their argument
- what arguments they might include
- what evidence they will use
- their sources of information which are referenced appropriately
- their preliminary introduction for the final essay
- an action plan for writing the final essay.

The briefing paper had two pedagogical aims. The first was to allow students to gain an understanding of the reading and writing processes involved in the writing of an academic paper. The second was to provide students with detailed oral and written formative feedback on their academic writing within two weeks of submitting their briefing paper. This was expected to improve performance in the second assessment.

For the final coursework essay, students are expected to take into account this feedback. Students are asked to submit a 2000-word individual paper drawing on their knowledge and understanding of the challenges facing contemporary organisations and the current issues facing HRM managers, choosing a topic from a previous list provided, together with a 500-word reflective piece evaluating their performance in completing the assessments for PMCC. The reflective piece presented the opportunity for students to comment on the feedback received from their seminar tutors on their briefing paper and to reflect explicitly on their learning with respect to academic writing.

In addition, the lecturer customised a generic LearnHigher CETL/ Learning Development essay-writing pack to produce a course-specific workbook for use in seminars and out of class which took students through key study and research skills focusing on writing their specific module essay and which was designed to encourage continuous engagement with the assignment and frequent writing activities.

▶ Challenges delivering PMCC in the first semester

Post-semester student evaluations of the first delivery of the module were encouraging as most students stated that they were happy with the module overall. In particular students seem to like:

- The idea of gaining formative feedback for their briefing paper.
- The introductory reading text which was edited by one of our London Metropolitan University colleagues, Wendy Bloisi.
- The structure of topics and effectiveness of the lecturers' styles and how relating people management theories to real life situations helped to further students' understanding of the subject.
- The overall organisation of the module including the teaching and learning materials for the lectures and seminar.

However, this enthusiasm was not matched by students' results and failure rates for the revised module remained high. This was in large part due to factors beyond our control, including late-starting students who missed early opportunities to engage with assigned readings for the briefing paper and students failing to attend lectures. We also experienced issues relating to the assessments. Although the teaching team used indicative assessment criteria, there were concerns about the disparities found in the marking of the briefing paper and the individual paper. This was due to the differences in opinions amongst tutors on whether high marks should be awarded for form, structure, and academic referencing or for original thinking and strong arguments, even with the absence of academic structuring and referencing. These are aspects we can learn from in designing future assessments, but they highlight the difficulty of such a collaboration between writing specialist and module leader in the case of a course which is delivered by a large teaching team and highlight the need for clarity and for bringing everybody fully on board and in agreement.

Following the relatively disappointing results, it was clear that—as we had expected—we would need to continue working on the module. We decided that, given the relatively high number of students failing to pass the module, it was important to learn from the students themselves what had worked well and what worked not so well. Based on the author's own observations and on several discussions with seminar tutors who had taught and marked the students' coursework, it was clear that some of the problems that students were experiencing with their writing were partly due to their difficulties with fulfilling the assigned reading which affected their gaining a better grasp of the subject. As noted by Hobson (2004), although reading skills are essential they are often ignored within the context of HE. Against this background the module leader decided to hold a focus group towards the end of the Spring 2009 delivery of the module exploring student experiences with reading as well as writing as part of the investigation of student experiences in the module.

A focus group interview was chosen since it was a convenient way of exploring the student's voice on reading and writing for PMCC. It is also a useful way of capturing broader data from students who are already familiar with each other. Eleven PMCC students from our City Campus volunteered to participate in a focus group study. Most of these students were international students from Asia, Africa, and Europe whilst only two were home students from the UK. The students who attended represented the academic range of students who completed the module. It is perhaps true that we really needed to hear from students who failed to produce assessments or attend lectures at all (see Gorard et al.'s 2006 critique of much widening participation research as too often neglecting students who fail to participate). However, we were convinced that it was important to learn from students and that this would be a good start to the investigation.

There was commonality between the focus group moderators (one of whom was the module leader and the other the Head of Teaching and Learning for the Business School) and these students who were keen to address the issues associated with student writing (Wall, 2001). Although the module leader provided the focus for the questions, the data stem from the students' interactions within groups (Morgan, 1997). Flip charts and post-it notes were used to facilitate the students' expression of ideas and solutions and to record key issues. The interviews were tape-recorded and transcribed. The focus group lasted 90 minutes and semi-structured questions were used to explore students' experiences of reading and writing. In the first part, students were asked questions about what they read, the usefulness of their recommended text, when they started reading for their assignments, and the difficulties they encountered with their reading. In the second part, questions centred around students' experiences of writing for the module, when they started writing for the assignments and the difficulties they encountered in writing their assignments. In what follows, we highlight what emerged from the group and its implications for our thinking about writing—and reading for writing—in this module.

▶ Reading for PMCC

With regards to the semi-structured questions on the issues students were facing with their reading it was pleasing to note that students found the main introductory text and recommended Web site useful and easy to understand. This may be because the reading was closely aligned with the characteristics of their assignment topics. Students seemed to like reading the introductory text and material from the CIPD (Chartered Institute of Personnel and Development) Web site as these were seen as clearly relevant to the course content (cf. Maleki and Heerman, 1992). However, with respect to the reading of other texts and journals students expressed less satisfaction:

> Some of the chapters are quite boring and not useful...when reading journals I found a lot of the journals useless as I found I had difficulty finding a useful reference or quote to use in my assignment.   (Focus group participant)

Such attitudes echo the view of academic reading and writing scholars who have found that the recommended reading texts in academia are usually designed for audiences who are highly skilled and specialised and as such these texts may seem irrelevant to novices such as first-year HE students (Maleki and Heerman, 1992; Leamnson, 1999; Bean, 2001; Hobson, 2004).

In addition, some students revealed that they faced problems with understanding the individual paper question and with assimilating information from their readings into their essays:

> There was too much information within the books regarding my chosen subject, so to make sure I was using the appropriate information was not always easy...Did not know which part of the information to extract. How much information to extract.   (Focus group participant)

Overall, it seems that the difficulties students encountered with their reading and assimilation of information link to various issues relating to their recommended reading list. This suggests that in some cases the required reading text adds little value to the students' learning process and the overall performance of the module (Hobson, 2004). Moreover, the fact that students have problems with understanding the individual paper question is a useful indication of the need to include sessions on understanding the assessments and the question well *before* students engage with reading the recommended texts. If students understand more clearly why they are being asked to read and what the purpose of the reading is for (being able to relate it to the essay they are writing), they may be more able to read actively and strategically and so feel in command of a reading list rather than intimidated by it.

There were also some issues with the timing of students' reading as most started to read for the briefing paper much later in the module than we intended (most starting around week 6), even though the briefing paper was due to be submitted in week 8. The same pattern occurred with reading for their individual paper. Moreover, some of the students acknowledged that engaging with the reading much earlier in the module would have helped to enhance their grades for their briefing paper which subsequently would have facilitated their individual paper. When we asked students why they started reading late their responses revealed issues associated with the lack of understanding of PM concepts and vocabulary, difficulties with assimilating information, note taking, and time management challenges. In this instance, it is important to note that for these students, difficulties associated with reading were more of an obstacle than lack of motivation to read.

The responses were a salutary reminder that practices which we take for granted in first-year students—for example, identifying readings which are relevant to an assignment and using them appropriately in academic writing—may in fact be skills which need to be acquired and reinforced. If this was the case for the students who completed the module successfully, it is likely to be even more the case for less successful students. This also suggests that attention to academic reading in the first year is likely to benefit all students and can be seen as something empowering rather than remedial, particularly if attention to reading is related closely to actual assignments students are working on. Indeed, such an approach might well resemble practices in many universities in a pre-modular era where development across a three-year course was often given more attention than in current programmes made up of discrete modules which often allow less scope for intellectual and practical scaffolding of the academic rigour of the degree years.

A particular finding seems to be that students cope generally quite well with the essential reading (e.g. textbooks), but find it harder to assimilate additional readings where the relevance of texts may be harder to gauge. It may be that in the first year, students need support in ascertaining the relevance of such additional reading and that an approach which leads to a few texts being well-understood—and where opportunities are given for students to actively and critically engage with such texts—may be more useful than intimidating reading lists which may lead to lower self-confidence and self-efficacy. This is in line with Australian research which emphasises the effectiveness of "preparing before reading", using class time to ensure students have the background knowledge needed to understand and engage with texts (Rose et al., 2008, p. 169, 178).

Our findings give impetus to future syllabus and pedagogical changes which will make the reading experience of first-year students more rewarding and also more formative for their future development as students where they will be expected to read more extensively. Indeed, reading activities have already been implemented for the current delivery (Autumn 2009) of the course, embedded in workbook and seminar activities. We should note that our findings in some respects support educational psychologists' work into reading. Nearly all such work relates to younger children, but an important finding is that motivation to read is a crucial factor in reading success (Guthrie et al., 2004 and 2006; for a useful overview of motivation theories in education, see Wang, 2008). And some educational psychologists have spoken of a "Matthew effect" (Stanovich, 1986), a vicious cycle whereby the successful at reading get further ahead and those who fall behind early on continue to fall behind. In such cases, bad learning experiences leads to lower motivation and reduced self-efficacy. It is not our intention here to make excessive claims about university students' reading, but—especially at universities with large number of widening participation and non-traditional students—it is important to bear in mind that many of our students may have had very bad learning experiences concerning reading and may be quickly alienated if they encounter negative reading experiences in their first weeks of university. Care taken to ensure that chosen texts—especially at the beginning of the first year—relate to students' experiences may lessen the risk of such alienation (see Rose et al., 2003, p. 43; also Guthrie et al., 2004 on choice of text and motivation for reading).

Experts suggest that motivation for reading is likely to increase where there are social and strategic elements to and active engagement involved in the reading activity (Guthrie et al., 2004, 2006; Wigfield et al., 2008)—perhaps involving group work where reading is carried out to fulfil a group activity (e.g. groups of students could use class time to choose a text from a reading list which they will read and report back on). This involves a recognition that many of our students may be extrinsically rather than intrinsically motivated (with "performance goals" rather than "mastery goals"; see Ames, 1992) and so need to see clearly the point of what they are being asked to read and how it will benefit them in writing their assessed papers. Workshop activities early in the semester perhaps need to be designed to allow reading to take place within a social context, and preliminary steps in this direction have been taken in the Autumn 2009 seminars. Such activities need to be part of an authentic and academic Business Management exercise and not seen as a "reading workshop" which may alienate students at both the high-achieving and lower-achieving end of the spectrum. Experts also suggest that disadvantaged students (who may lack the orientation to reading very often provided by middle-class parents; Rose, 2006, p. 40) may need reinforcement and affirmation that they are reading correctly in order to provide them with the confidence and self-efficacy to progress further themselves (Bandura, 1997 on self-efficacy; Margolis and McCabe, 2006 on the role of feedback—and also non-expert, peer modelling of successful performance—in fostering self-efficacy; Rose, 2006, p. 58 on affirmation as central to Vygotskyan learning theories).

The briefing paper can be used better in the future to bring about opportunities for such feedback but we think that any other activities (including class discussions and debates) where understanding of texts is manifested and acknowledged will be useful. In revising the module in the future, these are areas which we would like to continue to emphasise as part of an ongoing solution to these difficult problems (increasingly acknowledged by lecturers at most universities throughout the world; cf. Hendricks and Quinn, 2000).

▶ Writing for PMCC

With respect to students' writing for the briefing and the individual paper, the focus group indicates that students appear to face challenges with writing less than with reading, though once more we are aware that the students who formed the focus group are students who completed the module successfully. There seem to be very positive responses concerning students' experiences with writing. In exploring the students' perception on the importance of writing it was pleasantly surprising that students felt that academic writing was very important for studying Business Management as it develops their researching, their critical writing and referencing skills, aids their learning experiences, develops their organisation skills, and helps them to familiarise themselves with the vocabulary of business:

Good writing experience, did not have any major problems writing for this module... Writing made me see that I can do things that I never thought I will do. Like writing an essay and getting a B.... well done me!... I understand new ways of writing a business report. Get familiar with business terms and new key words and how to structure a report.   (Comments from focus group participants)

In particular, the briefing paper and the subsequent feedback seem to have been valued. The students who experienced problems with the planning of their briefing papers were able to plan their writing for the final paper because of the feedback they received from seminar tutors. Students also found that the action plan that they were asked to submit as part of their briefing paper was very useful. Verbal and post-it note responses echoed these views:

I think the action plan is helping me a lot during the process of writing. Feedback on the briefing paper was very useful... When I started writing for my individual paper I was more confident and I knew exactly what the assignment was asking me to do.... The feedback helped me write the final assignment, pointed me in the right direction and has showed me what I need to elaborate on and what was good about my briefing paper... The feedback from the briefing paper did help me to write the final assignment because I was told where I was losing marks in terms of writing, structure, punctuation and hence I know how not to make these mistakes.... Yes it helped me to understanding that I will need to be more specific when relating my theories with real life experiences managers had encountered.   (Comments from focus group participants)

Overall, the briefing paper was useful in terms of pointing students in the right direction, helping them to present their ideas and make use of relevant theories. There was a clear indication from the responses that the briefing paper was a success in terms of enabling students to reflect on their strengths and weaknesses which in turn helped them to progress in their individual papers.

However, similar to the responses on reading for PMCC, quite a few students indicated that they started writing for their briefing paper later than we intended, for example, in week 7 even though the briefing paper was due to be submitted in week 8. Once more, some students noted issues with assimilating information as their reasons for starting writing for their briefing paper and individual paper at such a late stage.

▶ Solutions for getting students to engage in reading and writing

Towards the end of the discussions students were split into two group to engage in a debate on what would they would do, as seminar tutors, to help students read for both assignments. Students drew a list of the following points which were then categorised as enablers and disablers.

Enablers

- Schedule extra reading lessons to allow more time for reading.
- Show students what reading is most useful for the coursework in order to get students excited about the subject.
- Getting students to focus on the question from the beginning of the module.
- It helps if tutors give encouragement and are passionate about the subject as this helps to engage students with their reading and to work harder. Most students revealed that the tutor's style was an important factor in helping students to gain success in reading for the assignments.
- Allow students to read a book followed by a set of questions.
- Compiling a list of recommended readings for the assignments.
- Discuss reading topics with friends or in group discussions.
- Action planning—this is already part of the individual paper.
- Attendance was seen as an important factor.
- Clear explanations on what is expected from students.
- Provide appropriate examples regarding the module assignments.
- Activities to engage students to research widely on their topic.
- Encourage students to submit drafts for tutor's feedback.

Disablers

- Tutors' just telling students to read for their assignments was not useful.
- Tutors not having a passion for the subject.
- Not giving students recognition for reading.
- Tutors' lack of explanation and clarity on a topic.
- Lack of encouragement.

We were pleased with the students' suggestions, as they paralleled our own feelings, particularly concerning the need to make the point of reading clear (as it relates to assignments) and also in providing feedback on reading and incorporating more reading activities into workshops. And we note that some students suggested that reading can take place in a social rather than isolated environment. It was also striking that students acknowledged the importance of the passion and enthusiasm of the lecturer and their need to be inspired. This brings us back to motivation as the key for students' reading and writing. It also supports the recent findings of Freeman and colleagues (2007) who show that academic motivation among first-year US students relates to students' sense of belonging and stress above all the role of the teacher in facilitating this—and in particular the importance of enthusiasm, openness, friendliness, encouragement of active participation, and good organisation. These are salutary reminders that a focus on writing only takes one so far and that the passion and competence of academic staff remain the key for student success. However, this suggests that well-designed writing and reading tasks and exhibiting enthusiasm for the value of academic reading and writing are likely to provide a positive experience for students writing their first university essays.

▶ Conclusion

This study has renewed our determination to continue to work on the module, and in future years we will focus in particular on more reading in workshops, taking into account our conclusions identified above: using authentic readings relevant to the assignment and in workshops involving a social element and providing feedback that encourages self-efficacy in reading. We will also continue with the briefing paper which seems to be working, although greater clarity is needed in terms of how this is assessed by a wide team of lecturers. This writing collaboration has been very useful in that it has enabled us to believe that we can attempt to tackle solutions which are often seen as systemic or something which somebody else should be taking care of. It is true that writing—and even reading—are not the only reason—and perhaps not even the major reason—for student failure. Nevertheless, focusing on these areas offers a constructive way to do what we can as lecturers to make our modules as conducive to student success as possible; and the very fact that we are engaged in the question of student writing is likely to mean that we exhibit a greater enthusiasm for the assignments we are asking students to do, which we hope in turn will lead to students who are more motivated to succeed. There may be quite a long way to go, but attention to writing seems to offer a uniquely rich vehicle for keeping us on track.

▶ References

ABS (2008) *Pillars of the Sustainable Economy*. Association of Business Schools. Available from http://www.the-abs.org.uk/files/ABS%20Pillars-Annual%20Report%2008.pdf [22nd February 2010].

Ames, C. (1992) "Classroom goals, structures, and student motivation". *Journal of Educational Psychology*, 84 (3): 261–271.

Bandura, A. (1997) *Self-Efficacy: The Exercise of Control* (New York: Worth).

Bean, J.C. (2001) *Engaging Ideas: The Professor's Guide to Integrating Writing, Critical Thinking, and Active Learning in the Classroom* (San Francisco: Jossey Bass).

Freeman, T.M., L.H. Anderman and J. M. Jensen (2007) "Sense of belonging in college freshmen at the classroom and campus levels". *The Journal of Experimental Education*, 75 (3): 203–220.

Gorard, S., Smith, E., May, H., Thomas, L., Adnett, N. and Slack, K. (2006) *Review of Widening Participation Research: Addressing the Barriers to Participation in Higher Education* (HEFCE report).

Guthrie, J.T., Hoa, L. W., Wigfield, A., Tonks, S. M. and Perencevich, K. C. (2006) 'From spark to fire: can situational reading interest lead to long-term reading motivation?' *Reading Research and Instruction*, 45: 91–117.

Guthrie, J.T., Wigfield, A., Barbosa, P., Perencevich, K.C., Taboada, A., Davis, M.H., Scafiddi, N.T. and Tonks, S. (2004) "Increasing reading comprehension and engagement through concept-oriented reading instruction". *Journal of Educational Psychology*, 96 (3): 403–423.

Haggis, T. (2006) "Pedagogies for diversity: retaining critical challenge amidst fears of 'dumbing down' " *Studies in Higher Education*, 31 (5): 521–535.

Hendricks M. and Quinn, L. (2000) "Teaching referencing as an introduction to epistemological empowerment". *Teaching in Higher Education*, 5 (4): 447–457.

Hobson, E.H. (2004) "Getting students to read: fourteen tips." IDEA Paper No. 40. Available from http://www.theideacenter.org/sites/default/files/Idea_Paper_40.pdf [23rd February 2010].

Holley, D. and Oliver, M. (2009) "Student engagement and blended learning: portraits of risk Computers in Education" (Elsevier Publishing). Available from http://dx.doi.org/10.1016/j.compedu.2009.08.035 [23rd February 2010].

Lea, M.R. and Street, B.V. (1998) "Student writing in higher education: an academic literacies approach". *Studies in Higher Education*, 23 (2): 157–172.

Leamnson, R.N. (1999) *Thinking About Teaching and Learning: Developing Habits of Learning with First Year College and University Students* (Sterling, Virginia: Stylus).

Leitch, S. (2006) *Prosperity for All in the Global Economy: World Class Skills: Final Report*. Norwich: The Stationary Office. Available from http://www.dcsf.gov.

uk/furthereducation/uploads/documents/2006-12%20LeitchReview1.pdf [23rd February 2010].

Lillis, T. (2001) *Student Writing: Access, Regulation, Desire* (London: Routledge).

MacAndrew, S.B.G. and K. Edwards (2002) "Essays are not the only way". *Psychology, Learning and Teaching*, 2: 134–139.

Maleki, R.B. and Heerman, C.E. (1992) "Improving student reading". Idea Paper no.26. Kansas State University.

Margolis, H. and P. McCabe (2006) "Improving self-efficacy and motivation: what to do, what to say". *Intervention in School and Clinic*, 41 (4): 218–227.

Morgan, D.L. (1997) *Focus Groups as Qualitative Research* (2nd edn) (Thousand Oaks: Sage).

Norton, L.S. (2009) *Action Research in Teaching and Learning: A Practical Guide to Conducting Pedagogical Research in Universities* (London and New York: Routledge).

Parmar, D. and Trotter, E. (2005) "Keeping our Students: Identifying the factors that influence student withdrawal and strategies to enhance the first year". *Learning and Teaching in the Social Sciences*, 1 (3): 149–168.

Parrott, G. (2010) "Redesigning the first year business curriculum at the University of Bedfordshire". *The International Journal of Management Education*, 8 (2): 13–21.

Rose, D. (2006) "Towards a reading based theory of teaching". *Proceedings of the 33rd International Systemic Functional Congress* (Sao Paolo), 36–77.

Rose, D., Lui-Chivizhe, L., McKnight, A. and Smith, A. (2003) "Scaffolding academic reading and writing in the koori centre". *Australian Journal of Indigenous Education*, 32: 41–49.

Rose, D., Rose, M., Farrington, S. and Page, S. (2008) "Scaffolding academic literacy with indigenous health sciences students: an evaluative study". *Journal of English for Academic Purposes*, 7 (3): 165–179.

Stanovich, K.E. (1986) "Matthew effects in reading: some consequences of individual differences in the acquisition of literacy". *Reading Research Quarterly*, 21: 360–407.

Wall, A.L. (2001) "Evaluating an undergraduate unit using a focus group". *Quality Assurance in Education*, 9 (1): 23–31.

Wang, S.K. (2008) *Motivation: A General Overview of Theories*. Available from http://projects.coe.uga.edu/epltt/index.php?title=Motivation [23rd February 2010].

Wigfield, A., Guthrie, J.T., Perencevich, K.C., Taboada, A., Klauda, S.L., Mcrae, A. and Barbosa, P. (2008) "Role of reading engagement in mediating effects of reading comprehension instruction on reading outcomes". *Psychology in the Schools*, 45 (5): 432–445.

Yorke, M. and B. Longden (2008) "The first year experience of higher education in the UK". The Higher Education Academy. Available from http://www.heacademy.ac.uk/assets/York/documents/resources/publications/FYEFinal Report.pdf [23rd February 2010].

8 Writing for Mathematics Education at Doctoral Level

Peter Samuels and Mary Deane

▶ Introduction

Although there is a growing body of literature on disciplinary writing development (Gottschalk and Hjortshoj, 2004; Somerville and Crème, 2005), most studies focus on ways of integrating writing development into undergraduate courses. This chapter addresses the relative lack of research into ways of supporting doctoral candidates in disciplinary contexts. It reports on a WiD initiative designed to foster a culture of writing for publication to assist doctoral researchers in mathematics education to submit their first journal articles (Samuels and Deane, 2008).

The students who took part in this initiative were at various stages in the process of producing a PhD, and this variety in their experiences was exploited to help build a community of mutual support. They were all under pressure to publish, which is not only an issue prior to gaining a doctorate, but also a demand that continues during an academic career. The ideas in this chapter are therefore adaptable to support any group of early career academics with their writing for publication.

This WiD intervention took the form of a series of three events co-led by Samuels, a mathematics education specialist, and Deane, a writing developer. Their work was conducted under the joint auspices of sigma, a Centre for Excellence in Teaching and Learning (CETL), and the Centre for Academic Writing (CAW) at Coventry University.[1] Sigma was initially funded by the Higher Education Funding Council for England (HEFCE) over a period of 5 years (from 2005 to 2010) which allowed the team to increase their research capacity and recruit several funded PhD students (Samuels, 2006). The Mathematics Education Centre (MEC) which encompasses the Mathematics Support Centre at Loughborough University expanded over the same period and recruited a number of PhD students in the field of mathematics education. Samuels and Deane brought these two groups of doctoral researchers together to foster their development of strategies for successful publication writing.

▶ Pressure to publish

Doctoral students are often under pressure to publish preliminary results of their research before submitting their theses for examination. It is advantageous for early career researchers to publish prior to submission because this helps them to gain standing within academic communities and boosts their confidence in preparation for the doctoral *viva voce*. Thesis examiners are concerned with whether a doctorate is "publishable", so it is beneficial for candidates to publish an element of their research to demonstrate the rigour of their work. Realistically though, doctoral research is a stressful endeavour and trying to publish before completing a thesis is often an additional strain for students.

Samuels was requested to organise training for a group of doctoral candidates to help them to obtain their research degrees and become more confident and fluent scholars. His aim was to support them in making the transition from postgraduate students to educational researchers. The training provided was contextualised and responsive to the needs of the students, and one of the areas in which they requested training was academic writing (Moriarty, 1997). Samuels and Deane collaborated to promote the researchers' self-determination as writers and researchers (Deci and Ryan, 2000). Their collaboration comprised a series of events as set out in Table 8.1.

▶ Mathematics education

The field of mathematics education research has an established community of practice with many conventional constructs (Mason and Johnston-Wilder, 2004) and research methods (Schoenfeld, 2002). However, the community has tended to concentrate on Mathematics

Table 8.1   Three mathematics education writing events for doctoral researchers

Event	Length	Topic
June	1 day	Abstract writing and critical thinking
December	1 day	Critiquing sources
June	0.5 day	Peer review

Education at the primary and secondary school levels, partly due to the complexity of advanced mathematical thinking (Tall, 1991) and partly due to a cultural divide between mathematicians and mathematics educators. Mathematicians generally find it hard to value mathematics education research that is not specifically relevant and helpful to their own (highly complex) activities and is not based on a research paradigm similar to their own (Mond, 2007). Therefore it is only relatively recently that Mathematics educators have sought to investigate undergraduate mathematics learning (Jaworski, 2002). The sigma and MEC PhD students were mostly researching issues in higher education, but the conventions of this field were not familiar to many participants, who came from a mathematical rather than an education background.

▶ Mathematics writing workshops

Samuels and Deane received initial suggestions from the students about the kinds of writing support they would appreciate, and as far as possible they involved the students in the design of training events. The sessions were scheduled to fit in with the sigma and MEC PhD training group, which held meetings approximately every 2 months. The philosophy and ethical approach adopted by the facilitators was to create a safe environment for developing professional academic writing competencies, which was influenced by the Non-Violent Communication (NVC) movement, especially Dannahy's use of NVC in mathematics teaching (Dannahy, 1998). As Samuels and Deane worked with a small group of researchers they could be very responsive to feedback and work with individuals on a one-to-one basis.

▶ Event 1: Producing journal abstracts

The first one-day event took place in June 2007 and was co-facilitated by Samuels and Deane. Their main aim was to encourage the researchers to appreciate key elements of relevant journal articles in order to motivate and equip them to improve the quality of their own writing for publication. The students were each asked to provide an example of an article they had read and appreciated, and these examples were critiqued by the other members of the group. This first event covered three main topics:

- Abstract writing.
- Critical thinking, including specific guidance on evaluation criteria for mathematics education journals taken from Lester, 'Crieteria to Evaluate Research' (1996).
- Integrating sources into an academic argument.

Each of these issues was underpinned by activities and examples of scholarly texts taken from the mathematics education context. The students read three different journal abstracts closely and analysed the key features. A list of criteria for evaluating the quality of journal articles was distributed to the students to offer them prompts in analysing these articles and thinking about the qualities they might wish to cultivate in their own writing for publication (see Table 8.2 for an example of criteria that could be used).

This event was well-received by the students (see Appendix 1) and their feedback indicated that they wanted more such writing

Table 8.2 Criteria for evaluating articles (based on Lester, 1996)

Features in article	Description of features
1. Originality	Clear contribution to knowledge in the field.
2. Logic	Clear link between the research question and data, methods, analysis, and so on. Coherence in the content of the article.
3. Theoretical framework	Well-conceptualised research, with appropriate use of theory to collect, analyse, and interpret findings, as appropriate.
4. Project design	Well-planned research, with appropriate acknowledgement of bias, assumptions, and limitations. Clear description and critique of research methods, allowing for use of these methods by other researchers in different contexts.
5. Ethics	Clear description of ethics approval obtained and relevant issues or implications, as appropriate.
6. Authority	Clear, credible, and appropriate use of data, secondary literature, and other evidence to back up claims and conclusions.
7. Communication	Well-structured reporting and discussion of research undertaken. Clear organisation of ideas and appropriate written style.

development, but they also made suggestions for the next iteration of writing support:

- The topics covered were helpful, but further training was needed on other key aspects of writing for publication.
- The time for thinking about the students' own work in progress was insufficient.
- The event covered too much information.
- The critical thinking advice had been helpful, but could have been further contextualised in relation to mathematics education.

Samuels and Deane used this feedback to design their next writing for publication event, which took place 6 months later in December. In particular, they sought to narrow the focus in response to the students' suggestion that they had covered too much material during the first event. They also took note that students felt there had been insufficient time protected for their own writing, so they built this into the next session.

▶ Event 2: Reviewing the literature

The focus of the second event was critiquing journal articles, and the goal was to offer students a constructive environment for exploring the literature and identifying some of the qualities and limitations in published work. Samuels and Deane hoped that by generating a shared understanding of the characteristics of publication writing, the students would gain more confidence as scholars by appreciating that no article is definitive or without flaws.

Another aim of providing training in critiquing articles was to help the students develop more awareness of the range of conventions and rhetorical devices that are conventionally employed by disciplinary scholars. Samuels and Deane dedicated time during this second event to highlight the features of effective research writing and giving the students time to practice adopting and adapting these features in their own draft journal articles. For instance, they discussed the concept of originality in research and experimented with ways of making claims to originality explicit within an article. Although the focus was writing for publication, the participants also asked questions about their writing for doctoral theses and compared the conventions of this genre with the shorter journal article form.

Prior to this second event the doctoral researchers were asked to provide extracts of their own writing-in-progress. If they were not yet ready to share their drafts, they were given the option of submitting a journal article with annotations critiquing this source, as shown in Figure 8.1.

The students implemented the strategies they had learnt during the first event to critique the articles that had been chosen by their peers. Samuels and Deane also selected a book review and prepared this for general analysis by adding annotations to highlight the strengths and weaknesses in terms of the content and written expression, as shown in Figure 8.2. This involved them collaborating to pool their expertise on the two issues of disciplinary knowledge and academic writing, from which they both benefited by learning to notice features they did not usually observe.

Samuels and Deane thought that book reviews might be a useful genre for the doctoral researchers to analyse during this event because they are brief enough to study in a relatively short time, yet they contain detailed critiques of a source and demonstrate some of the kind of critiquing that students require for their publication writing and doctoral

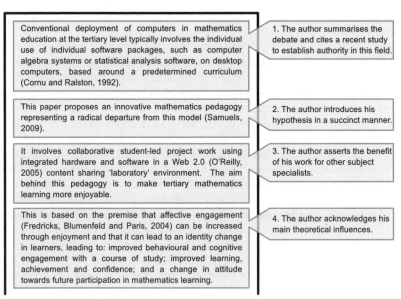

Figure 8.1 Journal article with annotations submitted by a doctoral researcher for discussion during Event 2 (Samuels 2010, p. 197).

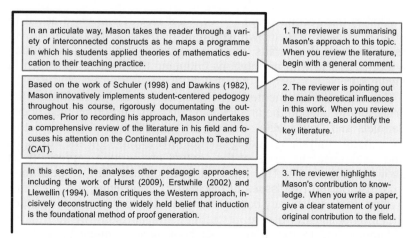

Figure 8.2 Annotated book review from the field of mathematics education (based on DALiC approach Purser et al., 2008).

work. During this second event, the students received annotated copies as shown in Figure 8.2 above to consolidate the book review with no comments and discussed the characteristics in pairs. They discussed the qualities of the review as a group, then received annotated copies to consolidate this analysis.

Bearing in mind the students' request for time and support to advance their own writing, Samuels and Deane created space during the second event for feedback on the work in progress that many students had taken the opportunity to submit. They introduced the concept of peer review and offered prompts for giving feedback to others based on the list of features they had discussed during the first writing event. They also shared examples of the criteria reviewers are given for articles that are submitted to journals, and suggested that students draw upon these both to support their peers and to reflect on their own plans for publication. Samuels and Deane read the students' work-in-progress prior to this event and they each spent time giving students individual feedback on the content and style of these drafts. Their goal was to foster a culture of peer review beyond this event to give students a growing appreciation of how to improve their own writing whilst contributing to a community of active research writers.

Also in response to feedback on the first writing for publication day, Samuels and Deane allocated time during the second event for students to continue drafting or revising the journal articles they were hoping to submit for publication. To prepare the researchers to use this time effectively, they offered them tips on goal setting for academic writing, including how to generate highly specific mini-targets of output per time period, for instance, the aim of generating 200 new words within an hour (Murray, 2005). They invited the researchers to set manageable objectives before they started writing and required them to report on their achievements after two hours. This guided practice at target-setting was intended to help students get to know their own rhythms of writing and enable them to feel more in control of the process of producing an article.

This second one-day event was especially well-received by the students (see Appendix 2), and their feedback indicated:

- Individual advice on writing-in-progress and detailed constructive critiques from tutors and peers were highly appreciated.
- Undertaking peer review was challenging, but helpful.
- The analysis and discussion of sample articles was useful.
- The time spent drafting and revising in a communal way during this event was appreciated by some participants, but not by others.

Samuels and Deane used the students' evaluations to design the third writing workshop, which took place 6 months after the second in June 2008. They reflected on the fact that some researchers wished to write independently, and others valued more structured writing time during the events. As their aim was to encourage students to explore models and methods that worked for them personally, they felt that the students' increased awareness of what they wanted and how they liked to work was a good result. Samuels and Deane thought that they were moving gradually towards their goal of supporting the development of a research writing community and creating ways for the students to support each other in their publication activity. This objective of fostering a writing community with diverse personalities and approaches was the main driver behind the third workshop, which was led much more explicitly by the students themselves.

▶ Event 3: Postgraduate conference preparation

The main goal for the third event was to assist the students in organising a postgraduate conference in the field of mathematics education. This conference was part of a wider programme of training in academic practice, yet Samuels and Deane were particularly keen to raise the profile of publication writing as an issue for the researchers to consider as they prepared their own papers or offered feedback on conference submissions. The principle behind the students organising this conference was to create a friendly ethos that encouraged the researchers to connect with scholars at other institutions and to view themselves increasingly as professionals in their field.

The third event was shorter because Samuels and Deane appreciated that some students wanted to protect maximum time for their own research, and they narrowed the focus to tips on reviewing paper abstracts because this was most relevant for the forthcoming postgraduate conference (Lores, 2004). This topic built on the work they had done during the first event on how to write a journal abstract and in the second on critiquing sources. The rationale for this incremental approach was to introduce students to explicit features in scholarly writing, they had guided opportunities to practice these, and then they were encouraged to implement the principles in their own ways.

Based on the WiD principle of embedding writing development within departments, Samuels took responsibility for this third event, applying the findings he and Deane had gathered throughout their collaboration. He was joined by Erik Borg, a writing developer from Coventry University's Centre for Academic Writing who helped to support the researchers as they reviewed conference paper abstracts. The researchers discussed the role of conference paper abstracts as a genre and examined key features in authentic examples (Swales, 1990; Berkenkotter and Huckin, 1994). They looked at how sample abstracts provide a synopsis of research, identify a target audience, hook the readers' attention, and claim a contribution to knowledge. They also looked at unsuccessful abstracts to identify common errors and develop more confidence as writers and reviewers.

The students were given different types of abstracts, and they were introduced to the formula "Introduction, Method, Results, Discussion" (IMRD) as one approach to organising ideas in a scholarly article (see Figure 8.3 below).

To help them review submissions for the postgraduate conference, students were given the following criteria for review:

- Relevance to the conference theme.
- Benefits to the conference delegates.
- Clarity of the argument.
- Originality of the research.
- Rigour of the methodology.

1 (Introduction) This article investigates EFL learner use of high frequency verbs, and in particular use of the verb MAKE, a major representative of this group. The main questions addressed are: do learners tend to over or under use these verbs? Are high-frequency verbs error-prone or safe? What part does transfer play in the misuse of these verbs? **2 (Methods)** To answer these questions, authentic learner data have been compared with native speaker data using computerized corpora and linguistic software tools to speed up the initial stage of the linguistic analysis. The article focuses on what proves to be the two most distinctive uses of MAKE, viz. the delexical and causative uses. **3 (Results)** Results show that EFL learners, even at an advanced proficiency level, have great difficulty with a high frequency verb such as MAKE. They also demonstrate that some of these problems are shared by the two groups of learners under consideration (Swedish- and French-speaking learners) while others seem to be L1-related. **4 (Discussion)** In the conclusion, the pedagogical implications of the study are discussed and suggestions made for using concordance-based exercise as a way of raising learners' awareness of the complexity of high-frequency verbs.

Figure 8.3 Example of an "IMRD" style abstract used in Event 3 (Altenberg and Granger, 2001).

The researchers worked both individually and in pairs to review the abstracts, which helped them to generate ideas and be more aware that there is an inherent subjectivity in the process of reviewing.

Feedback on this event was positive, in particular, students liked the direct link between their task of preparing for the conference and the support they received. They also appreciated that their feedback on previous events was incorporated into the design of the third event. In summary, the researchers responded:

- The tips on analysing paper abstracts were helpful.
- The group work was productive.
- The shorter length of the event was appreciated by some delegates, but not others.
- The session was relevant to students' needs at that stage.

▶ Findings

Feedback from this cohort revealed the students' appreciation of both the writing strategies they were taught and the space to experiment with their own styles as scholars. This collaboration helped Deane to increase her understanding of scholarship in mathematics education, and Samuels combined his authority as a subject specialist with a new repertoire of tips on publication writing. The students reported feeling more confident as writers and critically aware of the steps they needed to undertake to succeed within their discipline.

Samuels and Deane discovered through this WiD initiative that explicit tuition needs to tie in closely with what students are doing, and should be planned to offer advice at exactly the right time. This means that a range of provision should ideally be offered on a rolling programme to cater for students at each stage of the doctoral process. They discovered the importance of flexibility and of offering researchers alternatives in the type of development activities in which they participated. Most of all, it was clear that soliciting feedback and responding to participants' evaluations is essential to tailoring writing development to a cohort without being prescriptive.

▶ Conclusion

Samuels and Deane are continuing to implement opportunities for Mathematics Education doctoral researchers to become published authors, and their starting point has moved more closely to what the researchers request. This emphasis on listening and responding to the participants was Samuel's idea, and from the start of the collaboration he was the driving force behind planning events, including the postgraduate conference that engages and benefits researchers so much. The effectiveness of Samuels' approach is evidenced in the students' feedback, but it also testifies to the importance of subject specialists leading WiD initiatives, not only because they know their discipline, but also because they know their students and are best placed to encourage students to help each other to become better disciplinary writers (North, 1984).

▶ Acknowledgements

The authors wish to thank Ray Summers for his expertise in multimedia design and Erik Borg for his generous participation in this WiD initiative. They are grateful to Tony Croft, Director of sigma at Loughborough University, Duncan Lawson, Director of sigma at Coventry Universtiy, and Terry Hawkes, Associate Director of sigma at Coventry University, for their expertise and support.

▶ Appendices

Event 1

Appendix 1. Participants' feedback from Event 1

Student 1	Very well-thought out structure to the day.
	All talks were valuable to me and useful.
	Friendly staff abstract + critical analysis parts were the most helpful.
Student 2	Useful day.
	Very good venue, accommodation, food, resources—computers.
	Abstract content was well-covered.
	Critical thinking was well-covered.
	Interesting mix of presenters could also have covered:
	• Overall structure of a paper.
	• List of maths education journals.
Student 3	Very informative workshop, although I feel I have substantial experience in writing abstracts/papers, this workshop has been invaluable and much better than I originally anticipated!
	There is always room for improvement, and I am far from an expert in writing, but I have grown more confidence in my own abilities.
	An even longer session would be great to build up the skills further.
Student 4	Confidence boost, chance to talk about your problems interactively.
	Too much!!—meaning so may aspects, hard to narrow down what I need.
Student 5	Overall good/interesting.
	The session where we reviewed and so on papers was not what at least some of us expected—for example I thought we'd discuss strategies for revising/reviewing a paper rather than being left to it for 30 minutes—not overly productive.
Student 6	Range of activities
	Novelty—birthdays/height! Did a lot in a short time
	Atmosphere/location etc.
	Negative
	Not enough time for some exercises
Student 7	Useful variety of activities that touched on nearly all aspects of the writing process.
	A follow-up session may be to invite participants to bring nearly complete work for comment AND/OR a 2/3/4 hour exercise: write a group paper on an agreed topic.

Event 2

Appendix 2. Participants' feedback from Event 2

Student	Most useful	Least useful	Requests
1	Advice from knowledgeable experts in academic writing. Meeting such interesting people, all of whom are researching in the same field as me! Dedicated focussed time to write!!	Nothing—it was all very valuable.	Could the group be asked whether they are happy to read any of my writing, and I'm offering to read other people's work in return, like a sort of e-mail writing group.
2	The funnel analogy! And emphasis on thesis statement!	I would have preferred to work on my own/gotten feedback on my own work rather than an article I had chosen. I wasn't aware this was an option, but I know for next time!	Something about drafting/re-drafting or re-writing pieces of work?
3	Opportunity to gain feedback on my own writing. Suggestions for improving lit. review, especially introduction and conclusion.		Would welcome further opportunities to critically review own work.
4	Discussion with my paper and individual feedback. Emphasis on contribution to knowledge.		Some ideal examples of research papers and methodological critique or rationale on mathematics education related to ICT.
5	Early discussion on writing review = also "mapping" out of papers. Discussion with ... about the paper I submitted.	Work on own: I felt time could be better spent and work we did at the time could have been done in own time after session.	

▶ Note

1   Samuels and Deane benefited from the expertise of colleagues at Coventry University and Loughborough University, in particular Tony Croft, Duncan Lawson, Terry Hawkes, and Erik Borg who attended the events and contributed to the teaching.

▶ References

Altenberg, B. and Granger, S. (2001) "The grammatical and lexical patterning of MAKE in native and non-native student writing." *Applied Linguistics*, 22 (2): 173–95.

Berkenkotter, C. and Huckin, T. N. (1994) *Genre Knowledge in Disciplinary Communication: Cognition/Culture/Power*. Abingdon: Routledge.

Dannahy, P. (1998) "Maths and Non-violent Communication". *Maths Support Association Newsletter*, 8. Available from http://www.sigma-cetl.ac.uk/index.php?section=87 [22 July 2009].

Deci, E. L. and Ryan, R. M. (2000) "Self-Determination Theory and the Facilitation of Intrinsic Motivation, Social Development, and Well-Being". *American Psychologist*, 55: 68–78.

Gottschalk, K. and Hjortshoj, K. (2004) *The Elements of Teaching Writing: A Resource for Instructors in All Disciplines*. Boston: Bedford/St Martin's.

Jaworski, B. J. (2002) "Sensitivity and Challenge in University Mathematics Tutorial Teaching". *Educational Studies in Mathematics*, 51: 71–94.

Lester, F. K. (1996) "Criteria to Evaluate Research". *Journal for Research in Mathematics Education*, 27 (2): 130–32.

Mason, J. and Johnston-Wilder, S. (eds) (2004) *Fundamental Constructs in Mathematics Education*. Abingdon: Routledge Falmer.

Mond, D. (2007) "Mathematicians and Mathematics Educationalists: Can We Collaborate?" Mathematics Institute, University of Warwick, 26 January 2007. Available from http://www.warwick.ac.uk/~masbm/mvme.html> [22 July 2009].

Moriarty, M. F. (1997) *Writing Science through Critical Thinking*. Sudbury: Jones and Bartlett.

Murray, R. (2005) *Writing for Academic Journals*. Maidenhead: Open University Press.

North, S. M. (1984) "The Idea of a Writing Center." *College English*, 46 (5): 433–446.

Purser, E., Skillen, J., Deane, M., Donahue, J., and Peake, K. (2008) "Developing Academic Literacy in Context". *Zeischrist Schreiben* June 2008. Available from <www.zeitschrist-schreiben.eu> [10 January 2009].

Samuels, P. C. (2006) "Introducing the SIGMA Mathematics Support Research Programme". *MSOR Connections*, 6 (4): 12–13.

Samuels, P. C. (2010) "Motivating Mathematics Learning Through an Integrated Technology Enhanced Learning Environment." *International Journal of Technology in Mathematics Education*, 17 (4): 196–203.

Samuels, P. and Deane, M. (2008) "Academic Writing Training for Mathematics Education PhD Students". *Maths, Stats, and OR Connections*, 8(3): 41–44.

Schoenfeld, A. H. (2002) "Research Methods in (Mathematics) Education." In English, L. D. (ed.) *Handbook of International Research in Mathematics Education*, Mahwah: Lawrence Erlbaum Associates.

Somerville, E. M. and Crème, P. (2005) "Asking Pompeii Questions: A Co-Operative Approach to Writing in the Disciplines." *Teaching in Higher Education*, 10 (1): 17–28.

Street, B. (2005) *Literacies Across Educational Contexts.* Philadelphia: Caslon.

Swales, J. M. (1990) *Genre Analysis: English in Academic Research Settings.* Cambridge: Cambridge University Press.

Tall, D. (ed.) (1991) *Advanced Mathematical Thinking.* Holland: Kluwer.

Zevenbergen, R. (2006) "Book Review: In Search of a Pedagogy of Conflict and Dialogue for Mathematics Education" by Renuka Vithal. Springer Mathematics Education Library, Vol. 32, 2003, 416p., Hardcover, ISBN:1-4020-1504-6 in *Educational Studies in Mathematics* 62: 101–104.

9 Political Theory, Academic Writing, and Widening Participation

Birgit Schippers and Jonathan Worley

▶ Introduction

A frequently expressed view, widely articulated in the media, suggests that we are currently experiencing a decline of interest in politics, considered by some, even, as civic decay. A widespread voter switch-off from politics, and from the political process, as well as a pervasive cynicism among citizens are said to be key elements of this alleged decline. There is indeed compelling evidence that supports this assertion. Pattie and colleagues (2003), in a major study on civic attitudes and engagement in modern Britain, cite a downturn in electoral participation, a decline in party membership and a loss of trust in political institutions, as well as citizens' frustration with spin and corruption, as prime evidence to support this hypothesis of civic decline. Some of the most widely discussed recent texts within political studies, such as Colin Hay's *Why We Hate Politics?* (2007) and Gerry Stoker's *Why Politics Matters: Making Democracy Work* (2006), also engage, albeit in different ways, with the assertion of the decline of interest in politics, or political disenchantment. Two central points of contention regarding the current political condition inform their respective discussions: first, that politics is perceived as too difficult and complex to allow for widespread interest and to generate wide-ranging participation, and second that politics is seen as largely irrelevant to the concerns and interests of the majority of citizens. As Stoker (2006) contends, the professionalisation of politics, together with the required specialisation and expertise of its practitioners, as well as a consumerist and cynical attitude of citizens all contribute to the current "decline" of politics.

These concerns are of wider relevance to current debates on politics, but they also form the backdrop to our discussion in this chapter: we want to reflect upon the collaborative model of teaching political theory and the teaching of academic writing in political theory in which we currently engage. Key to our reflection is a consideration of student engagement with politics and with academic study, especially with academic reading and writing, and to this end, we examine three challenges. In the first part of the chapter, we want to suggest that student writing in political theory cannot be separated from broader student attitudes towards, and engagement with, politics, as these inform the motivation that students bring to the academic requirements of their degree. As we seek to demonstrate, Stoker's and Hay's respective assertions *vis-à-vis* the disenchantment with politics are reflected in large sections of the student cohort with which we are working. The theme of disenchantment also informs a second aspect of our discussion when we consider the methodological and epistemological challenges of political theory. There, we explore how these challenges may be addressed through the deployment of particular pedagogical strategies in the field of reading and writing. Central to this consideration is an emphasis on criticality, on the engagement with contested knowledge and the aligned requirement of close textual work. This leads to our third and final point: the location of our teaching practice in a widening participation agenda that aims to expose students to the world of political discourse while not expecting them to become expert practitioners within the discipline. This agenda, as we want to suggest, has implications for the teaching of writing, as well as for student willingness and preparedness to engage with political theory, and with politics more generally.

▶ Studying politics in an era of disenchantment?

We intimated above that the current political condition has been described as one of decline, decay, or disenchantment with the political process, especially in its electoral manifestation. As we suggested, commentators often refer to the well-documented decline in electoral participation and citizens' disillusionment with the political process and the political class (Pattie et al., 2003). If such a discontent exists in the wider population, it is particularly prominent among younger age groups, including those participating in higher education (HE). For example, it has been suggested that the term "politics" generates a negative response in young people (Tonge and Mycock, 2010, p. 182). Surveys of voter participation rates reveal that the age group of 18–24-year-olds seems most alienated from the political process, displaying the lowest electoral participation rate amongst all citizens (Electoral Commission, 2005). As we describe in more detail below, such an apparent lack of interest in politics is also expressed within sections of our student cohort, and it frames the extent of their engagement with politics, with the academic study of politics, and with their written work.

However, even though we regularly encounter a widely articulated lack of interest in politics in our classrooms, which corresponds to wider trends in the area of civic engagement and attitudes towards politics amongst young people (O'Toole et al., 2003; Tonge and Mycock, 2010), we believe it is necessary to take a closer look at such expressions of apathy and to distinguish between a lack of civic engagement and a lack of interest. The importance of such a distinction is repeatedly stressed in the critical literature on the topic. For example, Tonge and Mycock challenge what they term the "myth of political apathy". As they argue, a "disenchantment with certain politicians and aspects of the political system [is wrongly conflated] with a mass political 'switch-off' " (2010, p. 189). This assertion is shared by O'Toole and colleagues, who diagnose a "gap between falling political participation, on the one hand, and reported reasonably high levels of political interest on the other" (2003, p. 349). Our experiences in the politics and writing skills classrooms confirm these findings. Students' attitude towards politics in general, and towards the study of politics in particular, is framed by their association of politics with the realm of institutional politics, its focus on elections, macro-issues, and the dominance in this arena of professional politics. Hence, it seems almost inevitable that students perceive politics to be removed from their everyday experiences. Moreover, students new to the (academic) study of politics often conflate politics, as represented in the media and associated with well-known political figures and the formal institutions of government, with political studies; it is perhaps unsurprising that the latter, given its stress on rigour, continuous reflection, and methodical approach, poses a substantial challenge to newcomers. Further evidence for the distinction between engagement and interest was generated in a student citizenship audit conducted by Schippers in early 2009. This project aimed to establish more fully students' overall attitude towards politics, their degree of civic engagement, and their awareness of current affairs, above and beyond their engagement and participation in the politics classroom. While a majority of students did not identify themselves as being politically active, many considered taking up some form of engagement if and when it fit in with their lifestyles and wider interests. Moreover, almost all participants were able to identify several significant contemporary events; for example, they expressed a particular interest in the 2009 US presidential election and have followed at least some of the news coverage of this process. Familiarity with some headline-grabbing local events, such as the shooting of two British soldiers, was also mentioned frequently.

A further point is important to consider. As O'Toole and colleagues contend, little effort has been made to explore how citizens themselves, and young people in particular, define the political (2003, p. 350). An argument advanced by Tonge and Mycock further clarifies this point: they suggest that young people are often unaware of the political aspects of the decisions that they take (2010, p. 189). That is, young people pass judgement or take decisions that are implicitly political, but are not identified as such. This disconnect between civic action, or interest, and making explicit the political dimension of one's actions or judgements is frequently encountered in our teaching practice and can be usefully illustrated if we look at students' engagement with the concept of equality. Even though many students are reluctant to reflect in a deep and critical way about the concept of equality, including its historical origins and philosophical associations, they are passionate about the right to equality if and when it concerns their own lives. Young female students in particular are often dismissive of the continued relevance of feminism, yet they are adamant of their right to equal pay for equal work and are often shocked to discover discrepancies in pay between men and women. Equality also matters to students' lives in the context of the history of the North of Ireland. Whilst younger students have no direct experience of the Troubles, their collective memory is deeply attached to notions of fairness, equal treatment, and a vehement opposition to discrimination.

This willingness and demonstrated ability to engage with the personal dimension of politics should be welcomed (and can be teased out further through the use of relevant pedagogical strategies). However, it does not necessarily translate into an intellectual engagement with the challenging requirements of the academic study of politics, especially with reading and writing. It is this aspect that we examine in the next section. There, we suggest that the theoretical dimension of the study of politics, which lies at the heart of the politics classroom, raises particular challenges; these, as we discuss further below, are also pertinent to the widening participation dimension of the academic programme on which we are working.

▶ Political theory as critical theory

The study of politics, broadly construed, is concerned with the organisation of collective life, including the allocation and access to scarce resources and the distribution and control of power. Political theory, equally broadly construed, reflects on the ordering and organisation of collective life; it seeks to reveal and to assess underlying processes, normative assumptions and philosophical presuppositions, power constellations and ideological commitments. Central to the study of political theory is the recognition of its plurality, whether in relation to the methodologies employed, its wider epistemological commitments or its ontological assumptions. Hence, to attempt a definition of political theory, whilst of some heuristic benefit, would be an exercise in futility that runs counter to the essentially contested nature of all matters political. It is the very diversity of methodologies, subject matter, approaches, and underlying epistemologies which resist any such disciplining of political theory, that, in the eye of its practitioners, make it so fascinating. Yet, it is precisely this diversity, often perceived as slipperiness, with which so many students struggle and which turns many of them off. If political theory is perceived as difficult or removed from real-world politics, even for those students with an interest in political matters, then this is further compounded by its lack of a clearly defined subject matter and methodology. A further aspect is crucial: political theory's absence of definitions, its emphasis on debate and discourse, in short, the contested nature of knowledge, run up against the capacities and capabilities that students develop at secondary level and that they bring to HE. Its apparent distance from the real life experiences of the contemporary student body further undermines the potential for student engagement.

Clearly, there are pedagogical solutions to some of these problems (Sloam, 2008). Role play and classroom debates generate engagement, while credits given for seminar contributions aid student participation in the politics classroom. Besides, the choice of topics, especially those that students perceive as local, further helps to develop their interest: the conflictual and volatile nature of politics in the North of Ireland and students' intuitive attachment to a particular community and its broad-based political outlook may contribute to their curiosity. It should be noted, though, that this is not the case with all our students. Some sections of the cohort, while enjoying aspects of the course, do not get enthused about what they perceive as the sectarian nature of Northern Irish politics. Crucial to our context is a further consideration: their interest in political issues does not necessarily translate into an active engagement with the academic material and often leads to a regression into the mode of learning associated with the secondary level.

Our aim has been to stress the importance of teaching and studying political theory as part of a liberal education. The main reason why we accord such importance to political theory is grounded in its *leitmotif*: criticality. For political theorists, this stress on criticality underpins their methodological approaches and it informs their engagement with the world. The theme of criticality, which includes the development of a questioning attitude, is also central to any understanding of citizenship that seeks to re-constitute citizens' active engagement with their social and political world. For example, the American scholar Dana Villa advocates what he terms a Socratic conception of citizenship, that is, a form of citizenship that values contemplation, thoughtfulness and critique (Villa, 2001; see also Brown, 2005). Whilst this emphasis on contemplation and critique is central to the project of political theorists, it also connects with more practical and pragmatic considerations. For example, political theory constitutes, at least potentially, a useful training in criticality even for those students, such as ours, who are not reading for a degree in Politics (and it can extend the current government's agenda with citizenship education into third-level education). It is to this point that we turn to in the next section, where we provide a brief sketch of the educational context in which we work.

▶ Political theory on a widening participation programme: Liberal Arts in Belfast

In response to the challenges of the Dearing Report (1997), St Mary's University College Belfast, a former Catholic teacher training college in the North of Ireland, diversified its educational programme beyond the training of student teachers by establishing, in the year 2000, a Liberal Arts degree. The Liberal Arts degree, a broad-based social science and humanities degree, is aimed to partake in the government's drive to expand HE. As part of their degree, students take two compulsory courses in political theory at levels one and two. One of the major emphases of the degree programme, in line with the Dearing recommendations, as well as with current trends in HE, is the provision of classes in written and oral communications, ICT and, more recently, financial literacy. While the Liberal Arts degree places particular emphasis on the development of employability, it also provides for a liberal education in a classical sense, encompassing, among other things, the study of politics and philosophy, ethics, culture, and the economy.

A particular emphasis of the skills component of the Liberal Arts degree at St Mary's lies with the provision of academic support aimed at developing students' writing ability; this support includes, in the main, the writing centre and its affiliated programme of peer tutoring in writing. It is fair to say that these provisions are comprehensive and well-developed, including (compulsory) classes in written communications, and voluntary, drop-in sessions by students to the writing centre to meet with peer tutors. Yet, we were struck to see how few students initially benefited from or availed of this support. These admittedly anecdotal observations constituted the starting point of our exploration and encouraged us to develop a closer collaboration between the teaching of written communications and the teaching of Politics. This collaboration proceeded from the assumption that there is a close link between the level of motivation that students bring to their studies, the awareness of the requirements of studying at degree level, and the emphasis which students place on the development of their key skills. This connection, however, as we will discuss here, is complicated and confusing, particularly in relation to student motivation. Central to this puzzle seems to be students' engagement with politics, and in particular with the study of political theory.

Shortly after the inception of the degree, it became evident that the development of students' written communication skills needed to be more integrated into their subject study. To this end, we have developed a series of strategies for closer co-operation between classes in political theory and classes in written communications. This co-operation is located at level two, where students take a compulsory unit in Citizenship and Democracy and in Written Communications. Each year, before the teaching of the paired Politics and Written Communications courses, we meet to co-ordinate schedules and practices. We reach mutual agreement on the types of writing assignments to be deployed, we set due dates and we discuss and share key readings and lecture presentations. Tutorials in the written communications classes are tailored to provide effective support for the development of writing skills in politics, concentrating upon elements of reading and writing (discussed below): reading key texts with students and discussing how to interpret conceptual challenges of the discourse of political theory and writing about key texts together and discussing what is unique about writing in Politics. Discussions of epistemological considerations and conceptually difficult elements within the students' assigned political readings occur frequently.

The second year Politics unit consists of 12 lectures on a series of key themes in citizenship studies and democratic theory. These are accompanied by a series of seminars that discuss the content and themes of the lecture material in more detail and that centre on a required key reading. The seminars require a basic degree of student preparation that entails the reading of one prescribed key text, the willingness to engage in discussion, and the participation in an assessed group presentation. Perhaps unsurprisingly, the seminars that accompany the lectures generate challenges for both lecturer and students. Whilst students have already completed one academic year, many continue to resist the requirements of academic learning, specifically the emphasis on active learning. The level of preparation, especially for the first few sessions, is generally low. Many students proclaim to be struggling with the readings, but closer examination reveals that they often either fail to read the text, or, as is frequently the case, resist the effort involved in the reading of academic texts. This problem is a recurring issue in both politics and written communication classes and therefore needs to be perpetually addressed if student learning is to become effective.

Students also struggle to relate to the issues under discussion, though this differs from topic to topic. Generally speaking, the more contemporary and local the issue, the easier it becomes to spark students' interests. However, whilst they may willingly and often enough enthusiastically participate in a discussion on a given topic, this interest does not translate back into an engagement with the relevant critical literature. Finally, the wide range of interests and abilities represented in the cohort pose a further challenge for students and lecturer. It is probably fair to say that those students who struggle with the material are easily switched off, whilst others feel that the non-contributors inhibit and hinder their learning and academic progress.

Overall, we can summarise the challenges in the following way: first, a substantial minority of students have not accomplished the shift from a passive to an active mode of learning. This often goes hand in hand with a reluctance to engage with reading material, which is rejected, *a priori*, as difficult, and which is repeated in a failure to read for the essay. Finally, some students struggle to engage with issues, either because they are seen as uninteresting, or because they lack a wider general knowledge. As we intimated above, the Politics classroom deploys a series of pedagogical strategies to deal with these challenges. While these pedagogical tools go some way towards overcoming the resistance towards politics, they can run up against disciplinary conventions by trivialising complex issues. Moreover, they do not necessarily address the resistance to reading academic texts and writing on them. In the next section, we present the steps deployed in the written communications classes.

▶ Addressing the challenges of politics in the writing centre classroom

The challenge of developing effective written communications tuition for students studying Politics is multifaceted. Because of the commitment to widening participation on the St Mary's Liberal Arts Degree, the teaching of writing in Politics cannot be completely separated from a consideration of the student cohort. However, it would be a mistake to view the challenges our students face to be solely dependent upon the widening access background of many of its members. The more traditional, more accomplished students experience similar problems, if to a lesser extent. From a written communications perspective, these problems are fairly straightforwardly discussed in terms of difficulties with *both* reading and writing. With respect to reading political theory, students tend to be reluctant and unsophisticated readers without competent strategies for confronting texts that do not meet their expectations. With respect to writing, the rhetorical strategies that students deploy often revolve excessively around summary—or even less sophisticated forms of collecting information—which can be particularly inadequate for confronting the abstractions of political discourse. For example, one student showed me a page of notes from a Politics text: they were all direct quotations, and she didn't understand any of them.

▶ Reading: Understanding the discourse of political theory

When it comes to reading in Politics, lack of motivation and, even, passivity, can be compounded by the challenge of the text. Our students, in general, tell us that they are intimidated by subjects with which they have had little or no A-level experience, but when they approach the study of Politics, this lack of familiarity is complicated by additional epistemological considerations. Students who are used to a narrative deployment of knowledge (as in English literature) or a chronological one (as in history) now find these contexts largely absent. For example, in one of the core texts, David Held's *Models of Democracy* (2006), the organisation of chapters is roughly chronological, perhaps leading students to think they are dealing with a historical narrative. However, a survey of the book reveals that the content of each chapter is devoted to the explication of a particular political theory and its critique. While one chapter is laying out concepts of Marxism (pp. 96–124), for example, as a set of conceptual categories, students are at cross-purposes, latching onto dates and attempting to construct a chronological narrative. That Marx lived from 1818–83 will be given as much emphasis as any principal concept of Marxism, in part because dates have come to seem to students to be principally important facts, in part because dates do not present threatening concepts and may be memorised and in part because they fit into a chronological interpretive strategy. After reading the chapter, students will frequently write that Marx wrote *The Eighteenth Brumaire of Napoleon*, but not that that it "may be his most interesting work on the state", because their ideas of what constitutes "the state" may be an unfamiliar abstraction (Held, 2006, p. 106). Further, they will often reiterate the relatively sparse

biographical information on a theorist more readily than his or her political theories, attempting to construct a character narrative instead of
constructing the elements of a political theory. When Held offers a brief
aside about Marxism's relationship to feminism, students grasp onto
this because for them a simplistic feminist approach is a comfortable
approach to Marx: did he like women or didn't he?

Besides floundering while trying to understand the construction of
the text, student confusion when dealing with the abstractions of the
political vocabulary of Politics is also a problem. This problem is not
necessarily one of complex vocabulary. For example, the title of Held's
chapter on Marxist theory is entitled "Direct Democracy and the End of
Politics". Such a figurative description of Marxist ideology confuses students, and the uncertainty about what "direct democracy" or the "end
of politics" might mean prevents them from getting an initial purchase
on the chapter. After an initial reading of the chapter, students cannot in the classroom state the meaning of the title. In this case, for
example, "direct democracy" may signal the radical pruning of representative democracy, while the "end of government" may mean two
things: the withering away of the state or the aims of government
(which may include the government's withering away). More sophisticated readers would understand the need to interpret the allusive
nature of these phrases, and even, appreciate the creativity embodied in the title, but to the uninitiated student, Held appears obscure
even when using a relatively simple vocabulary. While the author of
the chapter is attempting to capture the reader's attention at a sophisticated intellectual level, students miss these particular encodings of
meaning and are left looking for more readily recognisable data, hoping to be rescued by classroom lectures that will present them with this
kind of simpler information. For example, in a lecture accompanied by
PowerPoint, students will faithfully copy down key points but entirely
miss the more sophisticated discussion to which these points refer.

Students' initial reading strategies should not be derided because the
attempt to establish a context for any new reading is probably a universal strategy, but where students fail at this point in their study of
Politics is in their reluctance to shift to new paradigms for what counts
as knowledge. If the text does not readily conform to their expectations
and previously established methods of understanding, they will discard
it before they can get a significant purchase on it. Students need to be
work at what they think counts as knowledge in Politics, and they need
to examine more closely elements of Politics texts to see how information is structured and encoded, beginning with introductory paragraphs
and proceeding to particular paragraphs from the body of the text.

They also need to be shown how to glean contextual clues—from
book and article titles, prefaces and introductions—from which they

can construct a provisional idea of what information will be presented, how it will be presented (epistemologically), and in what order information will be presented. In the Held text, for example, the preface and introduction say a great deal about the purposes for studying politics and the approach that the book takes. In Held's preface, he comments upon the way in which the "9/11" terrorist attacks highlighted the vulnerabilities of the democratic model, discussing the need to balance individual freedoms with collective security. This provides a concrete exemplification of Held's purpose in writing the book, and 9/11 can be element of shared experience to which the students will have a personal reaction. They can then compare Held's purposes to their own reaction. Another contextual clue may be found in the accompanying course materials (which students frequently lose and consider unimportant), including the statement of purpose provided to them in their course syllabus mentioning "the organisation of the collective life . . . the regulation and control of power . . . and the allocation and distribution of resources". These foci for the course can be developed and expanded with each additional reading, and each reading may be interrogated for its relevance to these central purposes.

As a final example of contextualising the reading, a study of the table of contents in the same book reveals that the writer is much more interested in contemporary political practices and that, consequently, Marxism is defined as a "classic model". Marx is not studied so much for the sake of Marxism as for what Marxism has to say about the contemporary political practice of democracy. If students can be persuaded that this is a principal purpose of the chapter, they may begin to abandon previous, unfruitful paradigms (such as narrative and chronology) for understanding the reading, and they may begin to see that Marx is being studied not merely so they can recite a few facts about Marx, but because they may be able to learn from Marx in what ways contemporary democracy succeeds or fails.

Before beginning a particular Politics reading, students are asked either to write about or discuss what they know already as a context for reading. We want to familiarise students with the building of contexts for understanding unfamiliar material. Often, on the subject of Politics, students will not know a great deal, but it is useful to sift through what they do know as a basis for developing how one should approach the study of politics. As a prelude to assigning students the above reading on Marx, students were vaguely able to discuss the way his name had pejorative associations. Teasing out those associations, which might link Marxism with the Red Scare, can help define what politics thinks about. Should discussions of Marxist theory be linked to past fears about Soviet aggression? If Held is calling Marxism "Direct Democracy", what is pejorative about either "direct" or "democracy"?

In other words, in these preliminary discussions, out of initial preju-dices, students can be guided to thinking in terms of what constitutes legitimate political discourse. In the above example, the discussions can become more about what constitutes legitimate knowledge in Politics and less about historical alignments. Students can be encour-aged to think about the abstractions of politics as a new frame of reference.

All of the above, of course, presuppose that students will actually read the assigned texts. As a sample of scripts from the 2008–9 cohort demonstrates, students frequently attempt to fulfil the demands of any written assignment based upon a reading by summarising material from that reading, principally through paraphrase but also through direct copying (which, of course, is how they quickly slip into pla-giarism, even with good intentions). Irrespective of the assignment question, students typically begin an assignment on a reading by sum-marising, starting at the beginning of a particular reading and stopping when they have approached the word limit for the assignment. A lec-turer could be reassured at the end of a marking session that the students were reading a great deal of the first few pages of a reading while subsequent pages had remained largely untouched. In an assign-ment that asked students to critique one chapter in terms of another, two summaries were often provided, and those summaries often only covered the beginning of each chapter. In an alternative strategy, one student admitted that he would only read and write about those parts of a reading that were easy to understand. This practice led to the bio-graphical strategy described above: the student, for example, discussed more about Machiavelli's origins than his politics.

Students are likely to resist readings on two levels. One level, as dis-cussed above, has to do with continued resistance to political discourse. But the other level has to do with the fact that students, of all abilities, tend to be reluctant readers. One of the most promising students on the Liberal Arts degree, who is in her final year, stated that she "hates to read". This is where more generic strategies to encourage reading need to be set into place. In the written communications course, students are regularly required to outline their readings, a task which initially they find unfamiliar and difficult to practice. The outlining process begins the task of turning reading into writing. Although the outlining of a reading can be a tedious and excessively structured exercise, (1) it forces stu-dents to complete a reading rather than to simply read a few pages, (2) it requires them to interpret difficult material by condensing and translating it into their own language, and (3) it encourages them to see a structure to the information presented in a reading. The poten-tially onerous quality of outlining a reading can also be alleviated by engaging in the pre-reading strategies mentioned above.

Unfortunately, because of the level of difficulty, students are often tempted into patterns of plagiarism. When outlining, students frequently attempt to repeat a familiar pattern of copying material. In the most recent set of writing skills classes, approximately 80% of the students attempted to subvert the demands of the first outlining exercise by simply copying one sentence from every paragraph of the text for each point in their outline. This practice, quickly spotted through use of a plagiarism detection service, resulted in students then having to rewrite their outlines translating and condensing the material into their own words. One student, who needed to learn how to condense material, balked at the assignment by writing a long e-mail in which he announced "regrettably" that he was unable to complete the assignment within the required word length.

The attempt to outline a chapter by simply copying elements of the chapter's text verbatim is another instance of students throwing up their hands in the face of a challenging reading in political theory, so the students need to be supported in their approach to the outline. They need to become as aware as possible how the material is likely to be useful, how it is structured, and why the writer finds the subject interesting. Preliminary questions which help the student to enter the text and assess it are also useful. Properly prepared, outlining has good potential for success. The practice makes students focus more intensively and thoroughly on the text and helps them to understand that a thorough reading is possible. If they can be further persuaded to include critical commentary within their outline, the task also becomes potentially more enjoyable.

In the worst-case scenarios, students have done very little independent reading at A-level. Instead, they tell us, their teachers have prepared them for exams by providing them with lecture notes and hand-outs. The concept of reading an assigned text, at all, is virtually unheard of among a significant number of our Liberal Arts cohort (students who studied for an English A-level can be an exception). In these cases, students have to be persuaded that doing any reading is a legitimate element of their educational experience and that to be independent writers they also have to be independent readers.

▶ Writing in politics: The rhetoric of criticality

When students are queried about the structuring of an academic essay, three dominant ideas are likely to emerge: (1) essays should have a beginning, middle, and end, (2) essays should not "waffle", and (3) essays should "flow". Despite repeated querying, our students rarely produce more concrete descriptors of academic writing. The stereotypical conventions of the "current-traditional" system of teaching writing in America, which tends to insist on introductory paragraphs with thesis statements and plans for discussion, followed by a structured series of developing paragraphs (making use of argument and evidence) and a summary conclusion are novel ideas for most Northern Irish students. These ideas are carefully introduced (to try and avoid the pitfall of having the students substitute structure for meaning) because they can become useful conceptions for improving coherence, shifting students away from using writing to simply provide a loose collection of evidence.

Exercises in writing of thesis statements before beginning critical essays can be extremely useful. Emphasis is placed upon what the student "wants to say" in their piece of writing and how they might relay that quickly in a conversation or interview. This begins the process of engagement. Thesis statements are also tested to see if they are written in the "language of politics". For example, if a student writes in the form of, "In my experience, women do not have political equality," a discussion needs to ensue about what counts for evidence in writing about politics. The statement needs to be reframed so that particular and legitimate evidence may be accessed, as in: "Studies of female MPs performance in parliament indicates that women are frequently co-opted by the practices of their male counterparts". Women may not have political equality, but the students need to frame this in terms of evidence of why this is true.

When students perform critical reviews of articles from journals in politics, they are presented with material that practices this use of legitimate argument and evidence and which also makes available to them legitimate argument and evidence for their own texts. Direct expression of personal experience in writing, by contrast, we tend to characterise as "pub talk". We want students to recognise that the emotional opinion, detached from evidence, is not what the discourse of Politics is about. (It may be the discourse of many politicians, an important distinction to discuss!) The transformation of emotional generalities into the discourse of political study enables students to gain a purchase on "what counts" in the discipline of politics.

When writing about readings, students apparently have been encouraged to provide a large body of information and then to conclude with a personal opinion at the end. This model, which appears to be practised extensively in their prior experiences of writing, is a very poor one for fostering critical engagement. Students remain alienated from the text throughout most of the summary and then are encouraged, in a manner relatively divorced from the text, to express a personal opinion. If students are shown how to make argument and evidence count with the main body of their text—not expressed in personal terms—the opposite from alienation, engagement, can occur, despite the apparent paradox that they are not using personal language. The deployment of argument and evidence within particular paragraphs is also practised in the classroom, and texts on the writing of paragraphs are used (Warriner, 1988; Belanoff, Rorschbach and Oberlink, 1993).

While students need to be educated in the need for an effective structure for their essays, the writing lecturer needs to be careful to negotiate a path between product and process: a less rigidly structured essay, particularly in an early draft, may reveal more clearly under what assumptions the student is operating, which may be the kinds of faulty assumptions mentioned above. Thus a two-draft system for every essay is potentially productive. Discussions of writing that make use of process models and activities can frequently be helpful in this regard.

However, the majority of students consistently fail to engage in significant revision. When students are required to revise rough drafts, their final drafts are checked for evidence of change. Comparisons of drafts frequently reveal that it is difficult to encourage students to move beyond perfunctory mechanical changes to a text. A very small percentage of students, less than 5%, will significantly reconceive and develop their texts. The remainder will add in a few sentences at the end of some paragraphs, correct a few obvious grammatical errors, or insert one-sentence responses to any marginal comments into the text. Students tend to regard a rough draft as a finished product, regarding it literally as if it were chiselled into a graveyard headstone, despite the fact that the student has probably not invested a great deal in the draft and does not regard it as a work to be preserved. Rather, students generally conceive of a rough draft as a kind of monetary token paid to a lecturer as the cost for passing a particular course. This reification of writing has its sources in "writing assignments", short requests for information. The writing in these exercises fails to assume the nature of an event or process occurring over time and involving critical reflection and engagement. In any discursive academic discipline, reflection and engagement are essential, but particularly when encountering a new and difficult subject, and for our students, the study of political theory is often the apotheosis of unfamiliarity.

If any activity is likely to encourage students to revise, it is an activity that intervenes in the rigidity of their conceptions about writing. The best opportunity for this kind of intervention lies in the one-on-one, student-centred writing tutorial, which occurs during peer tutoring. These tutorials are requirement in both the politics and written communications courses for every rough draft produced by our students, and the students are given marks for attending these sessions. On completion of their rough drafts, students must book an appointment with one of our student writing skills tutors.

The effort to embed the disciplinary practices of Politics into the teaching of writing occurs most clearly within the peer tutoring element of our programme. All departments recommend peer tutors to the writing centre, but politics has been particularly strong in making these recommendations. In addition, the politics lecturer serves as a mentor for the recommended peer tutors and discusses writing support needs with the tutors. While all tutors receive 10 hours of initial training and become qualified to teach in all subjects, part of their training requires them to develop a specialty in a particular subject area. During training, the disciplinary aspects of writing are discussed and tutors must go out into the departments to interview a lecturer. While some of the information they learn during the interview has to do with formal matters particular to a department, such as essay structure and bibliographic style, they are encouraged to concentrate upon matters of epistemology: what counts as knowledge within the discipline, how the discipline views itself as a "way of knowing", what it values, and what it contributes to the world of knowledge and learning. These visits are then followed by discussions during which tutor trainees share what they have learned in their interviews. As tutors become more experienced in tutoring writing in a particular subject, they are encouraged to write up what they have learned and add it to a folder publicly available in the writing centre containing information about the study of their subject. Finally, during the academic year, lecturers visit our peer tutor staff meetings (Politics lecturers come every year) to discuss the demands of particular assignments within their discipline and to discuss the discipline more generally. These meetings are written up and added to the subject folder.

When students book appointments with tutors, the tutor's subject specialty is listed next to their name, so that students can select a tutor with expertise in the subject on which they are writing. In the sessions, then, the peer tutor is likely to be familiar both with the subject material and the way in which knowledge is deployed within the discipline. Discussions of student texts, then, can consider content as well as form as a way of fostering engagement. Students studying politics who engage with tutors studying politics create an ideal situation in which the students, together, can construct an idea about what writing in Politics means. In the spirit of procedures established by Donald Murray at the University of New Hampshire (Murray, 1997) tutors will draw out students on particular topics by asking them to express their concerns and initially welcome personal language to facilitate comprehension of the more abstract discourse of politics. Thus, the transition from personal discourse to written, political discourse may be practised in the tutorial.

The Liberal Arts Degree at St Mary's seeks to foster an interest in a wide range of academic disciplines relevant to life and work. Despite our efforts, many students remain resistant to an engagement with Politics. When reviewing student evaluations of the writing course supporting their work in autumn of 2009, a few students registered keen enthusiasm for the study of Politics, a significant number registered having gained some interest, while another significant group remained resistant. A typical comment from resistant student is: "I have a strong dislike for politics and find it hard to be interested." A more receptive student said: "I wouldn't have a great interest in Politics—nevertheless, I feel my interest levels have increased as a result of the courses." Finally, a few students express marked enthusiasm, as evidenced in one of the more substantial comments:

> I have found Politics very interesting and not just the usual run-of-the-mill politics of Northern Ireland but a whole new rhetoric of political language and history. I would like to do political research for any political party, and democracy is a very valuable asset, especially in Northern Ireland, and the idea of consociationalism seems to be working.

Students who "find it hard to be interested" appear never to have made crossed over the threshold to new ways of learning, and we speculate that these students not only missed a significant number of their Politics classes, but also the writing classes designed to help them. We continue to develop and refine our strategies to encourage students, in concrete ways, to accept the challenge and "make the leap".

▶ Conclusion

In this chapter, we sought to demonstrate that the WiD challenges, for lecturers and students, are multi-dimensional. We identified and problematised a few of those challenges, which need to be set in the context of widening participation, the structural constraints of the degree, of teaching across modules, and the wider student engagement with politics. These considerations can make the teaching of politics and the teaching of writing in politics a frustrating process. Many of our students do not readily embrace the opportunity to learn new material—and politics is an excellent example of a new and challenging subject for them—or to improve their writing. They instead view academic learning as work to be resisted, "gotten through", or at least kept to a minimum. However, we believe that these attitudes are, at least in part, products of "deformed" earlier learning experiences that have inhibited creative and critical practices and prevented work from being transformed into more than drudgery (i.e. an endless sequences of lectures, hand-outs, and the consequent taking and memorisation of notes). The fundamental goal of teaching writing, therefore, is to help students reclaim an interest in actively pursuing new areas of learning, which, it could be theorised, is a more "natural" way of learning for human beings.

As we also argued, the teaching of Politics, as indeed the teaching of writing in Politics, is not removed from wider student perceptions of politics, and of the way they construe their civic identity. We encounter disenchantment, even "civic decay", but we also experience an ongoing interest in wider political issues, even though they are not always coded as political. The key challenge of politics must be to identify and make explicit "the political", that is, the everyday relevance of politics to students' lives. This in itself is not an easy task, and it can run against the competing challenge of complying with disciplinary conventions. Moreover, it is intimately linked with the development of students' intellectual and critical faculties.

Finally, it is fair to say that the collaboration between the teaching of politics and the teaching of writing skills undertaken so far has been promising, though there is undoubtedly room for improvement. At the moment, a similar form of collaboration between Written Communications and European Studies is occurring in the students' first year of study, attempting at an earlier stage encourages students to develop a critical ethos and to familiarise them with the expectations of academic writing. Further, the St Mary's Writing Centre now conducts over 650 writing centre appointments per year (in our first year of operation, 2002, we had only five students) but, of course, not all sessions succeed in encouraging students to engage with their work, or, even, to submit their assignments, as tutor and lecturer feedback attest. Clearly, there are particular challenges ahead—for tutors and for students alike—to foster a more widespread intellectual engagement with Politics.

▶ References

Belanoff, P., Rorschach, B. and Oberlink, M. (1993) *The Right Handbook: Grammar and Usage in Context* (Portsmouth: Heinemann).

Brown, W. (2005) *Edgework: Critical Essays on Knowledge and Politics* (Princeton and Oxford: Princeton University Press).

Dearing (1997) *The Dearing Report* (London: HMSO).

Electoral Commission (2005) *Election 2005: Turnout* (London: Electoral Commission).

Hay, C. (2007) *Why We Hate Politics* (Cambridge and Malden: Polity Press).

Held, D. (2006) *Models of Democracy* (Cambridge and Malden: Polity Press).

Murray, D. (1997) *A Writer Teaches Writing* (Belmont: Wadsworth).

O'Toole, T., Marsh, D. and Jones, S. (2003) "Political Literacy Cuts Both Ways: The Politics of Non-Participation among Young People", *Political Quarterly*, vol. 74, no. 3, pp. 349–360.

Pattie, C., Seyd, P. and Whiteley, P. (2003) "Civic Attitudes and Engagement in Modern Britain", *Parliamentary Affairs*, vol. 56, pp. 616–633.

Sloam, J. (2008) "Teaching Democracy: The Role of Political Science Education", *The British Journal of Politics & International Relations*, vol. 10, no. 3, pp. 509–524.

Stoker, G. (2006) *Why Politics Matters: Making Democracy Work* (Basingstoke and New York: Palgrave Macmillan).

Tonge, J. and A. Mycock (2010) "Citizenship and Political Engagement among Young People: The Workings and Findings of the Youth Citizenship Commission", *Parliamentary Affairs*, vol. 63, no. 1, pp. 182–200.

Villa, D. (2001) *Socratic Citizenship* (Princeton: Princeton University Press).

Warriner, J. (1988) *English Composition and Grammar: Complete Course* (New York: Harcourt).

10 Writing Design

Dipti Bhagat and Peter O'Neill

▶ Introduction

Figure 10.1 is a sample of student writing at level 1 (first year), indeed only 3 weeks into part of their new BA (Hons) curriculum in the School of Design at London Metropolitan University. It is a sample of what might be called design history or critical and contextual studies writing, here about a metal-framed rocking chair, as we can tell from the first sentence. (The rest of the paragraph may be divined to learn that it is a nineteenth century, British designed, metal-framed chair; currently on display at the Victoria and Albert Museum, in London.) We see that this text has involved more than one student; it shows erasures and re-inscription as part of the process of writing; it is handwritten and so appears to be quickly executed as a draft, hence its rather condensed and compacted appearance at the bottom of the page. The actual text is quite a compelling narrative about the importance of the material to the design of the metal-framed chair; indeed it even ventures to consider the contemporary consumption of metal-framed furniture. This short text might even be called a "critical" narrative, because it clearly deploys various types of evidence to evaluate the importance of the materials used in the design, production, and consumption of this chair. It tells a small story about an historical object, and its "rigour" is evidenced by the dispassionate—even if highly engaged and easy—style of writing, and the use of quotation, references, and footnotes, which in this text are deployed as more than mere "technical skills". This sample also evidences those somewhat hotly discussed aspects of the undergraduate curriculum in art and design higher education (HE); that is, design history and theory and its allied "academic writing" in British design education.

Indeed, the role of history- and theory-based learning and its concomitant academic writing in practice-led design education in Britain is a topic of significant recent interest and debate (Wood, 2000; Friedman, 2006; Tynan, 2006; Bhagat and O'Neill, 2009; Writing PAD, 2009). This discussion around academic writing and its relationship with and

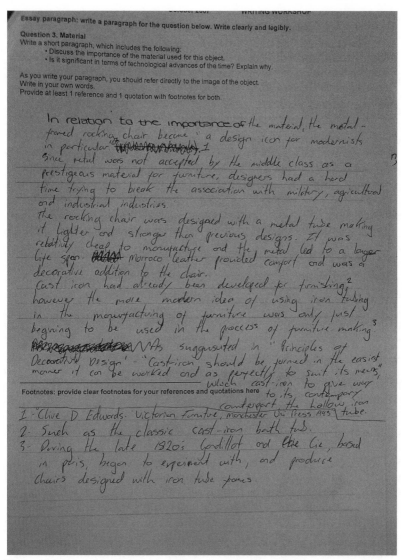

Figure 10.1 Example of Design student's writing from the workshops of *writingdesign*, 2007: object analysis of a "metal framed rocking chair", discussing the importance of material in the design—and even the consumption—of the chair.

relevance to courses predicated on designing, making, and producing visual and material culture (objects and images) reflects, in part, the shift from elite to mass education in UK institutions. New and diverse students in the academy have triggered varied concerns amongst lecturers about student writing. While some concerns have focussed on perceptions of student deficits in linguistic "skill" sets, others have grasped this opportunity to develop inclusive writing pedagogies that address and seek to assuage epistemic confusions experienced by *all* new learners. Widening participation, however, is merely the latest context to inform fresh dialogue about the form and function of academic writing in design education; these debates trace deeper concerns and qualms about the role of design history and theory and of academic writing in and for design education.

The context of widening participation has triggered discussion about how to engage so-called, non-traditional learners in discipline-specific, academic writing (Curry, 2006, pp. 181–184) so as to demystify this institutional practice. This chapter argues that elite approaches to "acculturation" into disciplinary academic writing are no longer tenable; and teaching generic—and de-contextualised—"study skills" *en masse* is inappropriate and insufficient (Ivanic and Lea, 2006). Rather, we insist, along with academic literacies theorists (e.g. Lea and Street, 1998), "Writing in the Disciplines" (WiD) initiatives (e.g. Monroe, 2002 and 2003; Bean, 2007) and widening participation researchers (e.g. David et al., 2009), that it is the disciplinary/subject specialist who is responsible for enabling students to understand and deploy disciplinary knowledge *through* a praxis that takes responsibility for and embraces writing as much as it does designing, making, and producing.

Approaches to academic writing pedagogy in design have sought to help students use writing to facilitate creative thinking and to bridge the perceived theory-practice dichotomy, especially where design students are seen as resisting or fearing the formality of design history and theory study and writing. Some have argued for the "rigour" of academic history and theory writing as an important underpinning of disciplinary study in design *practice* (Friedman, 2006) with positive implications for widening participation in the HE communities of practice (Bhagat and O'Neill, 2009). Others have sought alternatives to writing "traditional" academic, essayist texts (Wood, 2000; Writing PAD case studies, 2009). All respond to the QAA subject benchmark for design curriculum, which specifies that critical/theoretical and historical study of design is recommended as a means to achieve the appropriate *integration* of design practice and theory required to reinforce students' critical and intellectual engagement with their subject in preparation for their professional practice (QAA, 2002).

This chapter details and discusses *writingdesign*, an action-research collaboration between Dipti Bhagat (design history and theory lecturer and programme co-ordinator) and Peter O'Neill (director and writing specialist at Write Now CETL, both London Metropolitan University) initiated in 2007 with a focus on discipline-specific, academic, design history writing to underpin students' study of and in design. Our aim has been to enhance students' critical awareness of and practice in tackling the epistemological complexities (Lea and Street, 1998; Ivanic and Lea, 2006) of design history writing and knowledge. The project involved redesigning the module curriculum to encourage students' criticality through a discipline-specific methodology focussed on the contexts of design, a methodology that also offers the potential to circumvent, reject, and perhaps refresh canonical approaches to design history. The redesigned module was planned to be "writing intensive", with smaller writing assignments replacing the traditional end-of-module essay and assessment strategies designed to allow students' developmental progress. At the core of *writingdesign* were subject and assignment-specific writing workshops where students were able to practice their writing assessment collaboratively, learning disciplinary writing by "doing" it themselves in a social context (Bruffee, 1984). This chapter firstly discusses the context of design and academic writing within which we have developed *writingdesign*, our writing intervention at London Metropolitan University. We go on to detail *writingdesign* and then present our evaluation of the project through an analysis of student responses, which reiterate—quite powerfully—our argument for academic writing as an essential ally in the disciplinary study of design practice. We conclude with some reflections on the value of the multi-faceted collaborations fostered through this project.

▶ Design and academic writing

Recent research on widening participation in post-compulsory art and design education has sought to investigate, identify, and challenge the barriers to student access to, progression through, and success in further and HE (Gorard et al., 2006). In their report on the barriers of admissions processes in art and design HE institutions, Burke and McManus (2009), have drawn attention to students' interviews for entrance to some art and design degree courses, showing that admissions tutors' expectations and judgements of good writing and presentation "skills" are often core criteria for selection. Burke and McManus point out that such criteria may exclude applicants without the social and cultural capital of "well-schooled", so-called "traditional" HE entrants. They also draw our attention to academic literacies theorists who argue that adequate academic writing is less about taught "skills" than tacit understandings about how disciplines operate and express themselves and as such should be a matter for the responsibility of the lecturer rather than grounds for exclusion from HE. Academic literacy advocates point out that students' anxieties about writing should be alleviated not through a focus on their deficits but rather on undoing institutional "taken-for-granted practices and values" (Ganobcsik-Williams, 2006, p. 4) to develop effective pedagogies so students can *access* and deploy the conventions and epistemologies of their discipline and thus *participate* meaningfully in HE. These ideas speak well to widening participation research that argues for improving learning *through* or *by* widening participation. David and colleagues (2009) have argued persuasively that "[if] post-compulsory and higher education . . . is to be more equitable", this must be facilitated not only by "national policy contexts and institutional practices", but also by the development of "appropriate pedagogies to ensure social justice across disadvantaged, gendered and ethnic minority students" (2009, p. 5). Therefore, HE institutions and *all* members of institutions will need to adapt their teaching and learning practices to thoroughly embrace the principles of widening participation—that is diversity and inclusion (May and Bridger, 2010).

Working in the context of an inner city university such as London Metropolitan, we very much accept that it is the subject specialist's responsibility to help students understand and deploy disciplinary praxis. Our project is predicated on approaching academic writing as a *practice* or *process* equivalent to the way in which design students encounter their core learning in designing, making, and producing. Indeed, our title *writingdesign* suggests designing writing *into* students' design-specific learning. We see this as not only a challenge of embedding practices of writing in the discipline, but also of embedding academic writing of theory and history-based contextual learning within design education, where it is often contested and peripheral in a disciplinary study which focuses on practice for future work in the creative industries.

The current focus on the professionalisation of designers emerging from undergraduate courses is evidenced in studio and/or workshop-based teaching and learning methods, "live" industry projects and competitions invited into studios, and work placements as mainstays in design education. History- and theory-based learning about design and its attendant praxis of critique and academic writing is often perceived to occupy rather different "geographies" or learning spaces in the institution, being lecture- and seminar-based and usually comprising between 15% and 25% of the total degree course. This apparent distance from "the studio"[1] and this distinct percentage delimitation are said to have programmed a gulf or a split between practice and history/theory, between making and writing, between doing and talking (Candlin, 2001, p. 4). This curious blend—perhaps dichotomy—of vocational and liberal humanities models reflects, on the one hand, the sector's origins in the 1830s when specific practical education in design and the applied arts was viewed by the state as having the potential to enhance Britain's industrial competitiveness (Frayling, 1987; Tynan, 2006, pp. 41–42). On the other hand, the formalisation of art and design education by recommendations in the 1960 *Coldstream Reports* brought art and design education in line with other undergraduate degrees by introducing a compulsory academic element to be taught and assessed in the final diploma (Candlin, 2001, p. 3). While this eventually led to degrees in art and design subjects, many practitioners in the sector felt that the move to such formalisation was an implicit critique of the credibility of practice-based education (Candlin, 2001; Tynan, 2006; Lewis, 2009).

Before the *Coldstream Reports*—and since then, in the practice-based studio and workshop environments—teaching and learning in design was and remains focused on "making", on "doing", and on craft-based training borne of late-nineteenth century notions of experiential knowledge in the materials and processes of designing and making. The "value-added" component of history and theory-based learning was labelled variously as complementary studies, historical and theoretical studies, contextual studies, and often drew on cultural studies, design history, critical theory, and allied humanities disciplines. At the core of these was and remains the academic written assignment.

There are some vestiges of resistance among many studio tutors towards this place and role of academic writing in courses that are predicated on practice. Moreover, many design students may be unprepared for the academic rigour associated with the writing for their course. Indeed, one student we interviewed for *writingdesign* went so far as to suggest that her choice of design for university education was in part influenced by her perception that design was not writing focused, that writing is separate from, different from the *practice* of design. She explains her feelings when she first encountered the design history module in which the *writingdesign* workshops are embedded:

> I choose the course of Art [*sic*] because I had thought it was less writing. It's actually about design and to produce something, not writing. When I looked for the first time in this booklet, then I realized how much writing will be, I just was ... gob smacked.   (Student Interview, 2007)

Such attitudes are confirmed by the research of Caroline Hudson, who has also shown that the majority of art and design students express anxieties about academic writing associated with their practice-based degrees (Hudson, 2006).

Much attention has recently been devoted to pedagogies that will enable design students to use writing to facilitate creative thinking and as a means to bridge the perceived theory-practice dichotomy in design. This is particularly notable in the WritingPAD initiative (Writing Purposefully in Art and Design). This work has been stimulating, and it represents an embracing of writing for learning by many design practitioners and teachers. However, it has in general tended to look for alternatives to the rigour of so-called, traditional, academic essay writing in order to appeal to the perceived strengths of design students, many of whom are often seen to be reluctant academic writers. As Graves puts it, Writing PAD "explores strategies to achieve integration in art and design education—principally when it comes to writing" (2005, n.p.) so that writing is not perceived as a realm apart from students' practice and is an essential and "authentic" element of their creativity. WritingPAD in general attempts to bridge the practice-theory divide through a focus on *studio practice* informing writing practice. Indeed, although accepting that few pedagogical practices of WritingPAD are revolutionary, Rebekka Kill has even suggested that the work of WritingPAD offers a potentially subversive challenge to the "logocentric nature of the university" (2006, n.p.). This reflects John Wood's (2000) appeal for less emphasis on rigour, arguing that the idea of rigour (inherited from the Monastic tradition of "the Book", as Wood calls it [2000, p. 45]) as a guarantee or even supporter of truth is at odds with the task-based demands of design practice (inherited from the tradition of "the Crafts guilds") and the dynamic-situated actions, negotiations, and compromises they entail. Instead, Wood recommends less rigorous writing, and rather calls for more empathetic writing, a more embodied writing which is aligned with creative tasks—and which will take into account the audiences designers will one day work for and the situations in which they will find themselves.

Responses to Wood's argument from design researchers have been vigorous—and rigorous. Keith Russell suggests that Wood's misunderstandings of scholastic rigour are symptomatic of the "uneasy liaison" of the different knowledges of history/theory and the studio or workshop, which characterises the history of design education (2002, n.p.). Russell also draws attention to Wood's own use of devices of scholastic rigour to elevate and support the devices he sets up in opposition to rigour. Russell goes on to argue for "the uses of the culture of academic rigour, as a practice, in current and future design [education]" (Russell, 2002, n. p.). For Ken Friedman (2006, n. p.), Wood's "argument against the culture of academic rigour mistakes names for substance". Friedman and Russell suggest rather, that both the practice of academic writing and the practice of the design studio—or "the Book" and "the Guild" of Wood's terms—"are alike in their determinations of rigour ... [both are elevated] as a world of knowing with special features" (Russell, 2002, n.p.). In *writingdesign*, our goal has been to offer all students the opportunity to engage with the culture of academic rigour, as a *practice*, which we find to be inherent in discipline-specific writing. This is not to fetishise the "logocentrism" (Kill, 2006) of the university; rather we aim to demystify this institutional practice as a means to widen participation in practices of academic writing. And as Friedman reminds us, writing about the need for rigour in citation and referencing practices in all design research, the "worlds of scholarship . . . are based on a radical democracy of ideas" (Friedman, 2006, p. 22).

▶ Thinking about writing

From the initial stages of the collaboration, we saw our project as falling under the auspices of WiD. It appeared to us that much of the work in Britain on writing for design—including some of the WritingPAD work—was perhaps more akin to "Writing Across the Curriculum" (WAC) (McLeod and Maimon, 2000), with writing used to promote the critical and creative thinking of students (Bean, 2001, pp. 1–35). Our project emphasises the importance of enabling and supporting students to write firmly *within* the discipline of design history, in order to enhance students' critical and creative thinking about their specific design practices and design contexts.

In discussing our work, we were also influenced by academic literacies' advocates who have made a strong case for the need to embed writing within regular disciplinary teaching, pointing out that many of the confusions around writing are a result of confusions concerning disciplinary demands and epistemologies (Lea and Street, 1998). Such work implies the importance of the role of lecturers in enabling students to develop as academic writers; as Ursula Wingate asserts, "real understanding of the complexities of disciplinary writing can only be achieved within the subject and through explanations, modelling and feedback by subject tutors" (2006, p. 463). This resonated well with our investment in recent widening participation research that recommends lecturers embrace inclusive pedagogies to enhance student participation in communities of practice (David et al., 2009), in this case all practice components of design education—writing and designing.

Finally, building on the collaborative ethos of the *Write Now* London Metropolitan University Writing Centre—where undergraduate peer mentors work together with other students on all aspects of their writing (O'Neill, 2008; O'Neill et al., 2009)—we were keen to find ways for students to work together, to guide each other through some of the perplexing demands of academic writing, and to learn collaboratively through *doing*. Of course, our own collaboration (as writing specialist and design history lecturer) also relied on improving pedagogic practices in design history through *doing*: *writingdesign,* took the form of action research. Lin Norton (2001, 2009) has advocated action research in HE for several reasons: (1) it is aimed towards improvement: action research has the avowed intention of making things better than they were before, through embedding improved pedagogical practices. (2) Its ongoing, cyclical, nature is well-suited to the educational context: it engages with the idea of the process of teaching *and* learning as a journey. (3) It is underpinned by the idea of learning as a process of constructing knowledge and thus places both teacher and student at centre of creating meaning: academics carry out research into their own practice with a focus on how and what students are doing *and* on how and what they do when they teach. (4) It directly impacts on pedagogical praxis.

The appeal of action research for embedding inclusive pedagogies to widen participation in academic writing practice in design was and is abundantly clear. And we followed the recommended processes of action research: of planning, acting, observing, and evaluating to enhance students' experience in and confidence with academic writing.

▶ Planning: Curriculum re-design

All of the approximately 200 students a year, across 6 practice-based design courses (Design, Graphic Design, Textile Design, Interior Design, Furniture and Product Design, and Silversmithing and Jewellery Design) at London Metropolitan University were enrolled to take a compulsory, first-year module entitled "Context of Design", which focused on the co-constitutive relationships of design with its complex contexts between 1851 and 1945. This module serves as the University's required Higher Education Orientation module, designated to orient students into the demands of academic study in their disciplines. We interpreted this remit to involve the development of design students' criticality and disciplinary awareness *through* the development of their knowledge base that attends to the history of design in which design is contextualised as both practice and object.

The compulsory nature of this module allowed us to reach *all* design students at the start of their degree; it also allowed us to embed our practice to continue every year. As a result of our discussions concerning student writing, we replaced the traditional end-of-semester essay with four mini-essays written throughout the semester. Our aim was to provide a writing-intensive learning experience for students and to facilitate the idea of writing *practice* as continuous development, particularly as the mini-essay topics paralleled and reiterated the module programme of weekly in-class studying and thinking about design and its contexts. For each assignment students were asked to write mini-essays analysing an object of their choosing, from the period 1851–1945, the period of study through the module; all students were instructed to ensure that their choice of object must be a readily seen museum object—that is, the object was to form a primary source. In particular, they were expected to conduct detailed visual analysis of their chosen object and to consider its form through an understanding of the varied processes of production and consumption of their chosen object and to locate it within its historical, socio-economic, cultural, technological, and current museum contexts. Formative feedback between each mini-essay was offered in class, sometimes through using volunteered draft essays to frame weekly discussion. While all mini-essays were assessed, to address student writing as development, it was the best three of the four essays that were averaged for a final grade.

The focus on design objects and their complex contexts is informed by our efforts, on the one hand, to alleviate the still perceived dichotomy between theory and practice, and, on the other, to circumvent, reject, and even refresh a canon that focuses on great works, or even great "designers as heroes". The aim of the module curriculum is to allow very diverse students to relate their own work and practices within the world of ideas rather than seeing their own experiential knowledge as excluded or apart from a canon of so-called "great works". For, designing inclusive curricula is perhaps above all about *how* we teach design rather than *what* we teach. This follows Guillory's argument that great works must be recognised "as the vector of ideological notions which do not inhere in the works themselves, but in the context of their institutional presentation, or . . . in the way in which they are taught" (Guillory, 1993, p. ix). The module at the core of *writingdesign* looks to design, as object and as process, as co-constitutive with a complex of cultural, social, economic, technological, and political practices. This approach (a design history [e.g. Forty, 1986] and even, in part, a cultural studies [e.g. Grossberg et al., 1992] approach for the study of design and cultural work) aims to undo the "traditional investment in the moment of creativity [which] generates false categories of knowledge and power" (Tynan, 2006, p. 43). If, rather, design and its meaning is understood as produced and consumed through such a complex of socio-cultural, economic, technological, and political contexts, then, Tynan asserts, "the ownership of cultural production [design] is not easily pinned down" (2006, p. 43). Or rather, a contextual approach to studying design is less about acculturation into a canon or the acquisition of canonical knowledge than it is about facilitating diverse students participating in a "discussion about how culture [or design] works" (Tynan, 2006, p. 43).

▶ Acting: Writing as part of workshop practice

As well as regular, formative feedback, a compulsory, 90-minute workshop was integrated into the syllabus in week three; it was designed specifically to prepare all students to write their first mini-essay. The workshop was jointly developed by Bhagat and O'Neill and was delivered by all teaching staff on the module (see below on the nature of collaboration). Some of the teaching staff are hourly paid lecturers and in these cases the workshops were co-taught with either Bhagat or O'Neill in order to provide staff mentoring and development in academic writing pedagogy, an aspect of work in which the staff may otherwise have lacked experience. Ten workshops in total were held and student attendance was extremely high (in part because the workshops were held so near to the beginning of the semester).

The aim of the workshop was to provide space and time for the students to write with detailed guidance, a mini-essay. In the spirit of workshop practice we set a task for students to collaborate to model their *own* approach to the object analyses of their mini-essay assignments. This approach is in line with the insights of Margolis and McCabe (2006) who have shown that non-expert modelling of successful performance is a better vehicle to promote self-efficacy (Bandura, 1997) than providing models for imitation, a process that can be intimidating or counter-productive for many students (Harrington et al., 2010). The workshops were designed and planned to enable students to "try out", practice, and successfully complete the complexities of academic writing which often seem to be perplexing or intimidating, for instance: quoting sources, referencing, structuring material, and finding a focus for their writing.

In advance of the workshops, students were, according to their design specialisms, recommended a museum object to visit and to study and provided with several brief extracts from academic texts relating to the object. During the workshop, students were arranged to collaborate in groups, with each group responsible for writing one paragraph about their museum object in response to particular questions provided on a mini-essay template. We provided students with an introductory paragraph and then each group wrote paragraphs on:

- The object's description and function.
- The object's decorative style.

- Materials and technology used.
- The object's social context.
- The object's historical context.

They finished with:

- A concluding paragraph summarising the significance of the object.

The students had approximately 40 minutes to discuss and write their paragraph on the template provided (see Figure 10.2). Each template also tasked the student group to provide an appropriate caption and reference for the image of the object, to incorporate into their paragraph at least one quotation from their reading, correctly referenced, and to provide a bibliography. Students were also encouraged to evidence their visual analysis skills through the paragraph writing.

During the workshop, teaching staff circulated through the groups, briefly joining each group to explain and assist students through difficult tasks. Each group template was displayed one by one on a visualiser and various aspects of each group work were discussed. All the workshop paragraphs were collated and distributed to the larger group so everyone had a complete group-created "model" of a mini-essay to take away from the workshop (as well as the guidance for each of the paragraphs on the templates). Together, the paragraphs provided a coherent

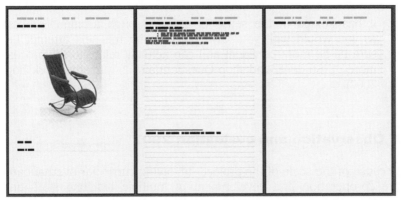

Figure 10.2 Sample of template distributed to each group: image of object on page 1, space to write a paragraph with references and footnotes on page 2, and space to list a bibliography on page 3. Figure 10.1, earlier, shows page 2 in detail as used for writing by a group of students.
Photo © Victoria and Albert Museum, London

approach to developing an argument about the object, which enabled students to make informed judgements using their visual skills. The resultant structure was perhaps somewhat artificial, perhaps somewhat haphazard; yet our intention was to *not* provide a polished, finished, or perfect—and intimidating—model of essay writing. Our workshop emphasised writing *practice*, through which students could encounter and work to solve typical problems of writing they might face with their assignment mini-essay. Students were quite clear that their own object choices would lead to unique object analyses.

As we expected, paragraphs were diverse: in length, style, how far they managed to incorporate such components as references and quotations, and the ease with which they managed to fulfil the tasks set. Figure 10.1, with which this chapter commenced, shows one student paragraph, in which we see that a group has written quite a sophisticated paragraph on the Winfield rocking chair, relating its materiality to its cultural and technological context and referencing and quoting confidently. Figure 10.3 reveals students' struggle with using quotations, while showing a rather well-considered conclusion.

However, our aim was not to assess the "quality" of student writing or indeed assess paragraphs or the "total" workshop mini-essay. While the group nature of the work took pressure off individual students, the workshop model offered all students an opportunity to learn from the strengths and weaknesses of every paragraph, which we projected on screen for the group to see and discuss. But above all the workshop was designed to show students that the mini-essay was *doable*. As one student said of the workshop:

> It has helped in the sense of going through a "mini" process as you would with your own object. With the next attempt I'm sure I'll be more confident as I can actually relate to the process more.   (Student Workshop Questionnaire 2: after the workshop, 2007)

▶ Observation and evaluation 2007

Because of the scale of the project—involving curricular overhaul and the co-operation and development of multiple teaching staff—and because writing design was a project designed to be embedded in the syllabus, we introduced pre- and post-workshop evaluation of students and their perceptions of academic writing and design, not least for reasons of internal validation of our approaches. Before and after the workshop, all students (+/− 200) filled out questionnaires on their:

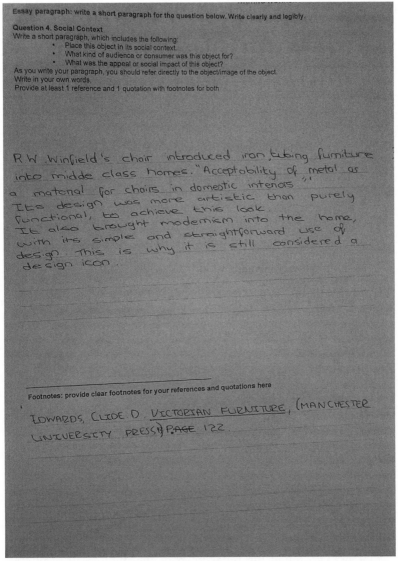

Essay paragraph: write a short paragraph for the question below. Write clearly and legibly.

Question 4. Social Context
Write a short paragraph, which includes the following:
* Place this object in its social context.
* What kind of audience or consumer was this object for?
* What was the appeal or social impact of this object?
As you write your paragraph, you should refer directly to the object/image of the object.
Write in your own words.
Provide at least 1 reference and 1 quotation with footnotes for both

R W Winfield's chair introduced iron tubing furniture into middle class homes. "Acceptability of metal as a material for chairs in domestic interiors". Its design was more artistic than purely functional, to achieve this look. It also brought modernism into the home, with its simple and straightforward use of design. This is why it is still considered a design icon.

Footnotes: provide clear footnotes for your references and quotations here

EDWARDS, CLIVE D. VICTORIAN FURNITURE, (MANCHESTER UNIVERSITY PRESS) PAGE 122.

Figure 10.3 Student paragraph: ask for a conclusion that outlines the key significance of the object based on the students' response to both the object itself and their research.

confidence in writing in their discipline of design; perception of their *integration* of practice and theory in their design education; perception of their own critical and intellectual engagement with their subject and its historical and theoretical context; progression and achievement; and the usefulness of the workshop for their learning. A thematic analysis of these questionnaires identified five themes around which students' comments cohered: skills for writing essays; writing for and in their learning about design; feelings about writing; writing through peer collaboration; and timing for writing.[2]

Theme 1: "Skills" for writing essays

Before the workshop many students revealed that they did indeed have considerable concerns about so-called generic skills, such as: referencing, quoting, writing bibliographies, use of language, appropriate writing styles, structure, grammar, and spelling. However, after the workshop, the majority of comments suggested that the template's provision for practicing footnotes, references, and bibliographies was surprisingly successful: many students commented on how they had learned to write a bibliography; they stated that they had learned to footnote and organise footnotes, and even why it is important to do so; and some felt they needed more time to learn the process of referencing or "referencing in more complex situations" (SWQ2, 2007). This speaks well to Ken Friedman's (2006) argument for rigour of citation and referencing as supporting a democracy of ideas; also here level 1 HE students tackle referencing in terms of its "mechanics" *and thereby* understand how to use the evidence to which citations refer in developing an argument (see Figures 10.1 and 10.3). As such, while many students may have faced anxiety about so-called "skills" before the workshop, the workshop practice—by integrating so-called "skills" into writing about the object at hand—enabled students to practice deploying writing conventions rather as part of developing a small design history discourse about an object of design.

These students' comments suggest that module-specific guidelines on referencing, citation, and constructing bibliographies (given in advance of the workshop) were read, *understood, learned* even, during the workshop, because students were able to discuss, practice, and observe each other's attempts, as part of the workshop process (Wingate, 2006). Admittedly, however, one student confessed to still being "lost and confused" in this matter (SWQ2, 2007).

Students also found the breakdown of the mini-essay helpful. As one said:

> Simply seeing it done and being part of the exercise helps you to understand certain aspects and importance of structure.   (SWQ2, 2007)

One student made an explicit connection between the focus on the object's "materials, social context and historical context" and under-standing ways to approach essay construction/ structure, pointing to a reciprocity between the practice of writing, and learning about design (SWQ2, 2007).

Theme 2: Writing for design

Overall, students articulated very well their understanding that writ-ing was relevant to design and even that it enhanced their thinking about design. For one student, history-based contextual learning about design helped him to "understand the social context of design" (SWQ2, 2007); for another, in the spirit of post-modern designers, it provided a resource to plunder: "understanding previous design and its history gives me a wider range of eras to study and items to gain inspira-tion from" (SWQ2, 2007). The potential for knowledge transfer was well-recognised, with students suggesting history and theory "gives the designer the ability to argue her viewpoint when discussing design" (SWQ2, 2007), or enables them to "learn about design and understand it properly in order to use the knowledge to be more successful in design-ing objects yourself" (SWQ2, 2007). The most ambitious student felt that history/theory learning could be "very helpful to write publications such as articles and explanations of your works. Maybe in the future if I decide to write a book about design I can use the knowledge gained at university" (SWQ2, 2007). No student hinted at writing being inessen-tial or irrelevant to their learning in and for design. Rather all found that writing and history serves—as the QAA recommends—their devel-opment as designers. Indeed, one student said: "now I understand that I have to look very carefully, see the details" (SWQ2, 2007), suggest-ing that the module assignment's object analysis enhanced her visual literacy.

Theme 3: Feelings about writing

As expected, before the workshop many students did express being "scared", "nervous", "anxious", "frightened" about, or "not that pre-pared" (SWQ1, 2007) for writing. However, it is equally important to notice that a notable number of students felt confident, even excited about the mini-essays, encouraged by the "interesting subject", and the opportunity to "choose my own objects" (SWQ1, 2007). These responses do not indicate that first-year design students had more antipathy towards writing than students in other subjects and therefore we should not assume *a priori* that design students will be unrespon-sive towards academic writing. Furthermore, the element of personal agency in the choice of objects to write about for the module assignment and the insistence that each object must be encountered first hand encourages students to assume both authorship *and* authority over their mini-essays. For, primary research, however introductory, demands that students think carefully about their questions they ask of their choice of object, for it is likely there may be no specific investigation already existing on their selected object: each mini-essay, or object-biography, has the potential to be unique.

Theme 4: Writing through peer collaboration

The majority of students found group work satisfying, commenting on the encouragement of working in a team, learning about "sharing ideas", "techniques", and "discussion" (SWQ2, 2007). Students indicated that the exercise had been "fun" and one even commented that learning about "human difference was the most beauty [*sic*] thing" (SWQ2, 2007). Student diversity was often valued as a strength: "with different ideas from different people, we had time to discuss how we can do something" (SWQ2, 2007). This reiterates the recommendations made by Lea and Street to replace the somewhat alienating "acculturation of students into academic discourse" (1998, p. 172) by an academic socialisation model where students aim towards a common, shared goal, that is, learning through practice, a specific academic discourse.

Theme 5: Time for the writing

Students also commented on the time available to write their paragraph. One student found the time available for writing in the workshops is "perfect" for a "first go" (SWQ2, 2007); another found it "constricting but motivating. It was good" (SWQ2, 2007). This matched our intention for the workshop: to reveal academic writing as enjoyable, accessible, and possible, as a practice that is not necessarily tortuous or drawn out. Inevitably—or even happily—some students wanted more time to write. But as *everyone* had actually produced some writing during the workshops, these comments suggest they were engaged with the activity and had developed a sense of writing as a process in time.

▶ Collaboration

Writingdesign involved a variety of collaborations that speak well to our emphases on writing in the disciplines, writing as practice, diversity, inclusive—and sustaining inclusive—pedagogies and knowledge construction. While collaborations seem par for the course in places of work and learning (academic and otherwise), it is worth revisiting and reiterating in this fresh context the value of collaborations articulated by Lunsford and Ede (1990, 1991). Following Lunsford, we can recommend at least seven clear benefits to students' learning of working collaboratively (Lunsford, 1991, pp. 5–6). Firstly, the writing tasks demanded peer collaboration to identify and solve particular writing problems set by the writing templates. Secondly, collaborating on and talking through their writing to highly defined tasks clearly enabled students to understand and work with such abstractions as "contexts of design". Thirdly, students worked in an interdisciplinary way, making highly articulate and sophisticated connections between the practices of writing and designing. Fourthly, they responded with combined energy to the task's demand for critical thinking—explaining, adapting, and defending as they solved the problems set up by the writing templates. This often led to a meaningful understanding of and between fellow students, who were diverse in myriad ways. Fifthly, peer collaborations generally led to higher achievement—*all* students had produced complete or near complete template tasks, and in some cases—sixthly—the collaborations promoted excellence where students learn from trial and re-trial, of their own and others' practice paragraphs. Finally, collaboration of this kind engages "the whole student and [encourages] active learning: it combines reading, talking, writing, thinking; it provides practice in both synthetic and analytic skills" (Lunsford, 1991, p. 6).

The implications of these specific benefits of the collaboration for staff are also easily seen, most obviously in the inter-disciplinary collaboration between design histories and theory lecturer and writing specialist, who, in part, embody this writing in the disciplines project. Yet our work highlights a further conceptualisation of collaborative work by Lunsford and Ede (1990). Figure 10.4 tabulates and maps out the hierarchical and dialogic nature of staff collaboration in *writingdesign*, after Lunsford and Ede (1990) and Lunsford (1991). We have worked seamlessly and equitably through a dialogic model through all aspects of *writingdesign*: curriculum re-design, assessment design, workshop planning, workshop leading, and research evaluation and dissemination. However, hierarchical collaboration was also necessary between the design history subject specialist and curriculum co-ordinator, and her design colleagues, all responsible for teaching the workshops and regular module delivery. As curriculum co-ordinator, Bhagat remains responsible for ensuring parity in the teaching and student learning experience and the necessary staff development that must result in implementing new pedagogical initiatives through a team of teaching staff. Furthermore, the prevalent practice in HE institutions of casualised, hourly paid teaching means that all development work on any new teaching initiatives is best and most equitably carried out by the permanently employed curriculum co-ordinator and not added to the preparatory burden of non-permanent teaching colleagues. This has immediate benefits for team cohesion and for parity of learning and teaching and equitable student experience of the writing workshops. Retaining authorship of the whole project with O'Neill, Bhagat is able to ensure that the workshop model can be implemented annually, regardless

Collaboration	Dialogic (Lunsford, 1991)		Hierarchical (Lunsford and Ede, 1990)
	Writing specialist practice Peter O'Neill	Design history specialist practice Dipti Bhagat	Design history staff practice
Curriculum design	Advice on integrating/ embedding workshops based on planned assessment item	Developing all weekly teaching and learning content linked to assessment item; devising detailed brief on assessment item; integrating time for formative feedback on mini-essays in teaching and learning schedule	Developing weekly teaching and learning content to demonstrate design in context, as instructed by subject specialist
Assessment item	Designing: 4 x mini-essay format recommending developmental assessment - best 3/4 mini-essays to be graded	Subject specific requirements, sample essay, assessment criteria and process	Briefing all students on: assessment, workshop as modelling assessment brief, potential for formative feedback throughout semester on each mini-essay

Figure 10.4 Dialogic and hierarchical collaboration in the *writingdesign* project. Dialogic collaboration is indicated by porous lines and hierarchical collaboration by non-porous lines.

		Structure, reading materials,	
Workshops	Structure, writing template to model assignment, facilitating/leading workshops together with teaching staff	and writing template to model assignment, facilitating/leading workshops together with teaching staff	Facilitating/leading workshops
Teaching and learning	Critical use of assignment-based content: workshop	Critical use of assessment-based content: lectures, seminars, and workshop	Critical use of assignment-based content: lectures, seminars, and workshop
Outcome	Research, evaluation of student feedback/interviews, writing for conferences and publication, sustained application of experience; embedding workshop in annual teaching of module, developing further workshops for further modules		Staff development impact: sustained application of training in further teaching, enhanced team cohesion

Figure 10.4 (Continued)

of non-permanent staff change, while also offering a powerful staff development experience to all teaching staff involved.

▶ Conclusion

Writingdesign began as a major project with ten workshops held for all first-year design students (approximately 200 students). It is now embedded and has become a flexible teaching model that can improve, adapt, and continue, and which underpins the students' 3-year curriculum: it places writing- and history- and theory-based contextual learning as central to the learning of all students in design practice at London Metropolitan University. The synthesis of writing and practice, of teaching and workshops, has emerged from the rich collaboration between writing specialist and academic subject specialist. The writing in disciplines approach of the project necessitated the development of the academic teaching team not only to make this first module, but also to sustain and develop this model for the rest of the 3-year curriculum. Therefore, writing in design resides firmly with the teaching team of design histories and theory specialists who are responsible for students' learning: it is our own "insider knowledge" (cf. Lillis, 2006) that directs students' writing in design.

In this project, we have been struck by the similarity of the almost peripheral spaces occupied by academic writing in design education and by writing development in academic departments. We have worked with shared pedagogical concerns. For design education at London Metropolitan University, the concern is primarily how to embed academically rigorous, history- and theory-based contextual learning and its concomitant writing practices into practice-based degree courses. For writing development, the concern is how to embed writing in the discipline and across the curriculum. *Writingdesign* addresses these shared concerns and we hope that it will support design students to write critically, confidently, and effectively about design in its complex and varied contexts and that this will in turn reinforce thoughtful and innovative design practice.

▶ Notes

1 In the context of mass education in art and design education in Britain, the singular and even hallowed space of "the studio" in which students work all day and all week is, arguably, not tenable. "Cost benefit analyses" regularly encroach on studio spaces; increased numbers of students results in staff deploying "innovative hot-desking" or larger spaces like lecture theatres or virtual learning environments; modular programmes insist on varied learning spaces; students juggle diverse commitments to jobs or parents or children. Thus design students are constantly negotiating myriad geographies during their time in HE, within which "the studio" is just one, and scarcely sustained experience.

2 Quotations taken from the questionnaires will be referenced as follows and where necessary: "Student Workshop Questionnaire 1: before the workshop", abbreviated to "SWQ1"; and "Student Workshop Questionnaire 2: after the workshop", abbreviated to "SWQ2". All questionnaires were anonymous and thus references are made to wither pre- or post-workshop questionnaires. Analysis was carried out for all +/− 200 questionnaires completed: all were first read to identify themes, and then all comments were tabulated against themes and coded as either before or after the workshop.

▶ References

Bandura, A. (1997) *Self-Efficacy: The Exercise of Control* (New York: Worth).

Bean, John C. (2001) *Engaging Ideas: The Professor's Guide to Integrating Writing, Critical Thinking and Active Learning in the Classroom* (San Francisco: Jossey Bass).

Bhagat, D. and O'Neill, P. (2009) *'Writingdesign:* A Collaboration between the *Write Now* CETL and the Sir John Cass Department of Art, Media and Design,' *Art, Design and Communication in Higher Education* 8(2): 177–182.

Bruffee, K. (1984) "Collaborative Learning and the 'Conversation of Mankind'," *College English* 46: 635–652.

Burke, P.-J. and McManus, J. (2009) *"Art for a Few": Exclusion and Misrecognition in Art and Design Higher Education Admissions* (National Art Learning Network report).

Candlin, Fiona (2001) "A Dual Inheritance: The Politics of Educational Reform and PhDs in Art and Design," *London: Birkbeck ePrints.* Available from http://eprints.bbk.ac.uk/738/ [26th February 2010].

Curry, Mary Jane (2006) "Skills, Access, and 'Basic Writing': A Community College Case Study from the United States," in Ganobcsik-Williams, L. (ed.) *Teaching Academic Writing in UK Higher Education: Theories, Practices and Models* (Houndmills: Palgrave Macmillan) pp. 180–192.

David, M. *et al.* (2009) *Improving Learning by Widening Participation in Higher Education* (London: Routledge).

Forty, Adrian (1986) *Objects of Desire: Design and Society from Wedgewood to IBM* (Pantheon: New York).

Frayling, C. (1987) *The Royal College of Art: One Hundred and Fifty Years of Art and Design* (Barrie and Jenkins: London).

Friedman, K. (2006) "Reference and Citation in Design Research," *Doctoral Master Class: Design Advanced Research Training* (Arts and Humanities Research Council, July 2006).

Ganobcsik-Williams, L. (ed.) (2006) *Teaching Academic Writing in UK Higher Education: Theories, Practices and Models* (Houndmills: Palgrave Macmillan).

Gorard, S., Smith, E., May, H., Thomas, L., Adnett, N., and Slack, K. (2006) *Review of Widening Participation Research: Addressing the Barriers to Participation in Higher Education* (HEFCE report).

Graves, J. (2005) "Reverie: Creative Conflict in Art, Design and Dyslexia". Available from www.writing-pad.ac.uk [Accessed February 2010].

Grossberg, L., C. Nelson, and P. Treichler (eds) (1992) *Cultural Studies* (New York: Routledge).

Guillory, John (1993) *Cultural Capital: The Problem of Literary Canon Formation* (Chicago: University of Chicago Press).

Harrington, K., O'Neill, P. and Reynolds, L. (2010) "Using Wikis and Blogs to Support Writing Development: The Online Evolving Essay Project," in Sabine Little (ed.) *Beyond Consultation: Staff-student Partnerships in Higher Education* (London: Continuum), 62–75.

Hudson, C. (2006) *CHEAD/ACE Research on Higher Education in Art and Design.* Available from http://www.chead.ac.uk/publications.html [25th February 2010].

Ivanic, R. and Lea, M.R. (2006) "New Contexts, New Challenges: The Teaching of Writing in UK Higher Education," in L. Ganobcsik-Williams (ed.) *Teaching Academic Writing in UK Higher Education* (New York: Palgrave Macmillan).

Kill, Rebekka (2006) "Travelling, Tinkering and Making the Kinds of Meanings We Really Want to Mean: WritingPAD in Context," Writing PAD conference 20th June 2009. Available from www.writing-pad.ac.uk [22nd February 2010].

Lea, M. and Street, B. (1998) "Student Writing in Higher Education: An Academic Literacies Approach," *Studies in Higher Education* 11(3): 182–199.

Lewis, J. (2009) "The written assignment in design education; a discussion of the significance of the historical background to current debates," *Writing Design*, 2009 Annual Design History Society Conference, University of Hertfordshire, September 2009.

Lillis, T.M. (2006) "Academic Literacies' Research as Pedagogy: Dialogues of Participation," in L. Ganobscik-Williams (ed.) *Teaching Academic Writing in UK Higher Education: Theories, Practices and Models. Universities into the 21st Century* (New York: Palgrave Macmillan), pp. 30–45.

Lunsford, A. (1991) "Collaboration, Control, and the Idea of a Writing Center," *The Writing Center Journal* 12(1): 3–10.

Lunsford, A. and Ede, L. (1990) *Singular Texts/Plural Authors: Perspectives on Collaborative Writing* (Carbondale: Southern Illinois UP).

Margolis, H. and P. McCabe (2006) "Improving Self-Efficacy and Motivation: What to Do, What to Say," *Intervention in School and Clinic* 41(4): 218–227.

May, H. and Bridger, K. (2010) *Developing and Embedding Inclusive Policy and Practice* (HEA report).

McLeod, S. and Maimon, E. (2000) "Clearing the Air: WAC Myths and Realities," *College English* 62: 573–583.

Monroe, J. (ed.) (2002) *Writing and Revising in the Disciplines* (Ithaca: Cornell University Press).

Monroe, J. (ed.) (2003) *Local Knowledges, Local Practices: Writing in the Disciplines at Cornell* (Pittsburgh: University of Pittsburgh Press).

Norton, L.S. (2001) "Researching Your Teaching: The Case for Action Research," *Psychology Learning and Teaching* 1(1): 21–27.

Norton, L.S. (2009) *Action Research in Teaching and Learning: A Practical Guide to Conducting Pedagogical Research in Universities* (Abingdon: Routledge).

O'Neill, P. (2008) "Using Peer Writing Fellows in British Universities: Complexities and Possibilities," in Brad Hughes and Emily B. Hall (eds) *Rewriting Across the Curriculum: Writing Fellows as Agents of Change in WAC. Across the Disciplines* special edition. Available from http://wac.colostate.edu/atd/fellows/oneill.cfm [25th February 2010].

O'Neill, P., Harrington, K., and Bakhshi, S. (2009) "Training Peer Tutors in Writing: A Pragmatic, Research-Based Approach," *Zeitschrift Schreiben* (*European Journal of Writing*). Available from http://www.zeitschrift-schreiben.eu/cgi-bin/joolma/index.php?option=com_content&task=view&id=75&Itemid=32 [25th February 2010].

QAA (2002) "Quality Assurance Agency for Higher Education," *QAA, Art and Design: Subject Benchmarking Statements* (Gloucester: QAA).

Russell, K. (2002) "Why the Culture of Academic Rigour Matters to Design Research: or, Putting Your Foot into the Same Mouth Twice". *Working Papers in Art and Design 2.* Available from http://sitem.herts.ac.uk/artdes_research/ papers/wpades/vol2/russellfull.html [26th February 2010].

Tynan, J. (2006) "Access and Participation: Rethinking Work-Based Learning on the Foundation Degree in Art and Design", *Art, Design and Communication in Higher Education* 5(1): 39–53.

Wingate, U. (2006) "Doing Away with 'Study Skills'," *Teaching in Higher Education* 1: 457–469.

Wood, J. (2000) "The Culture of Academic Rigour: Does Design Research Really Need It?" *The Design Journal* 3(1): 44–57. Available from www.writing-pad.ac. uk [26th February 2010].

Writing PAD (2009) "Case Studies". Available from www.writing-pad.ac.uk [accessed 12 December 2009].

11 From WAC to WiD: Trialling Writing-Intensive Pedagogies with Academic Staff in UK Higher Education

Rebecca Bell, Sarah Broadberry and Julius Ayodeji

Increasing student numbers has created challenges for many working in the UK higher education system and left some staff struggling to cope. Academics often have little spare time to engage with new approaches, but they are in desperate need of help in teaching academic writing to an ever-growing number of students. The "Writing in the Disciplines" (WiD) approach is proving to be a viable strategy that can help time pressed colleagues develop their students' academic writing. This chapter discusses a WiD initiative designed to support staff in developing their students' writing. It examines both the benefits and challenges of collaborating with colleagues and the issues faced when promoting writing activities to students. The chapter also discusses teaching strategies used by colleagues to manage and effectively implement the WiD approach in the classroom.

▶ **Introduction**

"Writing Across the Curriculum" (WAC) and WiD are less common in the UK than they are in the US. There are a few universities using some form of WAC- or WiD-based approach (for instance the Thinking Writing Project, Queen Mary University of London, and the Write Now CETL in the UK (Harrington and O'Neill, 2009; Mitchell and Evison, 2009). Nevertheless, the majority of institutions regard academic writing in terms of support rather than development. Responsibility for writing development and support often lies with individual departments creating a fragmented approach which can be confusing for both staff and students. Depending on the department, students who may be struggling with their writing are often referred to non-subject specialist support tutors to "fix" the problem (Lea and Street, 2000). As a learning developer based at Nottingham Trent University (NTU), Bell's role involves challenging this perception of academic writing identifying that it is not simply "a matter of mechanical skill, grammar or style" (Monroe, 2002). Academic writing is the format in which students are not only assessed, but also the medium by which they can express their ideas and as such develop their knowledge. It involves learning the language of the discipline in which students are studying and developing the ability to communicate effectively with their peers. By encouraging colleagues and students to think about writing in a different way it is hoped that many of their anxieties about academic writing may be allayed. Only once academic writing is perceived as a tool for learning as opposed to solely for assessment will students be able to begin to identify their own academic voice. By engaging with colleagues in the teaching of student academic writing, Bell's role aims to encourage staff to facilitate all students in developing their writing regardless of ability.

As a non-teaching member of staff with limited resources, convincing busy academics to trial WiD activities and offer feedback on their effectiveness was not an easy task. Bell began by promoting the approach as a year-long experiment entitled "The WAC Project" asking staff to come and take part in workshops that would help to develop their students thinking and enhance their writing. The US model of Writing Across the Curriculum was used as a template as there was very little work done that reflected the UK context. WAC as opposed to WiD was identified as the more useful term to promote the project as it is more widely understood and as an approach has a longer publishing history. Whilst the focus of WAC is on developing student learning of a subject through generic writing tasks, WiD, pays "greater attention to the relation between writing and learning in a specific discipline" (Russell et al., 2009, p. 395). Although the project began by focusing on WAC, the WiD approach project appealed to a wider range of colleagues who were able to develop students writing in close relation to their discipline and at all levels of study and it is the WiD strand of this project that will be discussed here.

The project consisted of a number of meetings that ran throughout the year and were open to colleagues from all departments. The meetings were established as a forum for discussing the issues colleagues faced regarding student academic writing. The sessions introduced the WAC and WiD approach, including what they could offer, the theory behind them and some sample activities. It has been Bell's role at the sessions to encourage sustainability within the WiD approach; this has been assisted by the fact that as a non-teaching member of staff she plays a limited role in the actual teaching of WiD activities. This can be initially difficult for colleagues who may have little confidence in their teaching of academic writing and as such would rather hand over to specialist. Using writing specialists can, however, create a fragmented approach undermining the WiD activities, portraying them as an add-on or study skills type session as opposed to an integral part of the learning process. Consequently, staff are encouraged during the sessions to develop and facilitate their own WiD activities as opposed to being dependent on specialist writing staff.

Although the sessions were attended by only a few colleagues from across the university, those that did come along were eager to trial activities. A small network of colleagues that shared, trialled, and created activities was soon developed. Activities trialled included "minute writes", "freewriting", "problem statements", and "the discussion starter" (WAC Clearing House, 2009). Whilst the activities used were reasonably generic, all took place in a subject-specific context and as such followed a writing in the disciplines approach. What follows are Bell's reflective experiences of the projects that she has been involved in personally and also the accounts of two academics who attended the WAC Project sessions and trialled some activities in their own lessons.

▶ Convincing colleagues to collaborate

Over the last four years as a learning developer, Bell has worked with a number of modules and programmes to facilitate the incorporation of writing instruction into student workshops and seminars.[1] Her involvement usually includes creating subject-specific resources for tutors and attending occasional sessions to observe and record how the staff and students engage with the activities. The observations and feedback recorded have provided an invaluable working knowledge of the WiD approach.

Over the course of the project, problems in incorporating WiD successfully have included attitudes of staff and students as well as practical issues of timetabling, room allocation, photocopiers, and Bell's own role. The staff development workshops she facilitated have often focused on how simple it can be for staff to create discipline-specific writing resources. The sessions often highlight how easy WiD could be incorporated into sessions:

> It's just a case of finding discipline specific writing examples, if you
> want students to learn how to draft an essay just find an appropriate
> essay question.   (S4, 2009)

However, it has become apparent that this can actually be quite difficult as it is not just about finding an essay question, it is about finding
one that will pull out the writing details students are expected to
learn about, one that is neither too easy nor too hard and that covers
material they have already learnt about. This can be a lengthy process and on one occasion it took approximately 3 hours to develop
the first writing activity of a 10-week term. This was made more difficult by the fact that Bell is centrally based and therefore has limited
access to discipline-specific material. As a result, it became apparent
that most academic staff would not have the time to develop these
resources and suddenly the rhetoric regarding writing in the disciplines
seemed flawed. The implication of WiD was not as easy as Bell had
promoted and it did take time, commitment, and interest. By negating
these aspects of the approach and oversimplifying the process staff had
been given false expectations of what the approach involved. It became
apparent that her previous discussions about WiD had been based
on knowledge but little experience, something she was determined to
counteract.

Colleagues involved in the project have found issues of their own with
the writing activities. As predominantly sessional or part-time lecturers,
they are often virtually un-contactable outside of seminar hours and
as such it can be difficult to communicate with them about activities.
Tutors often only check for the day's activity as they are beginning the
workshop and consequently any activity that requires preparation such
as photocopying is not possible. Last minute room changes and poor
attendance were also problematic, with many students missing sessions. As such it can be difficult to prepare activities that build on earlier
ones in the term as students have often missed the previous session or
lecture. Due to such issues as those mentioned above, the options for
the implementation of various writing activities become increasingly
limited.

The value placed on writing by both students and staff is also problematic. It is often apparent in sessions that both tutors and students
value the opportunity for discussion in seminars and workshops. Writing is often perceived as an activity related to assessment and as such
something tiresome, stressful, and difficult. Consequently students do
not tend to relish the prospect of writing activities and as such in some
instances tutors have asked students to "just tell me what you were
going to write" instead. This can be problematic in that it negates the
opportunity for students to practice writing outside of the pressure of

assessment and to challenge their perceptions of academic writing in general. Challenging staff perceptions that discussion is the most productive way to spend workshop time has proven difficult and is an ongoing issue.

Despite the problems raised above, one session recently turned the tide for some colleagues. The session included a short ten-minute activity based on the differences between writing and writing academically. Students were shocked to discover some of the conventions of academic writing with some stating:

> Why can't I write the way I speak in my essays? You understand me, don't you?   (S5, 2009)

Some colleagues reported that they were shocked at having to justify the notion of academic writing and from then on began to engage with the writing activities more fervently. Once tutors engage in dialogue with students about writing they often become more involved in the activities, suggesting areas of academic writing that activities could be based around.

Colleagues often believe that the students themselves will see little or no point in doing the writing activities, noting that students only engage with what is being assessed. Admittedly in some of the classes students often simply talk amongst themselves or doodle as opposed to writing, safe in the knowledge that the writing is not being assessed and therefore is not compulsory. Whilst it can be the case that students sigh or frown when the activities begin, some engage with the activities wholeheartedly and one student at the end of a session stated that:

> That was good I enjoyed that, mainly because I am leaving with some actual notes and usually I just forget everything we talk about.   (S6, 2009)

Staff are often encouraged therefore to simply give the activities a go without presuming how students will react to them.

As many seminar tutors are sessional, they are not paid to look at student writing outside of class time and therefore to give the writing clearer purpose I decided to trial peer feedback. In one instance, I asked students how they would feel if we used peer feedback with most responding that they would not like that approach:

> What if they were no better than me? They could be advising me wrong.   (S7, 2009)

Whilst discussing peer feedback and the writing activities, most students state that they feel confident about their writing and as such do not see the point in the activities. When asked if there are any areas they would like activities to focus on, most often state that they know all about referencing and most other aspects of academic writing. However, it is often once the first assessment results come back that it is apparent that they simply do not know what they do not know. A student who had recently received her first piece of feedback commented:

> I thought I was alright at referencing, but actually it's different here to FE. After I got a rubbish grade I thought right I'm going to ask for help next time!   (S8, 2009)

The students often find it difficult to identify the aspects of writing they struggle with, as they are often not aware what academic writing consists of. WiD activities therefore probably work best after students have received their first piece of feedback and are more open to looking at the problems they have encountered. This experience has been a learning curve and consequently the activities often focus on the basics a number of times throughout the term.

Despite the difficulties that have been faced throughout the project, there have been a number of valuable benefits that have outweighed the problems. Feedback from academics who engaged with the WiD initiative highlight that they found it useful in a number of ways. One of the main benefits was that the activities helped to highlight academic writing issues before assessment. Tutors became aware much earlier in the term of the level of writing students were currently at, whether there was confusion around the assignment and specific student writing issues such as dyslexia. Although some colleagues initially found the WiD initiative time consuming, once the activities and resources had been created they were often used numerous times in a variety of different contexts. Development of activities by the network of academics also helped to develop their confidence and knowledge surrounding academic writing empowering them to develop their students writing whilst reducing feelings of isolation. The most successful WiD initiatives have been those led by disciplinary academic staff as can be seen in the two accounts below.

▶ Using WiD to develop student writing

Incorporating WAC and WiD activities into disciplinary teaching has not only helped in the delivery of material, but also in the formative and summative assessment of subject-based outcomes.[2] WAC has helped in developing students' transferable skills: most notably effective written and oral communication. The ability to write scientifically requires students to initially demonstrate writing for clarification skills, further developing these into writing for communication. WiD activities, however, have proven to be a useful tool in encouraging students to develop their scientific writing by focussing more on the subject, as opposed to the writing itself.

The flexible nature of the writing activities means that as a lecturer Broadberry has been able to incorporate them into any learning situation, with limited preparation. This has allowed her the opportunity to conduct impromptu writing activities if it is deemed necessary to provide students with the opportunity to reflect on a new or challenging concept or to enable the checking of student understanding.

Simple writing activities such as writing down the main points from the previous or current lecture or from directed reading provide students with the opportunity to clarify concepts, reflect on prior learning in light of new information, and enable students to structure their thoughts and ideas (Fulwiler and Young, 2000). Activities such as freewriting can form the basis for peer discussions, engaging students in the subject and providing them with the opportunity to think and reflect. For disciplinary specialists, such activities can also aid in the identification of areas or concepts requiring further clarification and thus provide the opportunity to ensure learning outcomes are being achieved.

The ability to demonstrate an audience-adapted style of writing is a useful transferable skill for students of all levels. A poster assessment requiring students to communicate an area of recent research to the public/technicians aimed to develop a concise and clear approach to communicating science. This assessment employed a patchwork text approach to the assessment (Ovens, 2003) relying on peer engagement, peer assessment, and collaboration in the task, in addition to formative and summative feedback. The overall engagement with the task was high; with students advancing their knowledge of zoo nutrition, unaware that they were developing a transferable skill. This assessment proved so effective it has resulted in one student presenting their work at an international conference, where it was well-received.

Writing activities have enabled Broadberry to gauge student understanding of key concepts against their peers. This has also ensured early identification of concepts the students are struggling to grasp, allowing for immediate clarification or directed reading. It is suggested that using such activities may enable students to sharpen their memory recall, integration of ideas, and ultimately writing skills, thus benefiting exam technique, though quantification of improved performance is necessary to form conclusions about this. It may be that disciplinary writing tasks enable students to develop as both learners and communicators by taking responsibility for their own learning, a key element of effective learning identified by Biggs and Tang (2007), whilst building a culture of feedback on their learning within the context of their subject studies (Lindblom-Ylanne et al., 2006).

Writing activities have proved useful in ensuring lesson outcomes have been achieved, rather than assuming that learning has occurred. The opportunity for students to measure the learning distance travelled by recalling and reflecting during the activities adds value to the students' perception of lecture attendance. Such activities often encourage reflection and discussion with their peers and the lecturer, thus increasing student engagement in the subject whilst subtly developing their communication skills. Students responded positively to all writing activities employed and the general consensus was the more that writing activities were used the greater the benefit. Some students commented that the notes made during activities proved useful revision aids and provided greater opportunities for feedback, prior to submission of the final report.

The meetings with colleagues associated with the writing collaborations proved invaluable in sharing ideas for activities, as well as maintaining motivation to engage in the project. Through the Postgraduate Certificate in Higher Education course, Broadberry delivered a practice teaching session on WAC and WiD approaches to her group. The session opened with a WAC activity, asking the cohort to use freewriting to give an overview of their knowledge of WAC. This was followed by a ten-minute presentation, concluding with freewriting on the knowledge they had gained in the session. This exercise demonstrated not only that their knowledge of the subject had improved, but the process aided their learning and allowed the cohort to measure the development of their knowledge. The feedback on the session showed it was well received. There was some concern that the writing activities sounded like more hard work for the lecturer beyond their field of specialism. Yet, it is Broadberry's opinion that improved clarity of student writing within their subject studies makes marking student assessments much easier.

▶ Using WiD activities to meet learning outcomes

The WiD approach has also been trialled within the Multimedia Undergraduate BA Programme.[3] WiD techniques have been applied to the Successful Practice and Principles (SPP) modules in the first and second year of the Programme. The aim of these courses is to deepen students' contextual understanding of Multimedia. The Multimedia Programme has a common first year and its cohort come from a diverse range of study areas. One of the primary aims of this first study year is to develop a common understanding of Multimedia at Nottingham Trent University with students choosing their specialisations towards the end of the year.

The contextual SPP module seeks to provide skills that will allow each student to deepen their knowledge area, primarily in their discipline-specific area. It also looks to develop and deepen more generic skills, higher level skills as defined by Bloom (1956) and other skills such as analytical ability, critical awareness, and the ability to synthesise discrete elements of data. This SPP delivery takes place at the beginning of the academic year and consists of a weekly 1-hour seminar session delivered over a 10-week period. What follows is a discussion of the second-year SPP seminar WiD initiative.

The Multimedia second year cohort numbers 87 students. These students are divided into three approximately equal seminar groups where each group receives the same session in the same week. Ayodeji is the course leader for the SPP Module. He is also the lecturer responsible for the design and delivery of all of the sessions. The fact that he delivers the same session to three different seminar groups has proved invaluable as regards discerning the value of, reaction to, and engagement with each session.

The seminar sessions generally use a mixture of in-class written exercises and work prepared out of class which is then brought into class for sharing and discussion. The underpinning philosophy of the seminar structure design is how to use verbal discussion as a way of thinking about written discussion. This philosophy is designed to underpin the Learning Outcomes of the module, which include:

- To manage and communicate ideas confidently and persuasively
- To initiate and manage personal study.

The other major element of each session was its reliance on group discussion, peer collaboration, and the peer learning that is sought as a result of these methods.

A study conducted by the Australian Universities Teaching Committee discussed the universally recognised benefits of collaborative working (AUTC, 2002). This type of engagement might also lead to "transformation and internalization" (Fry et al., 1999, p. 21). Immediate usefulness of the learning greatly improves our motivation to learn (Fisher and Williams, 2000) so the sessions—whilst seeking to develop writing, analytical, and verbal discussion skills—were structured around activities to support the 2000-word assignment due at term end.

Many specialists in writing techniques such as Rabiger (2007) and Dancyger and Rush (2002) discuss the writing process. The importance of the ideation stage is consistently emphasised. Ideation is expressed as the process of developing initial ideas. The use of writing activities in this course allowed a format for the student's work to be developed along these lines. This development might happen before, during, and/or following the session.

One writing activity involved giving each student a week to write an abstract. They were asked to bring these to the seminar to be critiqued by the group in a round-robin style. Each abstract was analysed using criteria, with notes being taken. Each student read and analysed four abstracts on average and was also able to take away notes about their own work. The task was heavily reliant on collaborative learning as described by Gokhale (1995) in that the active exchange of ideas by group peers was designed to encourage interest in the task. The major element to evaluate is, perhaps, the question of openness with most of these methods. The lack of anonymity with the way sessions were delivered is potentially problematic for the student who is reluctant to share. A sample of some student feedback, included here, discusses the merits of this type of method:

> It was confusing to begin with, I thought it was a pointless task when writing it however, once in the seminar it made sense. Having seen the other abstracts being similar to mine really helps and gives me an indication of where people are in comparison to me.   (S1, 2009)

> I found the task fairly useful, it is helpful seeing how the rest of the group approached the abstract. Am now a bit more sure of what should go into my final abstract when I write it.   (S2, 2009)

The positive student feedback response outlined above arguably outweighs any concerns about anonymity. This particular task had a 70% uptake of the numbers who attended. Alterio (2002) discusses storytelling as a way to enhance student learning and as a Writer for Stage and Screen this method of engaging students, asking students to think through writing, sits well with Ayodeji's preferred method of teaching:

> I also enjoyed the informality of sitting round a table or in a circle, rather than sitting with my back to somebody. This at first feels slightly uncomfortable, but after a while everybody starts to talk, even the quiet ones.   (S3, 2009)

Ayodeji's ability to improvise and to be seen to respond to student queries is also beneficial when trying to introduce complexity to disciplinary assignment tasks. Writing intensive sessions will shortly be delivered to level one students. The aims and desired outcomes are similar to those in level two with writing seen as being integral to disciplinary thinking and critical analysis. To this end the sessions are similarly structured. The major assignment the sessions are designed to support is the writing of a visual essay.

▶ Conclusion

The above accounts of WiD activities have identified important benefits for students and disciplinary specialists. They have also highlighted issues for future consideration and ways to support students in exploring disciplinary writing. These WiD initiatives as a whole have brought academic writing into the classroom for discussion.

One of the key features of the WiD approach is that it begins to open up a dialogue between staff and students about disciplinary writing and the ways in which students' competencies and confidence can be developed. It gives students the chance to raise concerns, to identify areas where they feel confident, and to test that confidence in a non-assessed and relaxed environment. For disciplinary specialists, writing activities provide valuable markers of how the students are developing and allow for problems to be identified prior to assessment. The flexible and impromptu nature of the writing activities has proven to be a useful tool for increasing the learning opportunities of students, whilst enabling the embedding of writing-based and transferable skills in a subject-specific context. Such activities engage students in the learning process and provide feedback to both students and lecturers about whether learning is or (in some cases) is not occurring. Overall, WiD offers the opportunity to turn academic writing away from a solution focused assessed activity into a developmental productive process.

WiD initiatives have also allowed for greater collaboration between academics. The attention to disciplinary writing brought together academics from across the institution from programme leaders to PhD students in a shared endeavour. The disciplinary differences added to the rich and varied nature of the resources created and helped colleagues to think around and outside the restrictions of their own discipline. The project meetings also helped to create a network of interested and engaged colleagues who were willing to work with learning developers based more centrally in the institution to develop and trial resources.

Both Broadberry and Ayodeji and a number of other academics have helped to create a trickle down effect amongst their colleagues, thus increasing interest in WiD, and while some academics see the integration of writing development into their teaching as an increase in workload, many are now considering this as a viable way to support student writers.

Nevertheless, it has become apparent that WAC and WiD do not easily translate to a UK context. Whilst US colleagues have first-year writing seminars and a "long belief in the centrality of the teaching of writing" (Gottschalk, 2003, p. 23), in the UK writing is seen as very much a supportive process as opposed to developmental and as such lacks resources making the project difficult to sustain. Although the fragmented approach allows for a greater focus on one or two programmes, this also keeps the overall project fragile as it is always susceptible to failing interest from the few colleagues involved in the project. The lack of a holistic focus on academic writing from institutions may also prevent students and staff from recognising the value of disciplinary writing initiatives. The projects undertaken in the UK are, however, slowly helping to formulate a British version of WiD and the findings from such projects may provide invaluable feedback in moving forward.

Lessons learnt

A curriculum where assignments, teaching methods, activities, and assessment criteria are aligned creates a much more receptive student audience. The challenge of this for Multimedia students who might not enjoy writing is one where continual reflection is required. For instance, an assignment to create a report about person and professional networks was better framed around a discussion about placement opportunities. The students were aware of the importance of work experience in their industry so the assignment appeared less abstract than it might otherwise have done. Some of the tasks associated with writing (e.g. research, preparation, and drafting) could be better framed due to the broader acceptance of the *value* of the assignment. Another key implication of the WiD trial was the revelatory nature of the moment when students came to understand that writing was as much a demonstration of their thinking as of their knowledge and understanding. The bringing together of independent and classroom-based tasks was often about revealing to the student how their work could be seen to have met a number of the learning outcomes with usually only minor amendment such as being seen to try to substantiate claims, ideas and opinions, introducing alternate ideas, and working more depth into a thesis. The round robin nature of the peer sessions often revealed how this redrafting to make the essay, notes, and thoughts more *academic* might be practically undertaken by the student. This key idea of the student already having knowledge to bring is an important one.

From the perspective of a learning developer involved in promoting and creating writing resources, there have been problems in numerous areas. However, engaging unwilling or indifferent staff and students in WiD has been the greatest challenge and much more difficult than creating the activities themselves. The most important aspect (in Bell's experience) of incorporating WiD into sessions is to ensure the full commitment to trialling the approach from the staff and students. WiD should be promoted as a valuable use of class time and should challenge staff and student negative perceptions of what academic writing involves.

Practical suggestions

Abstract Writing Exercises (One hour)
Each student prepares an abstract for the same assignment outside of class. (The abstract should be 200–250 words maximum.) They then bring the abstract into class. Each abstract is read simultaneously (by pairs) and to criteria set by the practitioner leave a set of notes for the author of that abstract. Each pair then moves onto the next abstract. This should be a 10-minute process. At the end of the session each abstract should have four sets of notes. Reading of abstracts on the same assignment often reveals structure and reflection on ones own abstract writing process. This abstract exercise can be done pretty much at any stage of the essay writing process.

Essay Promise Exercise (one hour)
Start the session with a promise that by the end of the session each student who buys into the session, listens, contributes, and takes notes will have their essay structure for their given assignment by the end of the session. Start by recapping the expectations for the assignment and how the assignment will be assessed. Allow questions (10 minutes).

Split the class into three entitled Beginning, Middle, and End. Each section has 15 minutes to work out the structure of their section: What might go in the section and why? How does the content advance the argument? How might depth and complexity be introduced? Perhaps half way through the idea that the sections should interrelate is introduced and at this point one person in each group speaks to the other sections to get an idea of content for each section. This information is then fed back to their section (15 minutes).

After the 15-minute period each section feeds back to the whole class. This whole class discussion is facilitated by the practitioner. After each section three minutes is given over for each student to make notes about any points they specifically wish to follow up on. Continue until all sections have spoken. (30 minutes). End the session by getting each student to look at their notes. Challenge anyone to accuse you of breaking your promise!! (5 Minutes).

▶ Notes

1 Author: Rebecca Bell, Learning and Teaching Officer, NTU.
2 Author: Sarah Broadberry, Programme Leader and lecturer, Zoo Biology, NTU.
3 Author: Julius Ayodeji, Senior Lecturer, Multimedia, NTU.

▶ References

Alterio, M. (2002) *Using Storytelling to Enhance Student Learning*. Available from http://www.heacademy.ac.uk/resources/detail/id471_using_storytelling_to_enhance_learning, date accessed 11 November 2007.

Australian University Teaching Committee (AUTC) (2002) *Assessing Learning in Australian Universities*. Available from http://www.cshe.unimelb.edu.au/assessinglearning/docs/AssessingLearning.pdf, date accessed 14 December 2007.

Biggs, J. and Tang, C. (2007) *Teaching for Quality Learning at University* (Berkshire: Open University Press).

Bloom, B. (1956) *Taxonomy of Educational Objectives, Handbook1: Cognitive Domain* (London: Addison Wesley).

Dancyger, K. and Rush, J. (2002) *Alternative Scriptwriting: Successfully Breaking the Rules*. 3rd edition (Oxford: Focal Press).

Fry, H., Ketteridge, S. and Marshall, S. (eds) (1999) *A Handbook for Teaching and Learning in Higher Education: Enhancing Academic Practice* (London: Kogan Page).

Fisher, R. and Williams, M. (eds) (2000) *Unlocking Literacy: A Guide for Teachers* (London: David Fulton).

Fulwiler, T. and Young, A. (2000) *Language Connections: Writing and Reading Across the Curriculum* (Illinois: WAC Clearing House Landmark Publications).

Gokhale, A. (1995) "Collaborative Learning Enhances Critical Thinking". *Journal of Technology Education* (Urbana), 7: 22–30.

Gottschalk, K. (2003) "TAs and the Teaching of Writing at Cornell: A Historical Perspective", in Monroe, J. (ed.) *Local Knowledges, Local Practices: Writing in the Disciplines at Cornell* (Pittsburgh: University of Pittsburgh Press), pp. 22–40.

Harrington, K. and O'Neill, P. (2009) "Contributions of 'Top 10 Dissertation Writing Tips'", in Waldman, J. (ed.) *Doing Your Undergraduate Social Science Dissertation* (London: Routledge).

Lea, M. and Street, B. (2000) "Student Writing and Staff Feedback in Higher Education: An Academic Literacies Approach", in Lea, M. and Stierer, B. (eds) *Student Writing in Higher Education* (Buckingham: Open University Press), pp. 32–46.

Lindblom-Ylanne, S., Pihlajamaki, H. and Kotkas, T. (2006) "Self-, peer- and teacher-assessment of student essays". *Active Learning in Higher Education* 7 (1): 51–62.

Mitchell, S. and Evison, A. (2009) "Exploiting the Potential of Writing for Educational Change at Queen Mary, University of London", in Ganobscik-Williams, L. (ed.) *Teaching Academic Writing in UK Higher Education* (Hampshire: Palgrave Macmillan), pp. 68–82.

Monroe, J. (ed.) (2002) *Writing and Revising in the Disciplines* (New York: Cornell University Press).

Ovens, P. (2003) "Using the patchwork text to develop a critical understanding of science". *Innovations in Education and Teaching International*, 40 (2): 133–143.

Rabiger, M. (2007) *Directing Film Techniques and Aesthetics*. 4th edition (Oxford: Focal Press).

Russell, D. R., Lea, M., Parker, J., Street, B. and Donahue, C. (2009) "Exploring notions of genre in 'academic literacies' and 'writing across the curriculum': approaches across countries and contexts", in Bazerman, C., Bonini, A. and Figueiredo, D. (eds) *Genre in a Changing World: Perspectives on Writing* (Colorado: Parlor Press), pp. 459–491.

WAC Clearing House (2009) *Examples of Writing to Learn Activities*. Available from http://wac.colostate.edu/intro/pop5.cfm, date accessed 13 January 2010.

Part III

WiD and the Institution

12   Backward Design: Towards an Effective Model of Staff Development in Writing in the Disciplines

John Bean

▶ **Introduction**

In their important study of graduate students struggling to find their way into disciplinary discourse, Rienecker and Stray Jorgensen quote a representative PhD candidate at the University of Copenhagen, "If Lacan tried to hand this book in as a PhD project at my university, would he even pass? Am I supposed to write *like* Lacan, or *about* him, but in a very different style?" (2003, p. 106). Rienecker's and Stray Jorgensen's purpose is to compare their writing centre's methods of teaching writing—the "Anglo-American" approach using argument templates, genre instruction, problem-solving strategies, and explicit coaching—with the "continental" approach that leaves students struggling on their own. A particular version of the Anglo-American approach is at work in the writing in the majors project at Seattle University—a "Writing in the Disciplines" (WiD) initiative in which disciplinary faculty, working together as a department, try to create coordinated and sequenced assignments to accelerate students' growth as disciplinary thinkers and writers.

Partially funded by an assessment grant from the Teagle Foundation, disciplinary faculty meet for three brief workshops (one hour each over lunch) and then work together as a department on an assessment project focused on disciplinary writing. The lunchtime workshops are facilitated by a three-person team (me, the director of our writing centre, and a reference librarian). We use the Copenhagen student's question to illustrate that even PhD candidates can be baffled about disciplinary discourse. "So what is it that you want your undergraduates to do?" we ask disciplinary faculty at the first workshop. "What kind of papers would demonstrate undergraduates' ability to write and think like disciplinary insiders? Where do they learn these ways of thinking and writing? Could you as a faculty, working together, accelerate their progress?"

Disciplinary faculty members have both extrinsic and intrinsic motivation to participate in these workshops. Extrinsically, they are motivated by regional accrediting bodies, which mandate rigorous assessment of student learning in every department and program. At Seattle University we have adopted an approach to assessment that focuses on course-embedded assignments graded with a rubric, an approach that is particularly conducive to WiD (see Bean et al., 2005). Faculty discussion of strengths and weaknesses in student performance on a disciplinary assignment can lead to collaborative strategies for ameliorating weaknesses earlier in the curriculum. But faculty members are also motivated intrinsically by the satisfaction of promoting deeper and more engaged learning. Once teachers see assessment as a means of investigating students' ability to think and write like disciplinary professionals, they begin to see that better designed, sequenced, and co-ordinated assignments can lead to higher quality undergraduate research. The workshop discussions also help overcome instructor isolation—what Graff (2009) has called "courseocentrism"—and promotes faculty community.

This chapter describes the Writing-in-the-Majors project at Seattle University in ways that suggest its transferability to other institutions and settings. I present first the theoretical design for our three lunchtime workshops for departmental faculty. I then provide examples of how different departments at Seattle University, using the principle of backward design, have redesigned curriculum and instruction in order to teach disciplinary ways of thinking and writing. Finally, I describe and illustrate some shared principles for designing writing assignments aimed at teaching disciplinary discourse.

▶ Theoretical design of WiD workshops

There are many ways to design WiD workshops for faculty. In this section, I explain the particular approach that has evolved at Seattle University. Each of our three one-hour workshops focuses on a key WiD concept selected for its explanatory power:

- Workshop 1: MacDonald's concept of "expert insider prose".
- Workshop 2: Carter's concept of metadisiplines and metagenres.
- Workshop 3: Bizup's concept of the function of research sources.

These concepts, we have found, speak to the interests of disciplinary faculty and stimulate productive discussions leading to pedagogical innovation and change.

Expert insider prose

One of the perplexing frustrations that torment WiD advocates is the indifference of disciplinary faculty to the word "writing". Disciplinary teachers, of course, want students to write well, but teaching this skill is someone else's domain (the pre-university curriculum in Europe, first-year composition in the United States). Moreover, they regard writing as merely a foundational skill, acquired primarily through grammatical study, that enables the production of clear and fluent prose. According to this view, writing skills can be learned in stand-alone writing courses and then transferred seamlessly across the disciplines. To combat this view, WiD advocates have developed a repertoire of strategies aimed at reframing the word "writing". One approach is to link writing to critical thinking. If disciplinary faculty (and administrators who provide funding for writing initiatives) can see writing as a mode of thinking, they will appreciate the heuristic function of writing, thus broadening the narrow view of writing linked primarily to grammar and correctness.

In our writing workshops, we have found that an even more powerful way to reframe writing is to use a felicitous term from MacDonald (1994, p. 187)—"expert insider prose". For MacDonald, this is the final stage in her four-stage schema theorising students' growth from novice to expert in a discipline. Her schema, which we introduce at the very beginning of our first workshop, is as follows:

1 Non-academic writing.
2 Generalised academic writing concerned with stating claims, offering evidence, respecting others' opinions, and learning how to write with authority.
3 Novice approximations of particular disciplinary ways of making knowledge.
4 Expert, insider prose   (1994, p. 187).

MacDonald's schema is based on the American educational system in which students progress from high school into a university general education program (or core curriculum) and then into the major. Within MacDonald's schema, stage one represents students' high school experience where they write primarily non-academic or pseudo-academic prose such as personal essays or five-paragraph themes. Because American high schools typically don't demand or teach university-level critical argument, it is the goal of the ubiquitous first-year composition course to teach what MacDonald calls "generalized academic writing" (stage 2)—writing that introduces students to academic discourse without trying to teach disciplinary ways of thinking and arguing. What MacDonald emphasises, however, is that little of what students learn in first-year composition transfers directly into disciplinary courses. When students enter their chosen majors (stage 3), they essentially start over as writers with little sense of how the new discipline poses questions, gathers and analyses evidence, applies theories, or produces disciplinary arguments in conversation with other scholars. Appropriate writing assignments early in the major need to be aimed at teaching disciplinary ways of seeing, thinking, and making arguments. The last stage of MacDonald's schema describes students who eventually become acculturated into the discipline, learning to produce "expert insider prose" as defined appropriately by disciplinary faculty for undergraduates. Departmental assessment projects can help faculty monitor the strengths and weaknesses of senior projects and then develop ways to improve assignments, curriculum, or pedagogical methods to ameliorate weaknesses.

The particular insight of MacDonald is the importance of Stage 3—those early courses in the major where students begin to learn how scholars in their field conduct inquiry and make arguments. If students are not writing effective disciplinary papers as seniors, the problem cannot be solved by improving first-year composition but instead by helping students better navigate the "novice approximation" stage. In Seattle University's writing in the majors project, our WiD efforts focus specifically on writing assignments early in the major—assignments designed to teach disciplinary ways of seeing, question-asking, gathering evidence, analysing, and arguing.

How can we best identify and describe the skills needed for expert insider prose? We have found particularly helpful Beaufort's (2007, p. 19) taxonomy of the skills and knowledge that distinguish expert insiders from novices. She creates a Venn diagram in which a large circle labelled "discourse community knowledge" contains four smaller overlapping circles: "subject matter knowledge", "genre knowledge", "rhetorical knowledge", and "writing process knowledge" (p. 19). Beaufort's diagram, when combined with MacDonald's expert insider prose, powerfully reframes "writing", which now includes subject-matter knowledge—both conceptual and procedural—as well as knowledge of the discipline's primary genres. Of highest importance, shown in her Venn diagram's encompassing circle, is discourse community knowledge, which includes knowing the discipline's theoretical disagreements, its major players, its cutting edge versus old questions, its methodological controversies, its special terminology, its assumptions and warrants, its particular kinds of information literacy, its stylistic conventions, and its methods for positioning a writer's claims within a disciplinary conversation. In Burkean terms, disciplinary faculty "identify" with expert insider prose. "Writing" is no longer an isolated skill outside disciplinary faculty's range of interest, but a disciplinary performance under the purview of other disciplinary insiders. In short, disciplinary faculty "own" the teaching of expert insider prose in a way that they would never own the teaching of "writing".

Beaufort's diagram also suggests that disciplinary faculty have much to learn from writing scholars, who can help them teach the two remaining kinds of knowledge—"rhetorical knowledge" and "writing process" knowledge. Effective strategies for teaching rhetorical knowledge—for example, thinking like a reader, analysing the available means of persuasion, adapting message to audience, adjusting tone and register, linking new information to old information, and forecasting structure—have been developed by writing scholars. Meanwhile, academic writing centres are particularly effective at teaching (and coaching) "writing process knowledge"—brainstorming, planning, lowering expectations on early drafts, revising globally, and moving from writer-based to reader-based prose.

In our writing in the majors project, then, we have found that the first hour's discussion of MacDonald's four-stage schema and Beaufort's taxonomy of expert insider skills can be transformative for disciplinary faculty. Faculty members initially uninterested in teaching "writing" often become invested in designing a curriculum that teaches both subject matter knowledge and entry into disciplinary discourse.

Metadisciplines/metagenres
The next of our three lunch workshops focuses on Carter's (2007) concept of metadisciplines and metagenres. Based on WiD research into disciplinary practices at North Carolina State University, Carter produced an elegantly simple schema that maps similarities and differences among disciplines. (Table 12.1 shows my attempt to display his scheme in a chart format.)

Carter identifies four metadisciplines, which I have labelled in Table 12.1 as Problem-Solving, Empirical Inquiry, Interpretive/Theoretical, and Performance. As the table shows, disciplines with quite different subject matters can have surprising similarities in the kinds of disciplinary work they do. For example, professionals in such disparate fields as business and engineering both use professional expertise to solve problems for a targeted client. Their prototypical metagenre is the practical proposal. In contrast, the disciplinary work of both chemistry and psychology is scientific inquiry aimed at answering questions about the empirical world and advancing knowledge. Their shared genre is the empirical research report. Another metadiscipline—the humanities—generally focuses on interpretation

Table 12.1 Metadisciplines, metagenres

Metadiscipline	Explanation	Typical disciplines	Examples of ways of doing	Metagenre	Related genres
Problem-solving	Disciplinary professionals use disciplinary knowledge and procedures to solve real-world problems for a targeted client	Business, engineering, applied economics, and agriculture	Finance professional proposes ways to increase cash flow Engineering team designs a more effective battery	Practical proposal to solve a problem	Recommendation memo Technical report Feasibility studies White paper Management plan Technical documentation for engineering design solution Funding proposal
Empirical Inquiry	Researchers use disciplinary knowledge and procedures to advance empirical understanding of world Experimental empiricism Descriptive empiricism	Physical and social sciences	Biologist studies energy transfer within cells Psychologist studies effect of stress on test performance	Experimental Research Report with IMRD structure (introduction, methods, results, discussion)	Ethnography Technical description Scientific article Poster Conference presentation Research proposal
Interpretive/ Theoretical	Researchers interpret documents/artefacts/ cultural phenomena through various theoretical lenses with expectations that problems will be continuously debated rather than "solved"	Humanities and interpretive disciplines within Fine Arts (e.g. art history)	Literary scholar uses New Historicist theory to interpret *Hamlet*. Historian uses archival documents and feminist theory to reinterpret medieval queenship	Disciplinary journal article (no clear structural template)	Conference paper Conference presentation Book chapter Book
Performance	Ways of knowing result in performances	Fine arts, journalism, multimedia production, creative writing	Sculptor mounts a studio exhibit Journalist writes a feature article	Reflection/critique	Program notes Reviews

Source: Adapted from Carter (2007).

of human artefacts examined through the lens of various methods and theories. In Carter's terms, these disciplines conduct research by finding and examining primary sources (which vary according to discipline) and making arguments about them in academic papers—typically academic books, journal articles, or conference papers. Finally, the performance disciplines—dance, music, painting, creative writing, and journalism—produce creative works in various media rather than academic papers. However, they share a common metagenre—the reflection paper that aims to explore the artist's intentions and methods and offers a critique of the performance.

Our lunch discussions invite participants to locate their own recent research within Carter's schema; with only a few borderline exceptions, most are able to do so. Our discussions corroborate the findings of Thaiss and Zawacki (2006, pp. 14–16) that some disciplines are "compact" (most department members work within the same genres using similar methods) while others are "diffuse" (the department fragments into disparate sub-disciplines doing very different kinds of disciplinary or even metadisciplinary work). For example, on our campus, the psychology department is compact; the department achieved easy consensus that undergraduate psychology majors should learn to write an APA experimental report. In contrast, our political science department is a loose confederation of different metadisciplines. One of its members does theoretical/interpretive work in political philosophy; several do empirical inquiry using sophisticated statistical analysis. Still others do problem-solving work for government agencies or produce public policy proposals. Diffuse departments often have difficulty reaching consensus on what should count as expert insider prose for undergraduates. However, the discussion of Carter's taxonomy helps them articulate the special problems of deciding on the discourse communities that students need to join.

Function of research sources

Our third lunch discussion focuses on students' often *naïve* views of disciplinary research. In US universities, students are traditionally assigned the ubiquitous "research paper" or "term paper", a pseudo-academic genre, much attacked by WiD specialists, that leads students to think of research as going to the library or the Web to find articles to support a pre-determined thesis. According to one study, 87% of freshmen think of research as "going to the library and finding books and articles to use in my paper" (Ritter, 2005, p. 628). When they hear the word "research", in other words, students think of going to the library rather than of, say, observing migration patterns of butterflies, analysing longitudinal unemployment data in a certain region, or taking field notes in an art museum. Going to a library is one part of what happens when disciplinary professionals pursue research, but when, how, and why they do so varies by discipline. Our lunch discussions try to raise faculty awareness of what novices in a major need to learn about research in their new disciplinary fields.

We have found that a schema developed by Bizup (2008), based on the function of research sources, has significant explanatory power for students. Bizup refers to his schema by the acronym BEAM, which I summarise in Table 12.2 using my own explanations and examples.

In Bizup's schema, the "B" stands for any source the writer has used as Background—what the writer regards as non-controversial facts and pieces of information that set the context for a paper. Background information, which the writer assumes will be uncontested by readers, might come from encyclopaedias, reference works, news sources, textbooks, earlier research accepted as canonical, or other trusted disciplinary sources of shared knowledge.

Bizup's remaining kinds of sources—Exhibit sources, Argument sources, and Method/Theory sources—comprise the rhetorical heart of academic research. Exhibit sources are the actual data/phenomena/artefacts that the researcher is puzzling over depending on the disciplinary field—an unusual rock formation, the text of *Hamlet*, or the results of a questionnaire about workplace stress levels. Extracted material from the Exhibit sources often become evidence in support of the researcher's thesis.

What confuses novice students is that in some disciplines researchers go to the library to find their Exhibit sources, whereas in other disciplines researchers go to a laboratory or the field. A history major may conduct her exhibit research in a library working with archival sources while an economics major may need databases accessed through a library portal. But in other fields exhibit sources have nothing to do with libraries or Internet portals: A biologist may do exhibit research by observing plant fungi in a meadow or a civil engineer by taking soil samples at a proposed building site. Meanwhile a literature major may do exhibit research simply by sitting in a coffee shop re-reading *Hamlet*. Students need to understand that in all these cases, researchers are *doing research* by studying exhibit sources even though only some of the cases involve a library.

Bizup's next category is an Argument source—his designation for the work of other scholars or commentators who have studied the researcher's same question. Here researchers almost always go to a library or a library portal. Their goal is to position themselves in the scholarly conversation surrounding the topic—previous and contemporary scholars with whom the writer agrees or disagrees. The student researcher needs to learn how scholars in different disciplines

Table 12.2 A Taxonomy of source use by writers, adapted from Bizup's 'BEAM' (2008)

Source type	Explanation	Example (from literature) Question: How are we to regard Jane Eyre's marriage to Rochester? Liberation or loss?	Example (from sociology) Question: How does gender socialisation impact on college-age drinking behaviours and attitudes?
B Background sources	Sources which provide the writer with background or context information	Encyclopaedia article on historical context Biography of the author, Charlotte Brontë Articles on contemporary culture	Statistics on college-age alcohol consumption Articles on gender socialisation Cultural artefacts
E Evidence (or exhibit) sources	Sources the writer interprets or analyses Primary documents, primary data, contemporary images	Jane Eyre the novel Contemporary documents (diaries, pictures)	Qualitative data: for example, recordings of interviews or focus groups Quantitative data: for example, questionnaires (data must be based on and reviewed by ethical codes of practice)

Table 12.2 (Continued)

Source type	Explanation	Example (from literature) *Question: How are we to regard Jane Eyre's marriage to Rochester? Liberation or loss?*	Example (from sociology) *Question: How does gender socialisation impact on college-age drinking behaviours and attitudes?*
A Argument sources	Sources containing ideas the writer engages with, or to which the writer responds Sources contributing to the debate in which the writer is intervening	Journal articles and books on the novel The goal as a writer is to contribute to the scholarly debate with a new argument or interpretation	Scholarly studies and literature reviews The aim as a writer is to identify an unresolved problem or research question
M Method (or theory) sources	Sources from which the writer derives a method or approach. Theoretical texts or descriptions and evaluations of research methodologies	Theory written by or about scholars whose work is relevant to analysis of the novel	Theory written about relevant sociological issues and methodologies for data collection and analysis

Source: Copyright 2008. Adapted from 'BEAM: A Rhetorical Vocabulary for Teaching Research-Based Writing' by J. Bizup. Reproduced by permission of Taylor & Francis Group, LLC., http://www.taylorandfrancis.com

use their argument sources. In science writing, the conversation of different voices is usually placed near the beginning of the research report in the "review of the literature" section. In literary criticism, however, a writer often carries on a running argument with other scholars throughout the essay.

Bizup's final category is Method or Theory sources—references to scholars whose methods or theories the researcher is using. Thus a researcher might apply the ethical theories of Kant or Mill to an issue in genetic engineering, even though these philosophers themselves never examined biotech issues. In the humanities and social sciences, references to postmodern critical theorists are common (Foucault, say, or Geertz) while in the physical sciences scholars often employ specific methodological approaches or theoretical models that need to be documented.

Bizup's schema can either replace or supplement the more common terms of primary, secondary, and tertiary sources, which often seem confusing to students. Whereas the terms "primary" or "secondary" are defined by their degree of distance from the researcher's subject, Bizup's terms refer to the function of any source in the researcher's paper. Moreover the term "primary" seems to connote a document of some sort, whereas Bizup's term "exhibit" gives a name to natural or cultural phenomena that the researcher analyses. Thus the insects in the guts of trout could be an exhibit source for an aquatic biologist but hardly a "primary source" in our normal library or archival use of the term.

Workshop discussions of Bizup's BEAM can influence the way that faculty members subsequently design writing assignments early in the major. New majors need to learn what constitutes their discipline's typical exhibit sources, how these sources are analysed and interpreted, and how data from exhibit sources are used as evidence in arguments. Students also need to learn how to position themselves in a disciplinary conversation. Here they need to learn how to find and use argument sources to create literature reviews or to set up critical debates. Finally, they need to learn how to look through the lens of method/theory sources. The second half of this paper provides case studies of departments applying the insights derived from the discussions of Bizup's BEAM as well as from the first two lunch workshops.

▶ Departmental action: Assessment and backward design

Once departments have completed the three lunch discussions, their subsequent activities are motivated both by our university's assessment mandate and by their own desire, as committed teachers, to enhance student learning. The assessment process at Seattle University uses faculty-graded assignments already embedded in courses as a means of assessing specified learning outcomes. According to Walvoord (see Walvoord, 2004; Walvoord and Anderson, 2010, pp. 151–171), whose theoretical work on assessment has influenced our approach, the foundational assessment act is an instructor's grading of a student performance—an approach that validates an instructor's expertise and allows grades to be used productively for assessments so long as the grades are justified by reference to shareable criteria, usually through a rubric. We call Walvoord's method a "discourse approach" to assessment (as opposed to a psychometric approach) in that it relies for its effect on rich faculty talk about student performance on an embedded assignment, often leading to proposals for improving curricula or instruction. The assessment process is simple: Instructors grade an embedded assignment that focuses on a learning outcome and report patterns of strengths and weaknesses to a community of stakeholder faculty, who then plan ways that weaknesses in student performance might be ameliorated through improvements in instructional methods, assignments, or curricular design upstream from the assignment. This assessment approach doesn't rely on empirical research methods such as pre-post tests, treatment/control group studies, or statistical analysis of data. Although rubric scoring can yield data amenable to psychometric analysis, the discourse method thrives because (1) it validates a professor's judgement of student performance and alleviates fears that assessment is necessarily positivist or reductionist, (2) it leads to productive faculty discussions of curricula and pedagogy, (3) it focuses on improvement of student learning, and (4) it leads naturally to "completing the loop" by stimulating innovative improvements in assignments and teaching strategies.

This discourse approach to assessment provides a soft accountability structure for our writing in the majors project. A department's overarching assessment question is this: To what extent are advanced undergraduate students in our major able to produce "expert insider prose" as evidenced in some kind of capstone or capstone-like project? As we have seen earlier, expert insider prose requires a complex integration of different kinds of knowledge and skills: subject-matter knowledge (both conceptual and procedural), genre knowledge, discourse community knowledge, rhetorical knowledge, and writing process knowledge. Thus an assessment of expert insider prose is more than an assessment of writing; it is an assessment of a student's integrative ability to "do" the intellectual work of his or her discipline—in short to think and write like an historian, economist, chemist, political scientist, or nurse.

Using a discourse assessment approach, a department begins by deciding what would constitute "expert insider prose" for end-of-career seniors defined at an appropriate undergraduate level. It selects a senior-level course in which the designated kind of expert insider prose is required (the embedded assignment). The instructor grades the assignment using a rubric (sometimes departmental faculty work together to create the rubric); analyses rubric scores to uncover patterns of strengths and weaknesses in student performance; and presents the results at a department meeting, initiating faculty discussion. Finally, the department discusses strategies that might be implemented earlier in the curriculum to ameliorate weaknesses. This is the essential "feedback loop" stage of the assessment process.

In redesigning courses earlier in the curriculum, following the strategy of backward design, disciplinary instructors appreciate MacDonald's stage theory, which emphasises the importance of early courses in the major (MacDonald's Stage 3) for teaching disciplinary discourse. By identifying the skills needed to produce expert insider prose when students are seniors, faculty can design short, focused assignments or instructional modules early in the curriculum that can develop the needed skills. (In the last section of this chapter I show examples of assignments, which focus particularly on teaching students how to use disciplinary evidence or to work with the scholarly literature.) As can be expected from this decentralised approach, each department has its own assessment story. Here are some representative examples from our project that have already been reported in the scholarly literature:

- The history department, unhappy with senior papers that were often narratives without theoretical sophistication, changed its sophomore-level gateway course to introduce historical theory and to develop new kinds of assignments. Particularly, faculty wanted students to apply different theoretical perspectives to historical problems and to create thesis-governed historical arguments that draw evidence from archival sources. (See Bean et al., 2005.)
- The chemistry department decided that the typical lab report was "pseudo-academic prose" that didn't teach students to construct themselves as scientists. Two professors redesigned the labs for sophomore organic chemistry in order to eliminate cookbook experiments, engage students in the statistical analysis of error in data, and teach the empirical research report in the manner of professional chemists writing to professional audiences. (See Alaimo et al., 2009.)
- The English department redesigned its curriculum so that every 400-level literature course requires a researched literary argument informed by theory and aimed at presentation at an undergraduate research conference. Designing backwards, the department created an integrated sequence of writing assignments that increase in

complexity from 200- to 300-level courses, including one 300-level course that explicitly teaches students how to position their own views within a conversation of critics. (See Bean and Iyer, 2009.)

- The economics department discovered that economics majors, unlike professional economists, did not instinctively draw graphs on the backs of envelopes. The department's assessment focus has been on "rhetorical mathematics"—increasing students' ability to interpret graphs and to construct graphs that tell a significant economic story. This approach has led to new kinds of numbers-based writing assignments throughout the curriculum. (See Bean, "Quantitative Writing" a pedagogical Web site attached to Carleton College's Science Education Resource Center.)

- The finance department has defined its capstone projects as "short persuasive memos", addressed to specified audiences, arguing for a "best solution" to an ill-structured (open-ended) finance problem. Because finance professionals must frequently address lay audiences as well as finance experts, the department is especially interested in students' ability to shift audiences, constructing some arguments in an expert-to-lay context (with appropriate use of language and graphics) and some in expert-to-expert context. The department has developed short assignments in early courses in the major to teach these skills. (See Carrithers and Bean, 2008; Carrithers et al., 2008.)

For a closer look at the kinds of assignments used early in the major, I turn now, in the last section of this chapter to the principles of assignment design that inform our project.

▶ Designing powerful writing assignments

Throughout the writing-across-the-curriculum program at Seattle University, we try to link writing assignments to critical thinking, which we define broadly as the ability to formulate a problem with stakes, to enter the conversation surrounding that problem, and to make a contestable claim supported with reasons and evidence to an audience considering alternative views. We also encourage instructors to create a rhetorical context for students by specifying within the assignment an audience, purpose, genre, and motivating occasion.

The writing in the majors programme extends these general principles to discipline-specific writing. Good writing assignments invite students to confront what Bain calls "intriguing, beautiful, or important problems, authentic tasks that will challenge [students] to grapple with ideas, rethink their assumptions, and examine their mental models of reality" (2004, p. 18). The aim of a good writing assignment is to deepen and prolong students' engagement with such problems, to encourage critical thinking about disciplinary concepts and theories, and to teach use of disciplinary evidence to make arguments. Advanced assignments also teach students how to join the conversation of other scholars or professionals examining the same or similar problems.

At the senior level, when students are asked to produce expert insider prose, we usually expect them to pose their own beautiful problems; therefore a senior level assignment can often be short and generic: "Pose a disciplinary problem in an area of your choice, conduct the inquiry and research needed for you to address this problem, and, in an appropriate disciplinary genre, write a paper worthy of presentation at an undergraduate research conference." Earlier in the curriculum, however, when students are in MacDonald's "novice approximation" stage, short assignments can be designed to teach specific disciplinary ways of thinking and writing. Teachers of these early courses often design assignments specifically geared towards teaching students to work with exhibit sources and argument sources (see previous discussion of Bizup's BEAM).

Teaching students to work with exhibit sources

Exhibit sources are the phenomenon, artefacts, manuscripts, primary texts, or raw data that disciplinary experts analyse or interpret and then use as evidence in arguments. Entry-level students typically don't encounter puzzling exhibit sources in a field. Rather, they begin their studies by learning facts, concepts, and theories from textbooks, which present a discipline's accumulated knowledge, but often make invisible the field's actual knowledge-constructing practices. Textbooks typically don't show disciplinary experts wrestling with problems or making arguments based on disciplinary evidence. As Light notes in his study of teaching practices that enhance learning, "a surprising number of undergraduates describe learning how to use evidence to resolve controversies in their field, whatever their field, as a breakthrough idea" (2001, p. 122). When instructors devise writing assignments requiring students to wrestle with exhibit sources, they create powerful homework that supplements textbook learning by teaching disciplinary ways of thinking.

Teaching students how to use disciplinary evidence can be surprisingly challenging. New literature majors, for example, often think of evidence either as plot summary or as long block quotations from a literary text. Likewise, new finance majors think of evidence as Excel spread sheets attached to a memo or as an algorithmically derived "right answer" that needs no evidentiary support. The problem of teaching disciplinary evidence is at the heart of the revised organic chemistry lab mentioned in the previous section (Alaimo et al., 2009). Chemists Alaimo and Langenhan abolished the traditional "lab report" (typically based on cookbook experiments) because, among other things, such a report implies that chemists are satisfied with evidence derived from one run of an experimental procedure. They explain their thinking as follows:

> The problem with conventional lab reports is that they encourage students to think and behave like students rather than like professionals. Because students knew (or thought they knew) the expected outcome of the "cookbook" experiments, they chalked up any deviation from the expected outcome as "experimental error" with little thoughtful explanation... [The problem with lab reports] is that they focus on experiments that each generates a single datum. No scientist would follow such a process. In fact, few things are considered *less* scientific than to attempt to write a compelling, well-argued paper based on singular runs of an experiment. In short, the lab report develops habits that students must *unlearn* if they are going to think and write like professional chemists.   (2009, p. 20)

Alaimo and Langenhan revised the lab to require multiple replications of a procedure—a process that produced messy data that must be analysed statistically for error. Their revised writing assignment—to write a professionally argued scientific paper rather than a lab report— was aimed specifically at teaching students more sophisticated use of scientific evidence:

> The advantages of this simple change are dramatic. Students start to realize why doing an experiment only once is problematic. Because the redesigned experiments require multiple replications investigating several substrates, no single "right answer" emerges. Rather, laboratory work yields multiple trends in data that are often puzzling both to students and instructors and that may be contaminated by experimental error. To interpret their data—and to convince their audience that their interpretations are valid— students must learn how scientists determine experimental error statistically and how statistical analysis can be used to discard an erroneous datum... Confronting true experimental error puts students in the center of a discourse community—as active scientists puzzling over data with other scientists—where they learn

the important lesson that science is founded on reproducibility. (2009, p. 21)

Whereas Alaimo and Langenhan focused on the organic chemistry lab as a site for teaching disciplinary use of evidence, instructors in other fields can develop their own ways to engage students with their field's typical exhibit sources. Here is an example of a Stage 3 writing assignment designed for new economics majors:

> **Assignment Purpose**: A common task of economists is to use data to develop a conclusion and then support the conclusion in a written argument or report. The purpose of this assignment is to give you experience with this task.
>
> **Your Task**: A US senator has just given a speech in which she argued that the 2000s are the worst economic decade in the last 30 years. You are the fact-checker for a media outlet investigating whether the senator's claim can be justified with economic data. Your task is to write a memorandum to your boss giving your best argument as to whether the relevant economic data supports the Senator's claim.
>
> **Process**: Before you decide your own position, begin by collecting data for each year since 1980 on three variables: the growth rate of US real GDP, the US inflation rate, and the US unemployment rate. Put the data in a table, and create a chart to illustrate each variable graphically. You will need to incorporate these graphs into your memorandum. Then decide what conclusions you can draw about the macroeconomic performance of the economy during the 2000s compared with its performance in the 1980s and the 1990s. Do those conclusions support or reject the Senator's claim?
>
> **Product**: Write a two to three page, double-spaced memo to your boss. The memo should present your argument that the senator's claim is or is not justifiable based on your analysis of the data and referring to the tables and graphs as evidence. Attach copies of your tables and charts at the end of your memo; these do not count in the page limit. Give each table or graph an accurate title and refer to it in your memo.
>
> [My thanks to Professor Gareth Green, Department of Economics, Seattle University].

This assignment engages students with quantitative data, which constitute typical exhibit sources in economics. The assignment teaches students to use economics databases, to analyse the data, to construct rhetorically effective tables and graphics, to apply their analysis to a real-world problem with stakes, and to make an argument to a targeted audience in a workplace genre.

Teaching students to work with argument sources

Besides working with exhibit sources, new majors must also learn to work with the discipline's argument sources—the scholarly literature bearing on a disciplinary problem. Students must learn how to do disciplinary literature searches, how to summarise the arguments of other scholars, how to use disciplinary conventions for quoting versus para-phrasing, how to cite and document sources appropriately, and, most importantly, how to bring their own voices into conversation with other scholars.

One of the best ways to teach these skills is to ask students to write abstracts of disciplinary articles and to respond to them in ways that teach disciplinary thinking. In addition to assignments built around a single argument source (such as a journal article), teachers can design more complex assignments that ask students to summarise two or more articles and then analyse similarities and differences among their claims, points of view, and methods. Such assignments can be expanded further to teach the typical literature-review sections of aca-demic papers. In fields where literature reviews regularly appear in introductions, students need to learn how to write such a review. In fields where scholars typically take issue with one or more other scholars, students need to summarise the views they intend to push against in order to follow the template "Although some scholars think X, this paper argues Y".

Here are three commonly recurring kinds of literature reviews that can be easily adapted to undergraduate research assignments:

> *Literature Review Establishing a Controversy:* Here the writer's goal is to describe and analyze competing points of view on a disci-plinary problem. Such a review can be a stand-alone assignment or it might be one movement in a longer paper in which the writer takes sides in the controversy or attempts to resolve it through synthesis or through taking a new tack.
>
> Review the philosophic controversy on whether the earth has "rights".
>
> Summarize competing points of view on the question of whether alleged terrorists captured on U. S. soil (such as the Christmas Day underwear bomber) should be tried in civil or military courts.
>
> To what extent does Shakespeare's *The Tempest* help construct a colonialist world view?

Literature Review Explaining Current "State of the Art" Knowledge on a question: Here the writer's goal is to determine the current best thinking of experts on an issue or question, often as part of a proposal to solve a problem. In this role, the writer researches cutting edge knowledge on some contemporary problem in the discipline and reports, in either an academic or a popular style to a lay audience, what the experts currently think.

What is the current best thinking on the value of insulin pumps in managing Type I diabetes?

What is the current best thinking on the use of nanoparticles to create UV protection in clothes?

Literature Review Identifying Unknowns or Gaps in Current Knowledge: Here the literature review serves to show what is known and not yet known about a cutting edge problem, often as part of the introduction to a scientific paper aimed at filling the gap.

What is known and not known about the effect of sleep deprivation on short term memory?

What is known and not known about the use of interspecific chemical cues to advertise territory in competing salamander species?

▶ Conclusion

The writing in the majors initiative at Seattle University aims to enhance student learning by teaching disciplinary ways of thinking and arguing. A concomitant benefit is the way it stimulates productive talk about pedagogy among department faculty. As Graff has argued, professors often work as independent contractors in isolated silos, teaching their courses without much knowledge or interest in what their colleagues are doing. So long as the goal of teaching is to convey conceptual knowledge of a field, little collaboration is needed; once the disciplinary field is divided into agreed-on territories, instructors can work independently to cover their own assigned specialties. But the writing in the majors project changes the pedagogical focus from what students know conceptually to what they can do with that knowledge when confronted with new disciplinary problems. Once a department's goal is to produce disciplinary expertise rather than to cover the curriculum, cooperative collaboration becomes helpful. Based on her reading of novice/expert scholarship, Beaufort concludes that:

> [t]he single most distinguishing characteristic of those who gain expertise in a variety of skills domains are those who continually assign themselves more and more complex problems to solve.

> For educators this translates to a need for students to experience sequenced writing assignments within and across courses in which skills required to complete the task build upon previously acquired skills.   (2007, p. 184)

The goal of our writing in the majors initiative is to try to create this kind of sequenced curriculum.

Good assignments, we believe, engage students with disciplinary problems. Departmental collaboration aims to sequence these assignments so that students confront increasingly complex problems as they progress through the curriculum.

Does this approach require more faculty time? Is the workload too burdensome? Our experience suggests that for faculty who assign writing anyway (e.g. traditional term papers or reports), the amount of time can actually be reduced because many Stage 3 assignments can be short and can be graded quickly with a rubric. On the other hand, teachers often report an increase in the time they spend writing comments on drafts or conferencing with students. Also, in some cases an instructor's pedagogy begins to shift from mostly lectures to a more active-learning approach focused on in-class encounters with disciplinary problems. This shift can lead to reallocation of an instructor's class preparation time—from preparation of lectures to the development of sequenced problems for in-class discussion. It is thus hard to generalise about the impact of the writing in the majors approach on the total amount of instructor time devoted to teaching. To minimise workload concerns, we advise teachers to start slowly with a few small changes—such as the design of one or two short, purposeful assignments in Stage 3 courses. Even such small changes can lead to greater student engagement with course material and to their learning of disciplinary ways of thinking and arguing.

The writing in the majors project at Seattle University seems sustainable for the long run because most departments believe that students' ability to produce expert insider prose is an important learning outcome for the major. A senior capstone project is perhaps the best holistic indicator of a student's growth from novice to expert as a disciplinary writer and thinker. Also, the process of analysing student performance on embedded course assignments and using backward design to improve curricula and instruction goes a long way towards meeting a department's mandate for meaningful outcome assessment. Finally, the value of a professional community created by the cooperative demands of the project is another sustaining factor. Whether the Seattle University project can be adapted to other institutions is an open question. However, because the general principles behind our project seem to us grounded in sound theory and in harmony with

faculty desire to promote student learning, I am hopeful that other institutions can develop analogous projects that fit their institution's history,
context, and goals.

▶ Acknowledgements

I would like to thank my colleagues Larry Nichols, Director of the Seattle
University Writing Center, and Lynn Deeken, Reference Librarian and
Instructional Coordinator for the LeMieux Library at Seattle University,
for their partnership in facilitating the writing in the majors departmental lunches and workshops. My thanks also to the Teagle Foundation
for the assessment grant that has supported much of our work.

▶ References

Alaimo, P. J., J. C. Bean, J. Langenhan, and L. Nichols (2009) "Eliminating Lab
    Reports: A Rhetorical Approach for Teaching the Scientific Paper in Sopho-
    more Organic Chemistry", *WAC Journal: Writing Across the Curriculum*, 20,
    17–32.
Bain, K. (2004) *What the Best College Teachers Do* (Cambridge, MA: Harvard
    University Press).
Bean, J. C. and N. Iyer (2009) "'I Couldn't Find an Article that Answered
    My Question': Teaching the Construction of Meaning in Undergraduate Liter-
    ary Research" in K. A. Johnson and S. R. Harris (eds) *Teaching Literary Research*
    (Chicago, IL: Association of College and Research Libraries), pp. 22–40.
Bean, J. C., D. Carrithers, and T. Earenfight (2005) "Transforming WAC Through
    a Discourse-Based Approach to University Outcomes Assessment", *WAC
    Journal: Writing Across the Curriculum*, 16, 5–21.
Beaufort, A. (2007) *College Writing and Beyond: A New Framework for University
    Writing Instruction* (Logan, UT: Utah State University Press).
Bizup, J. (2008) "BEAM: A Rhetorical Vocabulary for Teaching Research-Based
    Writing", *Rhetoric Review*, 27.1, 72–86.
Carrithers, D. and J. C. Bean (2008) "Using a Client Memo to Assess Critical
    Thinking of Finance Majors", *Business Communication Quarterly*, 71, 10–26.
Carrithers, D., T. Ling and J. C. Bean (2008) "Messy Problems and Lay Audi-
    ences: Teaching Critical Thinking Within the Finance Curriculum", *Business
    Communication Quarterly*, 71, 152–170.
Carter, M. (2007) "Ways of Knowing, Doing, and Writing in the Disciplines",
    College Composition and Communication, 58.3, 385–418.
Graff, G. (2009) "It's Time to End 'Courseocentrism'", *Inside Higher Ed*
    (January 9) http://www.insidehighered.com/views/2009/01/13/graff.

Light, R. (2001) *Making the Most of College: Students Speak Their Minds* (Cambridge, MA: Harvard University Press).

MacDonald, S. P. (1994) *Professional Writing in the Humanities and Social Sciences* (Carbondale, IL: Southern Illinois University Press).

Rienecker, L. and P. Stray Jorgensen (2003) "The (Im)possibilities in Teaching University Writing in the Anglo-American Tradition When Dealing with Continental Student Writers" in Bjork, L., G. Brauer, L. Rienecker, and P. Stray Jorgensen (eds) *Teaching Academic Writing in European Higher Education* (Dordrecht, NY, and London: Kluwer), pp. 101–112.

Ritter, K. (2005) "The Economics of Authorship: Online Paper Mills, Student Writers, and First Year Composition", *College Composition and Communication*, 56.4, 601–631.

Thaiss, C. and T. M. Zawacki (2006) *Engaged Writers, Dynamic Disciplines: Research on the Academic Writing Life* (Boston, MA: Boynton/Cook).

Walvoord, B. E. (2004) *Assessment Clear and Simple: A Practical Guide for Institutions, Departments, and General Education* (San Francisco, CA: Jossey-Bass).

Walvoord, B. E. and V. J. Anderson (2010) *Effective Grading: A Tool for Learning and Assessment in College* (San Francisco, CA: Jossey-Bass).

13 Writing in the Disciplines and Learning Technologists: Towards Effective Collaboration

Celine Llewellyn-Jones, Martin Agombar and Mary Deane

▶ Introduction

This chapter examines the role of learning technologists in discipline-based writing development. It explores the nature of learning technologists' partnerships with colleagues to produce digital resources, and considers ways of fostering effective collaborations (Pilkington, 2009). The chapter argues that there are parallels between the roles of writing developers and learning technologists, especially in the collaborative nature of their work. However, it suggests that both learning technologists and writing developers should guard against loosing their voices as experts in higher education, and should work to ensure that they are not perceived as service providers rather than specialists in their own right. The chapter also makes a case for the value of writing centres as a locus for bringing different specialists together to support students' writing in disciplinary contexts.

▶ Learning technologists as integral to WiD work

The kinds of expertise that learning technologists might bring to a disciplinary writing intervention include the design and creation of multimedia resources that make the conventions of a particular genre explicit to students.[1] Such digital teaching materials are usually produced through a collaboration between a subject specialist and a technologist, although a writing developer might also advise (Smyth,

2003). Resources may be targeted at academics and integrated into curricula, or distributed directly to students via universities' Virtual Learning Environments. Some writing centres employ a dedicated learning technologist to focus on producing audio-visual materials that disseminate writing developers' expertise in virtual forms. Digital resources can be an invaluable way to meet the needs of students with disabilities and multi-media materials can also be tailored to suit different learning styles. They also help to scale-up the provision of writing support by catering for distance learners, offering out-of-hours support, and reaching students who do not seek advice in person for a range of reasons.

Learning technologists work at the intersection of education and technology. They bring to collaborations both practical skills and an understanding of how to think about users' needs. Having a background in highly technical areas as well as an interest in education, they often see beyond issues that preoccupy academics and offer fresh perspectives. For example, by developing multimedia teaching materials such as online quizzes for subject experts to populate with questions, technologists can help to engage students and introduce a means of measuring their understanding of key concepts. An advantage of such digital resources is that they can be reused or adapted for specific contexts and subject areas. A disadvantage of producing digital materials can be the time it takes to produce them, but by collaborating effectively and building on best practice it is possible to streamline this process.

To promote working in the most efficient manner, it is helpful to examine more closely what the learning technologist's role entails. In particular, the way the technologist's role is perceived by colleagues in the disciplines is relevant for subject-based writing development. As Oliver argues, success can be determined by the ways in which the learning technologist is viewed by colleagues, and if technologists do not establish credentials with colleagues, it is unlikely that fruitful dialogue will follow because they are more likely to be perceived as simply service providers (2002, p. 6).

Needless to say, learning technologists often make efforts to promote themselves as more than just service providers. In fact, they embody a wide-range of roles, which makes their job descriptions hard to pin down. According to Oliver, they represent a "rapidly growing group whose practices are little understood, even within their own community" (2002, p. 1). For example, a national survey of learning technologists' remits by Beetham identified 11 distinct roles (2000).

While these studies are not now new, a single definition of the learning technologist's role continues to elude academia. Many practices remain undocumented (Oliver, 2002), partly because much of what learning technologists consider central to their remit is frequently *ad hoc* staff development, training, or resource production that is not tied to courses or teaching loads in the conventional sense (Oliver, 2002, p. 2). This can make the technologist's role hard to quantify.

Oliver has studied the tacit practices and unofficial tasks of learning technologists through unstructured interviews. He has established five activities that are shared amongst the technologists he interviewed.

- Centring on collaborative curriculum development, usually initiated by an academic and focused on a particular piece of technology.
- Typically including additional administrative, technical, research, or management functions.
- Being educative, using discussion, case studies, and problems within the context of collaborations as the basis for reflection, and seeking to move the academic from the particular issues of implementation to more general educational issues.
- Being situated, drawing on the idea of communities of practice, and thus requiring the learning technologist to learn as well as teach during collaboration.
- Being responsible but without authority, relying on goodwill, expertise, and rhetoric to create opportunities (both practical and educational) and influence policy.   (Oliver, 2002, p. 7)

Based on this research, Oliver has developed a model of collaborative practice that he describes as "Legitimate Peripheral Participation" (LPP), as shown in Figure 13.1.

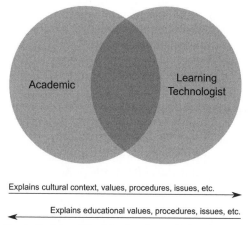

Figure 13.1 Legitimate Peripheral Participation (Lave, 1997; Oliver, 2002).

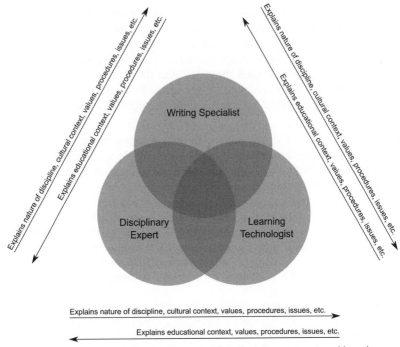

Figure 13.2 The related roles of writing specialist, disciplinary expert, and learning technologist.

This model of collaborative engagement could also be applied to the role of writing developers, who work with academics in departments in comparable ways to learning technologists. Based on this conceptualisation of learning technologists' interactions with colleagues, Llewellyn-Jones offers the paradigm for conceiving the potential of their role in disciplinary writing development, as shown in Figure 13.2.

▶ Challenges of collaboration

Collaborative work can be challenging as Andrea Lunsford points out, remarking that "creating a collaborative environment and truly collaborative tasks is damnably difficult" (1991, p. 3). The challenges collaboration can present include competing institutional demands, mixed agendas within a team of colleagues, and different expectations. These all potentially undermine learning technologists' work to enhance the teaching of writing through the use of multimedia materials.

At an institutional level, various pressures can impair working partnerships. Academics work in fast-changing environments and must manage the competing demands of teaching, research, and administrative tasks, as well as facing resourcing limitations. Although academics often acknowledge the need to improve their students' writing, and frequently would like to engage more with learning technologies, with competing demands on their time and resources individuals may lack the motivation to take on new projects. To make things worse, in many institutions the introduction of blended learning has been associated with cost-saving measures rather than a drive to enhance students' experiences at university. Academics may therefore be slightly suspicious of blended initiatives or suggestions from senior managers that they increase their dissemination of expertise to students via digital media.

Competing agendas

Even if subject specialists are able to overcome institutional hurdles, many pressures still challenge their engagement with a project to develop digital teaching resources. Such projects can involve a range of different parties, including students, writing developers, departmental colleagues, and learning technologists. This diversity can be a strength, but it also introduces a mix of agendas and perspectives which may clash or compete. The bigger the pool of partners, the greater the chances of misaligned expectations in terms of each person's role, way of working, needs, and goals.

Competing expectations

For learning technologists, this diversity of partners is a major challenge, and as a result, it can be difficult to achieve mutual understanding between a diverse range of skill sets as colleagues collaborate (Finnis, 2004, p. 9). Nevertheless, some harmonisation of goals is necessary to implement successful projects. As Finnis argues, without mutual understanding, subject specialists may reproduce their knowledge without attending to the demands of virtual environments or considering how to engage students with this learning environment (2004). In addition, academics may have unrealistic expectations of technologies, or be unaware of the potential digital resources might have for their teaching (Finnis, 2004, p. 9).

From the perspective of learning technologists, the misconceptions that might accompany a project depend in part upon who is involved. It is obviously crucial to establish the goals and methodology for a collaboration before it begins, but in doing so technologists should perhaps acknowledge their own ability to harbour misconceptions.

In this respect collaborative work can be about bridging gaps in understanding.

▶ Examples of collaboration

The four examples of learning technologists' roles in disciplinary writing development in this chapter illustrate the potential for their transformative influence upon students' experiences. Two examples are from London Metropolitan University, and two from Coventry University. At both institutions, dedicated learning technologists worked with writing developers on projects to enhance students' academic writing. All four projects were conducted under the aegis of writing centres, and operating in this specialised environment arguably helped to cohere with the goals and approaches of these interventions by focusing the participants' attention on the shared objective of enhancing students' confidence and competence as writers in their areas of study.

1   Business

As part of a *Write Now* Centre for Excellence in Teaching and Learning (CETL) research project, a senior lecturer in Business at London Metropolitan University responded to a call from the writing centre to participate in a disciplinary writing collaboration to support students' writing (see Chapter 7). This collaboration focused on the third-year course "International Purchasing". Plans for this project involved a learning technologist, a writing developer, and a subject specialist working together. The subject expert had clear goals for this WiD intervention, specifically, she was concerned that some of her students did not make the appropriate links between exam questions and the theory they had covered in class and she wanted to help them improve their exam performance.

In an initial meeting, a process of collectively seeking out a shared understanding of the main pedagogic problem began. The subject specialist was well-placed to present the case for this teaching intervention, and by virtue of working closely with her students she could make informed judgements about the nature of the issues they would need to tackle. Boundaries needed to be set at this first meeting, as Peter O'Neill, the writing developer, had to make it clear that he would not to be able to teach a session on the course because the ethos of WiD work is to facilitate subject-based academics' teaching of writing, and to pass on new strategies that colleagues can make their own. The writing developer agreed to give a five-minute talk to the students about this initiative and the provision they could receive from the writing centre. He also agreed to be present at the first workshop to support his colleague. They worked together to design a learning activity and teaching materials intended to help the Business students assess past exam questions and apply their knowledge of theory in appropriate ways. The informality of this meeting allowed potential disagreements to disperse quickly and painlessly.

Martin Agombar, a learning technologist at the writing centre contributed to this project and his role was to produce multimedia resources to support the intervention. During discussions, a common misconception arose concerning the proposed technological aspect of the intervention. The subject specialist had in mind an online resource that would address in general terms how an exam question should be approached. The problem was that a generic approach such as this would not serve the interests of the students, who needed discipline-specific theory presented in a way that was applicable for an exam situation.

The learning technologist used his expertise in accommodating users' needs to help guide the subject expert towards a better solution. The final outcome involved video clips of the Business expert explicitly discussing the theory students needed to apply in their exam answers, supported with text and graphics. The learning technologist also tailored an online Freewrite tool to allow the students to practice responding to exam questions using the theory they learnt in class. He used the tool Prezi to put this resource together. In this example, the three different experts interacted in a productive way as the subject specialist, the writing developer, and the learning technologist collaborated to support a cohort of students. All parties gained from the experience and developed a better understanding of the specialised knowledge their colleagues possessed. Students also benefited from the digital resources they produced.

2 Dyslexic learners

A second project at London Metropolitan University explored the potential of technologies to support participants on the Postgraduate Certificate course in Teaching Adult Dyslexic Learners in Further Education and Higher Education (TADLHE). The project emerged from a number of conversations about student writing, and a subject specialist from the Education department applied to participate in the *Write Now* CETL project to enhance the disciplinary teaching of writing. In this case the project had become oversubscribed, but staff at the writing centre worked with their colleague on an informal basis to support her teaching of writing through the use of technologies.

The Education expert identified a need to support participants on the TADLHE course with their academic writing, especially as many had been assessed as dyslexic themselves. She wanted to help these early career academics become more confident writers and find ways of enabling them to exploit assistive technologies in their teaching. Concurrently, Celine Llewellyn-Jones, a learning technologist at the writing centre, was researching assistive technologies and investigating ways of using them to support students' writing in disciplinary contexts. The Education expert and the learning technologist collaborated to find innovative ways of supporting the students without the writing developer's direct input in this instance.

This collaboration was based on the action research approach of starting with a specific challenge and trialling a solution. The problem in this case was how to use assistive technologies effectively, and to seek out solutions that involved participants on the TADLHE course. The early career academics on this course identified that their levels of confidence in using technologies were low, and this was an influence on their practice, so they decided to seek ways of building their familiarity and competence at harnessing assistive technologies to support their students. This cohort explored various techniques to meet their aim, including reading literature on assistive technologies, which they discussed via a private online communal space. They also trialled the latest assistive technologies as a group and evaluated the strengths and weaknesses of different tools for their own requirements.

At the start of this project the learning technologist had a technology-centred perspective, but the collaboration presented an opportunity to adopt a more student-focused approach, as well as gaining experience in educational research by participating in the evaluation of assistive technologies. Working collaboratively with a subject specialist and in direct contact with students afforded the learning technologist deep insights into the demands and opportunities of the TADLHE course and the potential role of technologies in staff and curricula development. The Education expert and the course participants both gained new competencies in using technologies to teach.

3   Paramedic Science

A third project at Coventry University aimed to offer writing development to distance learners in the field of Paramedic Science. This initiative also indicates the complexity of collaboration as the differing expertise of writing developers, subject specialists, and learning technologists converge. Ray Summers, the learning technologist at Coventry's Centre for Academic Writing, led this initiative to exploit technologies in pedagogically sound ways. He collaborated with the Paramedic Science course tutor Mark Garratt and the writing developer Mary Deane to produce a series of videos on key competencies such as referencing, reflective practice, and academic writing in this field.

Their goal was to support a cohort of 30 distance learning students studying for a Foundation degree in Paramedic Science. Many participants were unfamiliar with the demands of academia, and all were juggling the demands of study, shift work, and other commitments. There is relatively little dedicated guidance for writers in Paramedic Science, so this project involved the production of three short videos with animations and linked downloads containing samples of disciplinary genres and referencing advice. These were created by the Paramedics expert in collaboration with the writing developer, and were digitised by the learning technologist.

The videos were embedded into the course Web and integrated into the Foundation degree syllabus at relevant points. Students could thus discuss the concepts dealt with in the materials with their tutor in the relevant weeks and could use them to supplement their independent study. The downloads contained examples of strong and weak academic writing in this field, and to create this resource the team drew upon the Australian "Developing Academic Literacy in Context" project (DALiC) project (Skillen et al., 1999; Purser et al., 2008). They were also influenced project by Monroe's insights into the value of explicit teaching of disciplinary genres to foster learners' confidence and enjoyment of academia (Monroe, 2003).

In terms of tackling the challenges inherent in collaboration, this team had to deal with institutional pressures such as competing demands on their time and requirements to meet targets for diversity and income generation. These impacted on their individual agendas, for instance, the Paramedics expert was under pressure to design a distance learning course within a limited time, the writing developer was working to complete some publication projects, and the learning technologist's attention was also divided between a range of activities. As a result, their expectations for this initiative were not necessarily aligned.

Despite having different perspectives, these colleagues shared the goal of enhancing the Paramedics' confidence as writers, and on reflection they feel that coming together under the aegis of the writing centre helped to bring this objective to the fore. Nevertheless, feedback from course participants indicated that they wanted more personalised guidance on academic writing, in particular feedback on their work in progress.

4 Virtual writing tutorials for paramedics

A fourth initiative at Coventry University introduced virtual writing tutorials into the Foundation degree in Paramedic Science in response to the students' request for more individualised writing support. This work was also part of an investigation into ways of harnessing technologies to teach writing called the "Coventry Online Writing Laboratory" (COWL) Project funded by the Joint Information Systems Committee (JISC).

John Tutchings and Clive Teed, learning technologists from Coventry University's E-learning Unit, collaborated with the writing developers Mary Deane and Lisa Ganobcsik-Williams from the Centre for Academic Writing and the Paramedic Science course leader Mark Garratt. Together they planned a series of opportunities for students to participate in virtual writing tutorials to obtain feedback on their assignments before submission. They trialled two types of tutorials; the first type provided 50 minutes of real-time feedback via the Webconferencing tool Skype, and the second type offered delayed response feedback via e-mail that was accessed by students through the University's Virtual Learning Environment. Clive Teed enhanced the e-mail tutorials with Riffly which enabled writing tutors to record short videos as well as giving students written feedback.

Coventry's Centre for Academic Writing has a team of expert writing tutors who offer face-to-face tutorials to students in all disciplines and at all levels. These tutorials last either 50 minutes or 30 minutes, and the ethos is to teach writing strategies which students can apply throughout their studies. The tutors also aim to help students become more alert to the conventions of writing in their disciplines although they do not necessarily specialise in the subject areas they discuss. The tutors received training in both the Webconferencing software and the online tools to provide e-mail tutorials. They were allocated 50 minutes for face-to-face tutorials and 30 minutes for the email tutorials.

There were some initial technological hitches, but the medium of Webconferencing afforded a practical and personalised way of discussing potential strengths and weaknesses in the Paramedics' writing. The students appreciated this virtual opportunity to meet with a writing tutor to discuss their work in progress. They reported that it boosted their confidence and helped them to feel less isolated on the distance learning course. The Paramedics expert also valued the expertise offered by the team of writing tutors, who found Webconferenicng a relatively easy alternative to their face-to-face sessions.

The option of e-mail tutorials was less popular, and the Paramedic students did not all take advantage of this opportunity to submit their work for feedback. They valued the dialogic nature of the real-time tutorials and felt, although these were virtual, they could establish a working relationship with the writing tutors, which contributed to building their confidence and enthusiasm for academic writing. In contrast, the relatively impersonal exchange via e-mail was felt to be somewhat distant and inflexible, for instance, students could not easily ask further questions to clarify a point. This finding was contrary to the expectations of the project team, who anticipated that these busy students who were juggling their work and family commitments would appreciate being able to e-mail drafts and receive comments without the restrictions of setting a time to Skype with a writing tutor. The tutors themselves also felt that Webconferencing was more efficient than writing their comments or recording a short video summarising their advice.

As this collaboration involved a number of different parties, there were many points at which institutional pressures, differing agendas, and contrasting expectations affected communication and hindered the progress of the project. Regarding the important issue of expectations, the students expected to receive more opportunities for feedback than the writing centre could resource. The writing developers expected the choice of technologies to be relatively simple, and were challenged by the range of options the learning technologists presented to them. The technologists were surprised to find how much support the staff at the writing centre required in moving to virtual media to provide individualised writing development. Nevertheless, the team's shared goal of implementing technologies to enhance students' enjoyment of writing in the discipline of Paramedic Science brought them together and helped to make a positive difference to the students' experiences of academia.

▶ Collaborative aims

These examples of how learning technologists' expertise can transform the work of writing developers and support students in the disciplines suggest that, although collaboration is not straightforward, partnerships to exploit technologies are worthwhile. The challenges of competing institutional demands, mixed agendas within a team, and individuals' different expectations are seldom overcome completely, but this chapter has argued that a focus on disciplinary writing can help to make the various perspectives meet in the shared objective of enhancing students' engagement with subject-based discourse.

▶ Conclusion

These examples are relatively small scale, and it may be the case that team members engage with each other's agendas and expectations most successfully when projects are local, or when they are established on an *ad hoc* or informal basis. Even better, are long-standing partnerships between learning technologists and colleagues that lead to evolving ways of supporting students' discipline-based writing. However, there are strong arguments for formalising small-scale working, for instance because the results of informal projects tend to remain only locally known, with any benefits restricted to the original context rather than disseminated more widely. Similarly, whilst working with familiar colleagues can ensure productivity, this may also limit technologists' ability to promote the value of technologies to enhance students' writing further afield.

One of the biggest issues that can affect the goal of integrating the use of technologies into disciplinary writing development is the motivation of collaborators. Academics in the disciplines are extremely busy, and may be sceptical about the benefits of changing teaching practices which have proved successful over time. However, by aligning projects with the existing goals of subject experts, technologists can generate the most engagement and promote project success.

Positioning technology-based projects within an action research framework can be a powerful way to ensure that they are focussed on improving the student experience and developing academics' skills. Using case studies and examples of how technologies have been used to engage students and improve their disciplinary writing can be a good way to promote the benefits of this kind of approach. Yet, in order to reduce the pressures on individual academics, it is essential to find ways of encouraging institutions to recognise the value of technology-based projects by positioning them more clearly in terms of staff development.

In summary, this chapter has argued that learning technologists have an important role to play in writing in the disciplines work. However, they must be participants in a genuine conversation with subject experts and writing developers, and projects need to be achievable. Collaboration is indeed "damnably difficult", as Lunsford claims; but as she also attests, it is extremely worthwhile (1991, p. 3).

▶ Acknowledgements

The authors wish to thank Ray Summers for his expertise and guidance in producing this chapter. They would also like to thank Paul Summers for his advice on the remit of learning technologists.

▶ Note

1 There are examples of WiD resources produced by the leading learning technologist Ray Summers at Coventry University in Chapters 5 (a WiD initiative in law) and 8 (a WiD initiative in mathematics education) of this volume.

▶ References

Beetham, H. (2000) *Career Development of Learning Technology Staff: Scoping Study Final Report*, JISC Committee for Awareness, Liaison and Training Programme. Available at: http://www.jisc.ac.uk/publications/reports/2001/cdssfinalreport.aspx [Accessed 12 February 2010].

Finnis, J. (2004) Learning Technology: The Myths and Facts. *International Journal of Instructional Technology and Distance Learning*, 1(5). Available at: http://www.itdl.org/Journal/May_04/index.htm [Accessed 12 February 2010].

Lave, J. (1997) The Culture of Acquisition and the Practice of Understanding. In Kirshner, D. and Whitson, J. (eds) *Situated Cognition: Social, Semiotic and Psychological Perspectives* (Mahwah, New Jersey: Lawrence Erlbaum Associates).

Lunsford, A. (1991) Collaboration, Control and the Idea of the Writing Centre. *The Writing Lab Newsletter*. Available at: http://writinglabnewsletter.org/sphider/search.php?query=eodice&start=2&search=1&results=10&type=and&domain= [Accessed 12 February 2010].

Monroe, J. (2003) *Local Knowledges, Local Practices: Writing in the Disciplines at Cornell* (Pittsburgh: University of Pittsburgh Press).

Oliver, M. (2002) What Do Learning Technologists Do? *Innovations in Education and Teaching International*, 39(4), 245–252.

Pilkington, R. (2009) *Approaching Teaching Learning and Assessment*, JISC Committee for Awareness, Liaison and Training Programme. Available at: http://www.jisc.ac.uk/whatwedo/programmes/elearningcapital/reproduce/atlas [Accessed 12 February 2010].

Purser, E., Skillen, J., Deane, M., Donahue, J., and Peake, K. (2008) "Developing Academic literacy in Context". *Zeitschrift Schreiben*. Available at: http://www.zeitschrift-schreiben.eu [Accessed 13 July 2009].

Skillen, J., Trivett, N., Merten, M., and Percy, A. (1999) "Integrating the instruction of generic and discipline specific skills into the curriculum: a case study" in *Cornerstones: Proceedings of the 1999 HERDSA Conference* (Canberra: HERDSA).

Smyth, R. (2003) Concepts of Change: Enhancing the Practice of Academic Staff Development in Higher Education. *The International Journal of Academic Development*, 8, 51–60.

14 The Writing Centre as a Locus for WiD, WAC, and Whole-Institution Writing Provision

Lisa Ganobcsik-Williams

▶ Introduction

Writing development for all students is a concept that is taking root across the higher education (HE) sector in the UK.[1] Although scholars and support staff have worked with student writing in the UK context since the early 1990s,[2] the movement to teach and research academic writing has gained momentum as HE has moved into the twenty-first century. More than ever before, educational stakeholders are realising that university students benefit from explicit teaching in writing.[3] A key way in which writing scholars are moving debate forward on the topic of student writing is by outlining comprehensive whole-institution strategies whose goal is to build university cultures of writing that support students along a "continuum of writing development" (Ganobcsik-Williams, 2004, pp. 37–39;[4] 2009). One whole-institution approach that is proving to be successful in the UK is the writing centre.

This chapter introduces the idea of writing centres in UK HE and argues that university writing centres are an ideal location from which to build—along with other types of writing support—"Writing in the Disciplines" (WiD) and "Writing Across the Curriculum" (WAC) initiatives and programmes. While WiD focuses on the study and teaching of "disciplinary-related writing" (Bazerman et al., 2005, pp. 9–10), WAC refers to "efforts to improve students' learning and writing (or learning through writing) in all university courses and departments" (Russell et al., 2009, p. 395). This chapter proposes that the writing centre can function as a locus for writing development within universities and discusses ways in which WiD and WAC can be initiated and carried out through writing centres.

Specifically, the chapter examines how WiD and WAC collaborations stemming from writing centres can both engage with and enable an array of writing development opportunities for academics and students. To inspire informed discussion on the place of writing centres within universities and the potential benefits of developing initiatives such as WiD and WAC "from the centre" (Skillen, 2006, p. 140), the chapter analyses the model of the Centre for Academic Writing (CAW) at Coventry University. By examining the role of the writing centre, the chapter marks out a framework for an expanded definition of writing centre work in universities and seeks to promote further discussion of this model.

▶ A sense of possibility for writing development in UK HE

A sense of possibility exists for writing development in UK HE. In Autumn 2000, I conducted a national survey, the purpose of which was to ask staff across a range of disciplines and institutions a series of questions about their perceptions of students' literacy, their expectations of student writing, and their views on the explicit teaching of writing at the tertiary level.[5] To explore the perimeters of the field at the time, the survey posed questions on teaching discipline-specific writing, on generic ways of teaching of writing, and on writing tutoring and writing centres. Respondents overwhelmingly agreed that undergraduate students must mature in their ability to write over the course of their degree study, and, when asked if they felt it is necessary to teach writing to university students, 90 per cent of respondents said "yes" (Ganobcsik-Williams, 2004, pp. 12–13, 28). Staff responding to the survey also indicated that they saw a number of potential ways to develop student writing: through one-to-one tutorials offered by a university writing centre (93%), through optional professional development sessions offered to staff on the teaching of writing (92%), through optional courses taught by a writing specialist on subject-specific writing genres (91%), and through optional centrally taught writing courses for students from all disciplines (88%) (Ganobcsik-Williams, 2004, p. 28).

These early responses to the idea of support for all students engaging in writing at university provided me, as a writing developer, with a sense of optimism. The answers of some respondents to the survey were tempered, however, by the expectation that funding would be a major obstacle to realising any such provision. In other words, in terms of resource allocation, the idea of teaching students to write did not yet "play a major role in how UK universities conceive[d] of their mission as providers of education" (Bergstrom, 2004, p. 10).

For many of us who have worked in the area of writing development since this survey was conducted, much teaching and research effort has gone into convincing university managers that student (and staff) writing development is necessary and that it has real, long-term benefits for students, staff, and institutions. There are a variety of schemes, initiatives, and approaches that have been put in place in the UK over this time, ranging from an individualised tutoring scheme of Royal Literary Fund Writing Fellows administrated from outside the academy to a devolved model of Academic Skills Tutors at the University of Huddersfield, to an increasingly well-embedded WiD programme at Queen Mary, University of London, to a "Writing by Appointment" and associated student writing support programmes at the University of Dundee, to dedicated writing centres at Coventry University, London Metropolitan University, St Mary's University College Belfast, Liverpool Hope University, and the University of Gloucestershire.[6] In these diverse and locally contextualised ways, the sense of possibility for writing development is being realised.

Furthermore, as one UK writing specialist demonstrates when describing an undergraduate writing fellow mentoring scheme that he and his colleagues trialled from within a university writing centre, optimism about developing writing provision in UK universities continues to prevail:

> [This scheme] may not be the only approach to expanding disciplinary writing instruction in British universities, but I am convinced that [it] ought to be an important part of our curricular and pedagogical innovation. Indeed, [it] offer[s] so many benefits to students that it becomes tempting to see the "problem" of student writing as an opportunity to make improvements in an educational system that has resisted real pedagogical change for too long.   (O'Neill, 2008, p. 10)

This chapter, which will focus on the writing centre as a hub for organising and carrying out an array of writing development work, understands this sense of possibility to be an essential enabling factor for building comprehensive writing provision in HE.

▶ The influence of US and European theories and models of writing development

For many writing teachers and scholars in the UK, the sense of potential for tertiary writing development has been heightened by an awareness of the existence of US composition and rhetoric pedagogy and scholarship. Not only is the long-standing history of US composition pedagogy well-documented, but other US models of student writing support such as WAC, WiD, and writing 'centers' are becoming increasingly known to UK and European writing teachers and scholars. The knowledge that rhetoric and composition exists as a research and teaching field in its own right, with masters and doctoral degree programmes as well as academic posts, has inspired confidence in many UK writing developers that they are not working alone and that pursuing the impetus to set up student writing provision and to engage in the study and teaching of scholarly writing is recognised as a legitimate specialisation in other HE cultures.

As well as finding inspiration, UK writing developers have found in US writing scholarship fruitful points of comparison. In 1999, two writing teacher-scholars working at Richmond, the American International University in London, observed:

> [We] examine [...] the development of literacy practices in the United States, how they were shaped by cultural and historical forces, how they reflect the role of the university in American society, and how that changed over time. Why should that be of any interest to colleagues in the United Kingdom [...]? This is a moment when new debates are being engendered on the role of academic literacy in the university curriculum in the UK—a moment of possible invention or change. [...] This overview is offered not as a template, but as a means of widening the debate.   (Davidson and Tomic, 1999, pp. 161–162)

That emerging systems of writing development in UK institutions can be informed by US writing theories and practices without necessarily replicating them has also been pointed out by US writing scholar Joan Mullin. Because the UK is not hampered by traditions of writing support in the ways that US HE is, Mullin argues, there is more potential to set up new types of writing initiatives and programmes in UK HE than in the US context (Mullin, 2006).[7]

European writing scholarship has also been important to UK-based writing developers. Starting as early as 1988, European writing researchers and teachers founded organisations including SIG-Writing, a Special Interest Group of the European Association for Research in Learning and Instruction (EARLI), the European Writing Centers Association (EWCA), and the European Association for the Teaching of Academic Writing (EATAW) in order to bring together scholarly communities focusing on the study of writing.[8] The knowledge that European colleagues have begun to identify the writing of students and other scholars within the university community as an area meriting explicit teaching and research has further affirmed many UK writing developers'

belief in a shared interest and purpose across national and international
HE contexts.

▶ The writing center/centre

One US concept of writing provision that is being taken up across
Europe and in UK HE is the writing center.[9] Writing centres and writing
labs have played a role in American HE since the 1930s, and, since the
1970s, have been established in most colleges and universities across
the United States (Murphy and Law, 1995, p. xi; North, 1984). Histori-
cally, US writing centers have focused on offering students one-to-one
tutorials on the writing they do for their university courses, although
writing center pedagogy has responded to different institutional aims
and educational agendas throughout the decades (Boquet, 1999).

In the UK, the concept of the writing centre differs, perhaps in part
because it is an idea that seems full of possibility. As a prospective gathering place for prioritising, teaching, and researching academic writing,
the writing centre implies a locus whose activities are inherently far-
reaching. Furthermore, in UK HE "research centres" are highly valued,
and so an "academic writing centre" or "centre for academic writing" or
"centre for the study and teaching of academic writing" has, by virtue
of its name, a potential to share in that status.[10] Also, in more tangible
terms and in contrast to the US situation, other models of tertiary writing provision such as composition teaching do not exist, so UK writing
centres have the opportunity to take on more functions—and to take
them on more rapidly—in a university and public sector climate that
is eager to see standards of university students' writing performance
raised.[11]

A key example of the expanded definition of the "writing centre" that
the UK context can make possible is the Centre for Academic Writing (CAW) at Coventry University. Established in May 2004, CAW is
the first centrally funded UK university writing centre. From its start,
the aim of CAW has been to work with students, academics, and professional services staff in order to foster a holistic cross-university
culture of writing. In working directly with undergraduate and postgraduate students by offering face-to-face and online individualised
and small-group writing tutorials, paper-based and electronic writing
resources, and workshops on common topics such as 'the writing process', CAW operates within the student-facing ethos of a traditional
writing center. CAW's teaching of credit-bearing academic writing modules and its facilitation of "Protected Writing Time" sessions which
provide students with a place to work on their writing assignments are
localised variations that are also part of the traditional writing center

ethos.[12] As "an innovative teaching and research centre", however, CAW's mission is not only to enable students to become "independent writers", but "to equip academic staff in all disciplines to achieve their full potential as authors and teachers of scholarly writing".[13] This staff development remit enables CAW to work with academics and support staff on their own scholarly writing; for example, through individualised consultations, scholarly writing retreats, and dedicated writing events.

It is this staff development remit that also makes it possible for CAW, as a small department comprised of academic writing lecturers, tutors, and an administrative and learning technology team, to provide consultancy to academic and support staff across the university on how to teach writing and improve students' learning through writing (WAC) and on how to develop and teach discipline-specific writing genres and conventions (WiD).

▶ The writing centre as a base for WiD and WAC

Writing theorists and practitioners working primarily in US colleges and universities have produced a body of scholarship that explores connections between writing centers and WAC.[14] When accessing this scholarship, it is important to note that, although WAC and WiD are distinct concepts, US-based "scholars who talk about connections between WAC/WID and writing centers typically employ the umbrella term WAC" (Corbett and LaFrance, 2009, p. 3). As a movement to encourage the use of writing as a method of learning, WAC fits well within the traditional "liberal arts" or "general studies" curricula of US HE, with the potential for WiD initiatives to be introduced beyond the first or second year of undergraduate degrees when students begin to specialise in subject disciplines. In contrast, WiD has become the more prominent concept and "umbrella" term in UK writing development, because its focus on teaching and researching disciplinary writing genres aligns well with the early subject specialisation of UK universities and because academics teaching in this system may initially be more prepared to take responsibility for teaching disciplinary writing than for developing students' academic writing more generally (Ganobcsik-Williams, 2006, p. 52; O'Neill, 2010).

In Barnett and Blumner's seminal edited collection *Writing Centers and Writing Across the Curriculum Programs: Building Interdisciplinary Partnerships* (1999), Barnett and Rosen link WAC/WiD with the aim of creating a whole-university culture of writing, by suggesting that a university-wide "writing environment" has the potential to engender "recognition that writing is central to students' intellectual development and to their success in the wider world" (Barnett and Rosen, 1999, p. 1).

Such an environment would mean "that writing is visible, understood, and accepted as a valuable tool for teaching and learning across the disciplines. A campus-wide writing environment implies ongoing dialogue about writing and its relationship to thinking and learning among faculty as well as students" (Barnett and Rosen, 1999, p. 1).

Barnett and Rosen propose that a viable way to create and sustain university-wide writing environments is through collaboration between writing centers and WAC/WiD programmes. On the face of it, WAC/WiD may appear to be incompatible or even at odds with writing center work, in that the remit of most writing center tutors is to work with individual students outside of their disciplinary classrooms while the point of WAC/WiD is to shift the responsibility of teaching writing to academics across the university in order to offer teaching and practice in writing to all students. However, many prominent US scholars, such as Childers, agree with Barnett and Rosen that writing centers can serve ably as a hub for WAC/WiD consultancy, and that writing center staff, "rather than mostly working with students, [can] become more of a resource, guide, and facilitator for faculty research, discovery, and risk taking with writing, thinking, and learning across the disciplines" (Barnett and Blumner, 1999, p. xii; Childers, 1999). Emphasising the importance of both writing tutoring and the explicit teaching of writing across the curriculum, Waldo contends that WAC/WiD activities can be situated most logically in a writing center that "reaches out to faculty through a well-designed consultancy and provides students with a comprehensive tutoring program" (Waldo, 1993, p. 16). McLeod and Maimon take this point a step further:

> Although it is possible to run a WAC (/WiD) program without such an entity, *our experience is that to sustain a WAC (/WiD) program, a writing center is crucial.* Students need audiences other than their peers in the classroom or their teacher to respond to their writing, and faculty need the assurance that when they assign writing in their classes, there will be a place on campus where knowledgeable tutors can respond to drafts of their students' writing. The most successful writing centers work with faculty in the disciplines, asking for copies of assignments and helping faculty refine them [...]. (2000, p. 581, italics added)

As testified by McLeod and Maimon, therefore, writing centres can not only enhance the work of writing specialists in collaborating with academics across and in the disciplines, but can also be viewed as fundamental to the sustainability of WAC/WiD initiatives and programmes.

At Coventry University, WiD has been part of the remit of the Centre for Academic Writing since its founding. One of the main duties stated in the department Head's job description is to "organise staff development activities to assist academic and academic-related staff in helping students to improve their academic writing" (Coventry University, 2003, p. 1), and in 2006 this responsibility was written into the University's *Learning and Teaching Strategy* as a WiD initiative (Coventry University, 2006, pp. 2, 8, 10). At CAW, academic writing lecturers aim to cascade the teaching of writing by collaborating with discipline-based academics to formulate strategies for teaching writing more explicitly in subject modules. WiD at CAW typically begins with an individual or small-group consultation between a writing specialist and one or more colleagues who teach in a subject area or department, and focuses on priorities such as identifying the aims of the module or course being taught by the colleague(s), discussing types of assignments or assessments that will best meet those aims, drafting or revising assignment briefs, and setting or revising assignment marking criteria. CAW's proviso is that academic writing lecturers are not able to teach writing *for* colleagues but rather that they are available to provide staff development and support for colleagues in the teaching of writing.

During a WiD consultation at CAW, a writing specialist and subject experts use a *WiD Consultation Record* sheet to agree and record details under categories including "degree programme and modules relevant to consultation", "names of collaborating colleagues", "stated focus of subject specialist", "stated focus of CAW lecturer", and "project management: action to be taken, by whom and by when" (Centre for Academic Writing, 2009, pp. 2–3). The breadth and duration of the collaboration—for example, whether the planned intervention will take place within one module or be spread across a degree course—are also considered. CAW has found that WiD consultations assist colleagues by guiding them to think about how to assign and teach writing genres purposefully and incrementally in their modules and degree courses. An additional outcome of WiD collaborations is that they have the potential to result in joint research into discipline-specific writing pedagogies and may lead to publication opportunities for disciplinary academics and writing specialists in academic writing and disciplinary journals.

The benefits of WiD are exponential, because a WiD collaboration between one writing specialist and a core module leader can result in the revised teaching practice of an entire team of lecturers, thus providing discipline-specific writing instruction to students on a large scale.[15] However, while CAW promotes WiD as a pedagogical approach that effectively disseminates expertise in teaching discipline-specific writing throughout the university, CAW lecturers have also experienced the following limitation: WiD collaborations can be time-consuming, especially if they are ongoing over terms/semesters or even academic years, and it is not possible for writing centre staff to engage in more than a small number of collaborations at one time. Gradually, therefore, CAW staff have also begun to explore what we see as the broader and less discipline-specific scope of WAC pedagogy, with the aim of offering strategies to colleagues who want to motivate their students to write more and to use writing as a tool for learning.

In drawing on WAC principles, CAW facilitates staff development workshops that introduce "writing to learn" concepts and techniques (Bazerman and Russell, 1994, p. xiv). CAW writing developers also discuss with academics how to focus, as in a writing centre tutorial, on writing as a process of inventing, planning, drafting, and revising. "In this process of taking drafts to successively higher levels, the student learns to analyze her own writing style", and finds ways of dealing with problems and of building on strengths (Corbett and LaFrance, 2009, p. 5). In this manner, a WAC ethos contributes to the work of the writing centre, and writing centre pedagogies inform WAC classroom teaching practices.

The CAW model demonstrates how useful, reciprocal connections can be forged between writing centres, WiD, and WAC. This integrated provision for writing development means that the writing centre can be involved in writing development for academic and professional staff as well as for students at all levels, and that writing specialists can work with students and colleagues to create a flourishing, intellectual whole-university culture of writing.

▶ Key challenges and strategies

This chapter has outlined a number of benefits that a writing centre can bring to a university or college. In doing so, the chapter has countered two arguments that are often raised against writing centres: that writing centres only provide remedial help to students and that writing centre provision is not scalable. The chapter has shown how WiD and WAC initiatives can broaden the reach and impact of writing centre work and ensure that it addresses the needs of all students along a continuum of writing development.

By focusing on the writing centre as a base for WiD and WAC, the chapter has articulated a model for implementing writing provision in HE institutions. A major challenge for writing developers in the UK, however, is that at some institutions there may be many hurdles that need to be overcome in order to establish a writing centre. In facing this challenge, writing developers must be prepared to argue for resource allocation and to convince senior managers and other colleagues that a whole-institution writing strategy is worth investing in. Writing developers also need to work within their own local institutional contexts and to build on writing or learning development initiatives that may already exist at their institutions. As the examples of provision cited in the second section of this chapter demonstrate, WiD, WAC, and writing tutoring work can come into being and operate in many different ways. What this chapter is suggesting is that it can be extremely beneficial to pull together or join up writing provision within institutions and that writing centres are valuable sites from which to organise, house, and promote WiD, WAC, and other types of writing development work.

▶ Conclusion

This chapter has focused on the strategic development of WiD and WAC from within the context of a writing centre, and has argued that university writing centres are an ideal location from which to build systematic WiD and WAC interventions and programmes as well as other writing-related initiatives. Although HE institutions in the UK and Europe may be well-placed—and currently poised—to develop and implement an expanded definition of the traditional "writing center" concept, growth and change are also afoot in HE cultures with longer-established traditions of student writing development. This chapter is intended to serve as a thought-provoking contribution to ongoing scholarship examining and championing the connections between WiD/WAC/writing centres and whole-institution writing provision.

▶ Notes

1 "Writing Development" is the term used in UK HE to describe the work carried out by teachers, tutors, and researchers of academic writing.
2 A convergence of factors led, in the early 1990s, to the beginning of a movement to develop student writing at university level (Ganobcsik-Williams, 2006, pp. xxi–xxvi). These factors included an unprecedented increase in student numbers that started in the late 1980s and a concomitant diversification of educational and cultural backgrounds in the student population of UK HE institutions (Scott, 1995, pp. 1–5). Since that time, this diversification has been intensified by the burgeoning agendas of internationalisation and technologically enhanced learning. Whilst attention to the writing of Non-Native Speakers of English in HE pre-dated the broader "writing development" movement, the work of teachers and scholars in supporting and studying the writing of Non-Native Speakers of English informs the

pedagogy and research of colleagues working with student writing in the mainstream.

3   In the UK, calls for institutions to take responsibility for teaching and supporting writing have come from both inside and outside of HE. Educational stakeholders include graduate employers, academics, university managers, government policy makers, and funding bodies. See, for example, Bergstrom (2004) and Ganobcsik-Williams (2006, p. Xxii). Also see "Flying Start", a HE Academy-funded project involving four institutions whose aim is to study ways of "bridging the 'separate worlds' of writing and assessment at pre-university and undergraduate level" www.hope.ac.uk/flyingstart; the "Write Now" Centre for Excellence in Teaching and Learning (CETL) http://www.writenow.ac.uk/, which focuses on tertiary writing development and is grant-funded by the Higher Education Funding Council for England; and the COWL Project http://cuba.coventry.ac.uk/cowl, funded by a grant from JISC (the Joint Information Systems Committee), whose aim is to develop and disseminate a sustainable, systematic model of online student writing support.

4   On comprehensive institutional strategies for writing development, also see Dai Hounsell's keynote address, "Developing Students' Writing Expertise: Strategic and Institutional Dimensions", given at the 2008 Writing Development in Higher Education (WDHE) conference: http://www.writenow.ac.uk/wdhe/presentation/Hounsell.pdf and http://www.writenow.ac.uk/wdhe/wdhe2008.html; and Sally Mitchell's keynote address " 'Now you don't see it; now you do': Writing Made Visible in the University", given at the 2009 European Association for the Teaching of Academic Writing (EATAW) conference http://wwwm.coventry.ac.uk/eataw2009/Pages/KeynoteSpeakers.aspx.

5   The six-page questionnaire entitled "A National Survey of Staff Perspectives on the Teaching of Academic Writing in Higher Education" was posted, in paper format with return envelopes, to a cross-section of 450 staff within all universities and colleges of HE in England, Wales, Scotland, and Northern Ireland. The number of questionnaires returned was 137 (30%), revealing a substantial interest in the topic of student writing (Ganobcsik-Williams, 2004).

6   The Royal Literary Fund Fellowship Scheme (http://www.rlf.org.uk) has expanded greatly since its launch in Autumn 1999. For the devolved Academic Skills tutoring model at the University of Huddersfield see: http://www2.hud.ac.uk/academic_skills/tutors.php and Hill and Mullen (2007); for the "Thinking Writing" programme at Queen Mary, University of London see: http://www.thinkingwriting.qmul.ac.uk/; for the "Writing by Appointment", "Just Write" and "Write Right" initiatives at the University of Dundee see: http://www.dundee.ac.uk/aatu/writing.htm; for the Centre for Academic Writing at Coventry University see: http://www.coventry.ac.uk/cu/caw; for the London Metropolitan University Writing Centre see: http://www.londonmet.ac.uk/depts/dops/writing-centre/writing-centre.cfm; for the St. Mary's University College Belfast Writing Centre see http://www.stmarys-belfast.ac.uk/writingcentre/; for the Liverpool Hope University Writing Centre see: http://www.hope.ac.uk/writingcentre; and for the Centre for Academic Writing and Numeracy Skills at the University of Gloucestershire see: http://resources.glos.ac.uk/departments/lis/lcd/openstudy.cfm.

7   For one example of international cross-fertilisation of ideas on teaching writing in HE, see Donahue in this volume.
8   See http://www.sig-writing.org/, http://ewca.sabanciuniv.edu/eng/, and http://www.eataw.eu/. Also see the *Journal of Writing Research* (*JOWR*) http://jowr.org/ and *Zeitschrift Schreiben* http://www.zeitschrift-schreiben. eu/, two European journals devoted to the study of writing.
9   Recognising that writing centers are being set up in a number of countries, the National Writing Centers Association (NWCA), founded in the US in 1983, has changed its name to the International Writing Centers Association (IWCA). See http://writingcenters.org/.
10   I would argue that a subtle difference in meaning exists between the terms "centre" and "unit", with "centre" enjoying a higher status in UK HE. In contrast, the "academic writing unit" or "study skills unit" appears to have more remedial connotations.
11   The first documented attempt to set up a writing centre in UK HE took place at Newcastle Polytechnic (now the University of Northumbria) in 1979 (Hebron, 1984). This writing centre was not sustainable in terms of securing university funding, perhaps because it pre-dated the increased need to teach writing explicitly that was brought about by the "massification" and "universalisation" of HE described in endnote 2 of this chapter, but also because it perhaps tried to follow too closely the traditional US model upon which it was based (Hebron, 1984, p. 87) and did not attempt to stimulate additional types of systemic writing provision across the university.
12   For a map of CAW's activities in support of student writing, see: http:// cuba.coventry.ac.uk/cowl/files/2009/05/caw-current-model-v1-23-04-09-final.pdf.
13   CAW's mission statement appears in full at: http://www.coventry.ac.uk/cu/caw.
14   See, for example, the Spring 2009 special edition of *Praxis: A Writing Center Journal*, which is devoted to exploring the relationship between WAC and writing centers (http://projects.uwc.utexas.edu/praxis/?q=node/268). Also see, for example, Wallace (1989), Pemberton (1995), Barnett and Blumner (1999), and Mullin (2001).
15   For example, see details of a WiD collaboration between the writing centre and the Department of Physiotherapy and Dietetics at Coventry University that involved a team of lecturers on a core level one module (Ganobcsik-Williams and Toms, 2005).

▶ References

Barnett, R. and J. Blumner (1999) "Introduction", in R. Barnett and J. Blumner (eds), *Writing Centers and Writing Across the Curriculum Programs: Building Interdisciplinary Partnerships* (Westport, CT: Greenwood Press), pp. ix–xiii.

Barnett, R. and L. Rosen (1999) "The WAC/Writing Center Partnership: Creating a Campus-wide Writing Environment", in R. Barnett and J. Blumner (eds), *Writing Centers and Writing Across the Curriculum Programs: Building Interdisciplinary Partnerships* (Westport, CT: Greenwood Press), pp. 1–12.

Bazerman, C. and D. Russell (eds) (1994) *Landmark Essays on Writing Across the Curriculum* (Davis, CA: Hermagoras Press).

Bazerman, C., Little, J., Bethel, L., Chavkin, T., Fouquette, D. and Garufis, J. (2005) *Reference Guide to Writing Across the Curriculum* (West Layfayette, IN: Parlor Press and the WAC Clearing House).

Bergstrom, C. (2004) "The Status of Writing in the University", *English Subject Centre Newsletter*, 6: 10–13.

Boquet, E. (1999) "'Our Little Secret': A History of Writing Centers, Pre- to Post-Open Admissions", *College Composition and Communication*, 50 (3): 463–482.

Centre for Academic Writing (2008) "Centre for Academic Writing (CAW) Mission Statement", Coventry University. Available from http://www.coventry.ac.uk/cu/caw [16th October 2009].

Centre for Academic Writing (2009) *WiD Consultation Record Sheet.* Unpublished document: Coventry University.

Childers, P. (1999) "Writing Centers or Experimental Center for Faculty Research, Discovery, and Risk Taking?", in R. Barnett and J. Blumner (eds), *Writing Centers and Writing Across the Curriculum Programs: Building Interdisciplinary Partnerships* (Westport, CT: Greenwood Press), pp. 177–186.

Corbett, S. and M. LaFrance (2009) "From Grammatical to Global: the WAC/Writing Center Connection", *Praxis: A Writing Center Journal*, 6 (2) Available from http://projects.uwc.utexas.edu/praxis/?q=node/254 [6th September 2009].

Coventry University (2003) *Job Description: Co-ordinator, Centre for Academic Writing.* Unpublished document.

Coventry University (2006) *Learning and Teaching Strategy, 2006–2009.* Coventry University internal publication.

Davidson, C. and A. Tomic (1999) "Inventing Academic Literacy: An American Perspective", in C. Jones, J. Turner and B. Street (eds), *Students Writing in the University: Cultural and Epistemological Issues* (Amsterdam: John Benjamins), pp. 161–170.

Ganobcsik-Williams, L. (2004) *A Report on the Teaching of Academic Writing in UK Higher Education* (London: Royal Literary Fund).

Ganobcsik-Williams, L. (ed.) (2006) *Teaching Academic Writing in UK Higher Education: Theories, Practices and Models* (Houndmills: Palgrave Macmillan).

Ganobcsik-Williams, L. (2009) "Supporting Students along a Continuum of Writing Development". *Bridging the Gap: Transitions in Student Writing* symposium hosted by Flying Start, Write Now and Learn Higher. 10th June 2009. Keynote address. Available from http://www.hope.ac.uk/latest-news-and-progress-reports/writing-symposium.html (video of conference presentation and PowerPoint) [10th November 2009].

Ganobcsik-Williams, L. and Toms, J. (2005) "Helping Academics Assess and Teach Writing: The Writing Center's Role". European Association for the Teaching of Academic Writing (EATAW) Conference, Athens, Greece. Abstract of conference presentation. Available from http://eataw2005.hau.gr/pages/list_01_day1.htm#29 [12th December 2009].

Hebron, C. (1984) "Newcastle Polytechnic's Writing Centre and is Origins: A Description of an Innovation", in R. Williams, J. Swales and J. Kirkman (eds), *Common Ground: Shared Interests in ESP and Communication Studies* (Oxford: Pergamon Press), pp. 87–98.

Hill, P. and Mullen, J. (2007) "Writing Skills—An Integrated Approach". 4th LDHEN Symposium: "How Do Students Engage with Learning?" Bournemouth University. Available from http://www.aldinhe.ac.uk/bmth_papers/hill_files/frame.htm (PowerPoint of conference presentation) [12th November 2009].

Hounsell, Dai (2008) "Developing Students' Writing Expertise: Strategic and Institutional Dimensions". Writing Development in Higher Education conference. Keynote address. Available from http://www.writenow.ac.uk/wdhe/presentation/Hounsell.pdf (PowerPoint of conference presentation) and http://www.writenow.ac.uk/wdhe/wdhe2008.html (video of conference presentation) [10th November 2009].

McLeod, S. and E. Maimon (2000) "Clearing the Air: WAC Myths and Realities", *College English* 62 (5): 573–584.

Mitchell, S. (2009) " 'Now you don't see it; now you do': Writing Made Visible in the University". European Association for the Teaching of Academic Writing conference. Keynote address. Available from http://wwwm.coventry.ac.uk/eataw2009/Pages/KeynoteSpeakers.aspx [10th November 2009].

Mullin, J. (2001) "Writing Centers and WAC", in S. McLeod, E. Miraglia, M. Soven and C. Thaiss (eds), *WAC for the New Millennium: Strategies for Continuing Writing-Across-the –Curriculum Programs* (Urbana, IL: NCTE), pp. 179–199.

Mullin, J. (2006) "Learning from—Not Duplicating—US Composition Theory and Practice", in L. Ganobcsik-Williams (ed.), *Teaching Academic Writing in UK Higher Education: Theories, Practices and Models* (Houndmills: Palgrave Macmillan), pp. 167–179.

Murphy, C. and Law, J. (1995) "Introduction: Landmark Essays on Writing Centers", in C. Murphy and J. Law (eds), *Landmark Essays on Writing Centers* (Davis, CA: Hermagoras Press), pp. xi–xvi.

North, S. (1984) "The Idea of a Writing Center", reprinted in C. Murphy and J. Law (eds) (1995), *Landmark Essays on Writing Centers* (Davis, CA: Hermagoras Press), pp. 71–85.

O'Neill, P. (2008) "Using Peer Writing Fellows in British Universities: Complexities and Possibilities". *Across the Disciplines* [Special Issue on Writing Fellows]. Available from http://wac.colostate.edu/atd/fellows/oneill.cfm [11th November 2009].

O'Neill, P. (2010) *Personal email to Lisa Ganobcsik-Williams* [13th January 2010].

Pemberton, M. (1995) "Rethinking the WAC/Writing Center Connection", *Writing Center Journal* 15 (2): 116–133.

Russell, D., Lea, M., Parker, J., Street, B. and Donahue, T. (2009) "Exploring Notions of Genre in 'Academic Literacies' and 'Writing Across the Curriculum': Approaches Across Countries and Contexts", in C. Bazerman, A. Bonini and D. Figueiredo (eds), *Genre in a Changing World*. Perspectives on Writing series (Boulder, CO: Parlor Press), pp. 459–491.

Scott, P. (1995) *The Meanings of Mass Higher Education* (Buckingham: Open University Press).

Skillen, J. (2006) "Teaching Academic Writing from the 'Centre' in Australian Universities", in L. Ganobcsik-Williams (ed.), *Teaching Academic Writing in UK Higher Education: Theories, Practices and Models* (Houndmills: Palgrave Macmillan), pp. 140–153.

Waldo, M. (1993) "The Last Best Place for Writing Across the Curriculum: The Writing Center", *WPA: Writing Program Administration* 16 (3): 15–27.

Wallace, R. (1989) "The Writing Center's Role in the Writing Across the Curriculum Program: Theory and Practice", reprinted in C. Murphy and J. Law (eds) (1995), *Landmark Essays on Writing Centers* (Davis, CA: Hermagoras Press), pp. 191–196.

Conclusion: Ways Forward for WiD

Mary Deane and Peter O'Neill

Writing in the Disciplines has brought together a range of perspectives on disciplinary writing development with the aim of stimulating debate about fresh ways of supporting students. The book's premise is that students who are offered opportunities to learn how to use disciplinary discourse are often more engaged and confident writers. Here we want to highlight three themes which emerge from this volume: the role of collaboration in disciplinary writing development; the importance of staff development in disseminating good practice; and the value of researching disciplinary literacies. We conclude by considering the potential of WiD as a means to revive neglected traditions of rhetoric in university education.

▶ Collaboration

As demonstrated in Parts II and III, partnerships between subject experts, writing developers, and learning technologists can take the strain from all parties as they work together to enhance students' experiences of writing at university. The challenges of collaboration include finding like-minded colleagues and protecting time to plan and execute WiD teaching strategies. Yet, the benefits can outweigh these efforts, as often partnerships are best at generating innovative ideas and a collaborative approach to improving students' writing provides a strong support base. For senior managers, a more strategic approach to academic support is resource-efficient, and one of the lessons of the case studies collected in Part II is that a co-ordination of goals can maximise the effectiveness of teaching interventions.

▶ Professional development

The case studies in Part II are mostly based on one or two colleagues working together, and a possible critique of this small-scale collaborative model is that the impact can remain local, and may be put at risk if one of the key players withdraws from the collaboration. This could be addressed by more systematic implementation of the WiD approach, as outlined by Bean in Chapter 12, where he details a form of staff development and curricula design that leads to a coherent pattern of writing assessment across a department. As Harrington points out in Chapter 3, the core remit of assessing students that is shared by every academic represents another avenue for co-ordinating an effective approach to student writing development, although as Horne and Peake suggest in Chapter 6, such an approach needs to be used with care.

As Ganobcsik-Williams argues in Chapter 14, a centralised unit for writing development can prove to be a valuable mechanism for working towards the collaborative disciplinary writing research and practice that *Writing in the Disciplines* aims to promote. As she indicates, there are alternative models to the North American-style writing centre, and such a centralised approach can be usefully adapted to accommodate institutional agendas in other national contexts. The advantage of the writing centre as a base for research and staff development is that this puts writing on the map alongside a myriad of other key issues such as widening participation, retention, and student satisfaction which are inextricably connected with students' success.

▶ Research and publication

More work is needed to analyse the features of writing in different disciplines and to communicate these principles to students at various levels. We think it could be helpful if the results of more pedagogic collaborations are published, and if the resources created by subject experts and writing developers could be made available to colleagues across the sector, for instance via digital repositories as Llewellyn-Jones and colleagues discuss in Chapter 13. Thinking about WiD collaborations in terms of a research project, perhaps using action research framework, or as a publishing opportunity is likely to encourage discipline-based academics to participate in carrying out this important work, since this makes it part of appraisal mechanisms and means of promotion.

▶ WiD and rhetoric

We want to conclude by focusing on a fundamental aspect of writing development that has not been explicitly discussed in this volume: the relationship of WiD to rhetorical theory. Worley and Schippers touch on this issue in Chapter 9 as they explore teaching writing in Politics as a means of engagement with the subject and with civil society. Yet, in general the case studies in Part II focus on solving practical problems surrounding student writing and attempting to promote a more successful writing experience. However, attention to academic writing is inevitably going to involve attention to rhetoric, the art of persuasion, which formed the basis of ancient education and remained central through the Renaissance and into the early modern period. We want to end this book by suggesting that WiD could be more ambitious still, and become a space for exploring what a contemporary rhetoric in higher education (HE) might look like.

According to the classicist Tom Habinek:

> Rhetoric, whatever its challenges and limitations, is the discourse of citizens and subjects, in all their glorious specificity, struggling to recompose the world.   (Habinek, 2005, p. vii; see also Touraine, 1997)

This reminds us that through attention to the art of writing and persuading, we are not merely providing a key skill that will help students to become more effective communicators and better prepared to be economically productive. We are also helping them to become more confident citizens and better able to participate in modern democratic life. This point places students as social actors (Touraine, 1997) at the heart of a vision of a modern democratic culture fostered by communication and discussion.

This is a rather grandiose claim, and a degree of scepticism is doubtless in order. Sharon Crowley, for example, has questioned the extent to which—for all its claims—rhetoric plays a genuine part in courses that teach writing as a generic skills divorced form the content and purpose of arguments:

> Any theoretical discourse that is entitled to be called "rhetoric" must at minimum conceive of rhetoric as an art of invention, that is, it must give a central place to the systematic discovery and investigation of the available arguments in a given situation. Furthermore, it must conceive of the arguments generated by rhetorical invention as both produced and circulated within a network of social and civic discourse, images, and events. As ancient rhetors such as Gorgias and Cicero argued in theory and personified in practice, any practice entitled to be called "rhetoric" must intervene in some way in social and civic discursive networks.   (Crowley, 2003, n.p.)

Crowley draws attention to the work of Charles Sears Baldwin and his adherence to Aristotle's conviction that the moral nature of rhetoric means that it should never be divorced from subject matter that really counts, and who showed that attention to the speaker at the expense of the message has led repeatedly throughout history to sophistry. For Crowley (and Baldwin), for genuine rhetoric, *inventio* (the process of discovery, and the first of the five classic canons of rhetoric) should be more than a matter of simply selecting a topic, and *dispositio* (the process of arrangement, the second canon) should be more than adopting a structure for writing. Rather, the urgency of the subject matter and the importance of the message drive discovery and arrangement to enable the moral importance of rhetoric to manifest itself.

In the UK as academics often teach subject-based rather than generic courses, there is an opportunity to promote assignments where rhetoric matters, and indeed becomes fundamental to education, underlying the studied content and enabling students to construct living arguments with moral seriousness. Writing is perhaps the most powerful means we have with which to fully engage our students with their studies. Yet, it is often seen by students as an obstacle, and academic writing can be an activity ridden with fears of failure or plagiarism. Even the brightest students often write more to please a tutor or to show off their knowledge than because they are fully engaged in their work. In order to engage students, writing assignments need, where possible, to be designed in such a way that they encourage students to adopt a committed position, to develop an argument that is expounded logically with the best supporting evidence available.

Such principles of good writing are not always explicitly articulated to students, and some academics may not see explicit value in them. Yet, these aspects of writing lie at the root of Aristotelian rhetoric, and at the heart of theories of rhetoric and composition. The more we are able to persuade colleagues of their value, the better, and we believe that the outcome could be a more engaged experience for all students as they write in the conviction that their work matters. It is possibly the case that students who struggle in academia are the most likely to switch off if they do not see the point of what they are being asked to do. Those who are more familiar with the academy may be more at ease in fulfilling requirements to succeed, but all students can benefit from being challenged to interrogate their own positions and identities more fully.

As Michael Halloran suggests, the issue at stake here, "is one of existential commitment to the implications of an argument, or more simply of the seriousness with which one takes an argument" (1975, p. 626). Attention to writing can bring about this seriousness and the engaged commitment that it implies. Halloran brings in the importance of *ethos* (ethical character) here, the most important of Aristotle's modes of rhetorical appeal, and perhaps the most important today:

> In our time of fragmentation and isolation, *ethos* is generated by the seriousness and passion with which the speaker articulates his own word, the degree to which he is willing and able to make his world open to the other, and thus to the possibility of rupture ... ethos is the measure of one's willingness to risk one's self and world by a rigorous and open articulation of them in the presence of the other. (Halloran, 1975, p. 628; on *ethos*, see also Halloran, 1982)

This reminds us of what Kenneth Burke calls rhetoric as identification (1950), where rhetoric goes deeper than its traditional art of persuasion, and is the reaching out of humans to each other to forge connections in a world of separateness and division; "identification is affirmed with earnestness precisely because there is division. Identification is compensatory to division" (1950, p. 22). As Halloran points out:

> It is only through the existential risk of rhetoric that one transcends the boundaries of immediate experience, and thus it is through rhetoric that the self and its world are constituted. Not to engage in rhetoric is not to be human. (Halloran, 1975, p. 626)

This potential aspect of WiD is aspirational, especially in an increasingly mechanised HE environment. Nonetheless, disciplinary writing development is a vehicle through which rhetorical theory can be engaged with and through which the role of this tradition in education can be enhanced. Above all, these ideas help switch agendas from a remedial approach, to teaching writing, to viewing it as a vital activity with which all students need to be given the best opportunities to engage. We think that discipline-based writing research and teaching is the best way of meeting government requirements concerning skills and graduate attributes for all students. But we think too that WiD work has the potential to go way beyond such requirements, and that academics should refuse to be limited by them. It is through understanding this potential that we are most likely to give explicit attention to writing, which, in the long run, is likely to have a transformative effect on HE in the UK and beyond.

▶ References

Burke, K. (1950) *A Rhetoric of Motives* (Berkeley, CA and Los Angeles, CA: California University Press).

Crowley, S. (2003) "Composition is Not Rhetoric." *Enculturation*, 5.1 <<http://enculturation.gmu.edu/5_1/crowley.html>>. Date accessed 25/02/2010.

Habinek, T. (2005) *Ancient Rhetoric and Oratory* (Malden, MA: Blackwell).

Halloran, S. M. (1975) "On the End of Rhetoric, Classical and Modern." *College English*, 36.6, 621–631.

Halloran, S. M. (1982) "Aristotle's concept of Ethos, or If Not His Somebody Else's." *Rhetoric Review*, 1.1, 58–63.

Touraine, A. (1997) *What is Democracy?* (Boulder, CO: Westview).

Afterword—and Onward!

Cheryl Glenn

Writing in the Disciplines reaches your hands at a propitious moment. The British, Australian, and US contributors to this collection showcase sophisticated delivery systems for the teaching of writing that are flourishing around the world, not just in the US. Thus, this collection handily dislodges the long-standing belief that only we US compositionists find value in student writing, only we have multiple systems of teaching writing, and only we have developed writing programs (a mistaken belief that John Bean and Christiane Donahue wisely point out).

Of course, it has been easy to cling to yesteryear, to that US-centric story of college composition where it all began. Scholars simply hearken back to nineteenth-century America, to Harvard (no less), where the most privileged of young men found themselves in need of additional instruction, having not yet mastered the felicities of good writing. As mentioned in the Introduction, in the late 1800s, Harvard's English A was launched as the way to help young men master correct spelling, grammar, punctuation, expression, and even the simple sentence in English before they would be permitted to open a text in Latin or Greek. English A also sparked the field of rhetoric and composition in higher education here in the States. The vibrant essays in this collection speak to the challenges, promises, and achievements of present-day writing instruction, with two essays focusing on the States and the rest on the exciting curricular initiatives taking place abroad.

Writing holds the key to academic success for our students, regardless of where we live in the world. But for a number of reasons, the teaching of writing has, since the days of English A, too often been considered only a remedial endeavour. With the continuing influence of collections like this one, showcasing the dynamic spectrum of advanced, successful writing instruction, the perception of writing instruction as remediation will surely fade away.

Yes, our students come to us in need of our help, our teaching. Yes, some come to us as inefficient readers and writers, with fluency in languages and dialects other than Standardised English, with weak discipline-specific foundations, with heavy commitments to family or work, and with marked age or income differences from their classmates. Yes, some students—in the States, in Australia, in Britain, everywhere!—arrive with so-called deficits. But many of our students appear in our classes fully prepared and committed to move quickly ahead.

After 12 years or more of compulsory schooling, all these students elect to continue their schooling because they have faith in education to change lives. They may not come to us prepared in all the ways that make our teaching—or their learning—easy, but they come with all the life experience and knowledge that their 18, 25, or 40 years have earned them. They come to us with the same notion we have long held for our own, better-educated selves, that education (that our teaching) will change their lives, that their lives might be better than their parents', and that the lives of their children might be better than theirs has been. For these reasons (and many more), we would all be wise to follow the pedagogical advice Lisa Ganobcsik-Williams shares in this volume. She tells us that our writing pedagogies would be ever so much more successful if, instead of focusing on what our students cannot do or do not know (their deficits), we encourage our students to learn, to do, and to participate meaningfully in their classes. Every essay in this volume aptly puts her advice into practice.

Like writing professionals everywhere and throughout time, all of these contributors celebrate writing as the lynchpin of academic learning and success. Mary Deane and Peter O'Neill argue, "Writing is perhaps *the* most powerful means we have with which to fully engage our students with their studies." Ursula Wingate recognises that "academic writing cannot be learned in separation from disciplinary knowledge". And thus, chapter after chapter, these contributors demonstrate the many ways they engage their students: through Writing in the Disciplines (WiD) programs, Writing in the Majors (WiM), Centers for Excellence in Teaching and Learning (CETL), and writing centres.

Throughout these chapters, the contributors illustrate intellectually challenging and successful models of writing pedagogy, long- and short-term strategies that acknowledge the ways disciplinary knowledge and engagement coupled with writing practice almost always lead to good writing. (After all, the greater the student's engagement, the greater the investment, one that often has exponential growth and compound interest!) Whether these authors speak to issues of the writing process, technologies, or any of a wide-range of subjects and genres, each author speaks to innovative writing initiatives and programs that completely revitalise and transform whatever remnants of nineteenth-century English A remain. The teaching of writing is a long-term endeavour, one best anchored to a whole-university culture of writing energised by interdisciplinary partnerships that provide supportive yet demanding writing instruction.

Shoulder-to-shoulder and heart-to-heart, these writing and subject specialists work together to develop student writers who use the deeply mysterious, endlessly adaptable technology called writing in order to explore, discover, learn, develop their academic literacy in context (DALiC), and showcase their disciplinary expertise. Together, students collaborate, reviewing one another's written work, establishing criteria for writing assignments (and specific genres), and reviewing discipline-specific information. Together, they blossom with the realisation that through writing they can learn about their disciplines, about themselves, about their families, and about their communities. They come to believe that "language is power", that when they are "released into language" (as Simone Weil so elegantly put it), the power that is writing becomes central to their intellectual development and to changing the real, material circumstances of their lives. This fine collection of essays looks forward and moves onward. May you be as inspired as I have been to continue teaching writing, for these stories of writing and teaching motivate me teach myself and my students into a future we might all want to inhabit.

Index